A Chinese Look
at Literature

A Chinese Look at Literature

The Literary Values of Chou Tso-jen in Relation to the Tradition

by DAVID E. POLLARD

UNIVERSITY OF CALIFORNIA PRESS
Berkeley · Los Angeles

UNIVERSITY OF CALIFORNIA PRESS
Berkeley and Los Angeles, California

© David E. Pollard 1973

ISBN 0-520-02409-5

LC 72-97732

CONTENTS

INTRODUCTION

I started reading Chou Tso-jen seriously in 1961, on the advice of Professor D. C. Twitchett of Cambridge University and Dr. J. D. Chinnery, now Senior Lecturer in Chinese at Edinburgh University. As a major figure in modern Chinese literature who had been largely ignored since the war because of his collaboration with the Japanese, he clearly deserved to be 'written up'. But I soon realized that his essays were such a mine of information on Chinese culture, and his views such a mixture of modern rationalism and age-old Chinese bias, that to do a 'life and works' study, though necessary, could only touch on the many issues which 'meddled with his thoughts' (to quote Miranda, in *The Tempest*) without exploring any thoroughly. Fortunately Dr. Ernst Wolff completed a very sound thesis on Chou's life and works for the University of Washington, Seattle, in 1966, (since published in book form as *Chou Tso-jen*, New York, 1971), and the way was open for this more specialized study of Chou's ideas about literature.

For all his esteem for 'scientific thought' Chou Tso-jen was not a scientific critic. His theoretical propositions were not carefully thought out or very logically expressed; they were mostly generalized responses (he preferred latterly not to personalize his arguments) to contemporary issues, put in too absolute terms (a pardonable fault in essay writing), and clothed, often, in traditional Chinese dress. They were also repeated unchanged in different essays. If some of his ideas ran along particularly Chinese lines, his literary values – that is, what determined his likes and dislikes in literature – were wholly Chinese, which is not to say that some are not universal too. It is this coexistence of traditional Chinese values with a determinedly modern cast of mind and an extensive education in Western learning that makes him such an interesting subject for study.

Because of the constant need to refer for comparison to traditional Chinese literary concepts I was obliged to acquaint myself to some extent with the vast corpus of critical writings of the past. There has been no systematic attempt to survey this field in any European language, and the task would have been quite impossible without the aid of three works in Chinese, namely Kuo Shao-yü's *Chung-kuo wen-hsüeh p'i-p'ing shih* (A History of Chinese Literary Criticism), Lo Ken-tse's book of the same name, and to a lesser extent Chu Tung-jun's *Chung-kuo wen-hsüeh p'i-p'ing shih ta-kang* (Outline of the History of Chinese Literary Criticism). I have mostly referred to these books, and other secondary works, as sources for passages from classical authors quoted, rather than to the enormous encyclopaedic collections, as is usual, because I like to pay my debts where they are due; I do not want to give the entirely false impression that I have spent my days and nights sifting the *Ssu-pu ts'ung-k'an* for critical nuggets. I also have in mind that readers of this book who know Chinese are more likely to have a copy of Kuo Shao-yü's 'History' at hand than the same *Ssu-pu ts'ung-k'an*.

Apart from conducting a general and inevitably rather superficial study of certain themes in Chinese criticism by these means I have given special attention to two schools of literature, the Kung-an of late Ming and the T'ung-ch'eng of the Ch'ing dynasty, because they figure so prominently in Chou's essays and lectures; summaries of their characteristics are included as appendixes.

I found very little of this material easy to understand, not being a classical scholar. I was therefore very fortunate that I could refer to Prof. D. C. Lau those points which most puzzled me. He has saved me from several errors which in any other field would be egregious. Doubtless, though, there will still be things about which my confidence in my correctness has been misplaced.

Since quite a lot has now been written about modern Chinese literature in English I have not filled in the background to any considerable extent. Even more selectively, I have concentrated on the middle period of Chou Tso-jen's career, when he was withdrawn from active involvement in national affairs, and conversely more absorbed in the problems of his art and cultural heritage. It would not be sensible, however, to impose any absolute chronological limit, since what he wrote before, in the May Fourth period, and after, when the Sino-Japanese war was in full swing, can naturally throw light on the opinions he expressed during the middle period. I have therefore observed no such limit. On the other hand, different problems did exercise Chou's mind in his May Fourth period, so this book is not a complete study even of his ideas about literature. For that period I might refer the reader to my essay 'Chou Tso-jen and cultivating one's Garden', in *Asia Major*, XI, pt. 2, 1965. To avoid giving too partial an impression on the present occasion, however, I have included a chapter entitled 'Perspectives'; besides attempting to provide what the name denotes, that chapter contains enough generalized description and comment to excuse me from more of the same here.

As to the bibliography, I have listed only those books quoted or cited. There may be other Chinese books and articles which have either informed or influenced me, but I am not conscious of any further indebtedness. Among Western books the reader will notice that M. H. Abrams' *The Mirror and the Lamp* gets very frequent mention. The reason is not that it is the only Western work on literary criticism I have read – though it is certainly the best – but that there are remarkable coincidental correspondences between Chinese lyricism and European Romanticism, the subject of Abrams' book. Again the material is in the book for the reader to judge.

For the sake of convenience I append here a short biography of Chou Tso-jen. A fuller one, compiled by Dr. William Schultz, can be found in Howard Boorman's *Biographical Dictionary of Republican China*, vol. I.

Chou was born in 1885, the second of three brothers who between them were to restore, in fame at least, the fortunes of a family brought low by the arrest of his grandfather, a prominent official, on a corruption charge. His elder brother, Shu-jen, became better known as Lu Hsün, and his younger brother, Chien-jen, a biologist by training, rose to a high political position in the People's Republic. In Tso-jen's boyhood, however, the family were impoverished, and he had to pursue his education by going to the government-financed Kiangnan Naval Academy in Nanking in 1901. The naval expertise he learned there was never put to use, but he did begin to learn English, a link with the outside world, and more important, he was set on a course that led to further study in Japan from 1906 to 1911, where he shed his embryonic military role and took up in earnest the study of foreign literatures. He also found himself a wife, one Hata Nobuku, in 1909.

In 1911 he returned to his native province of Chekiang and worked in the educational service. The turning point in his life came in 1917 when he went to Peking and was appointed to the staff of National Peking University, the power-house of what came to be known as the 'new culture movement'. Previously Chou had published some unnoticed translations, mostly of Slavic literature; now he made a name for himself as a writer of essays in the new medium of the vernacular on social and cultural questions. He also tried his hand, successfully by contemporary standards, at writing poetry in the vernacular, though these poems are forgotten now. He was particularly active in promoting and supporting literary societies and magazines, being a founder member in 1921 of the Literary Association (*Wen-hsüeh yen-chiu hui*) and the *Yü Ssu* magazine (1924), and patron of the student journal *Hsin Ch'ao* (New Tides) – 1919.

In the mid-1920s Peking, which had been the intellectual centre of reform and revolution, became a backwater, as a result of repressive warlord measures. Progressive publications were banned and individuals were hounded down. The dissident intellectuals were faced with the alternatives of fleeing south or shutting up: Lu Hsün chose the former course, Chou Tso-jen the latter. He ceased to write overtly on current affairs; most of his subsequent essays were on literary, scholarly or antiquarian questions, and it is as a writer on these harmless topics that he is remembered by the majority of Chinese.

When the Japanese invaded China in 1937 Chou was again faced with the choice of seeking refuge elsewhere in China or staying in Peking under an oppressive regime. His decision to stay led him this time to incur lasting obloquy in the eyes of his compatriots, for he eventually yielded to extreme pressure from the Japanese to join the ranks of the collaborationists. From 1941 to 1943 he was head of the Bureau of Education in the puppet government. For this act he was tried by the Chinese government after the war, sentenced to life imprisonment, and pardoned in 1949 as the Communists moved south. Under the People's Republic he was allowed to live in retirement in Peking. According to report, he died during the Great Cultural Revolution.

CHRONOLOGICAL TABLE OF CHINESE DYNASTIES

Spring and Autumn period (Ch'un Ch'iu)	770–475 BC
Warring States Period (Chan Kuo)	475–221 BC
Ch'in	221–206 BC
Western (or Former) Han	206 BC–24 AD
Eastern (or Later) Han	25–220
Three Kingdoms (San Kuo)	220–280
Western Chin	265–316
Eastern Chin	317–420
Six Dynasties (Liu Ch'ao)	222–589
Southern and Northern Dynasties (Nan Pei Ch'ao)	420–589
Sui	581–618
T'ang	618–907
Five Dynasties (Wu Tai)	907–960
Northern Sung	960–1127
Southern Sung	1127–1279
Yüan	1279–1368
Ming	1368–1644
Ch'ing	1644–1911

1

THEORIES OLD AND NEW

Chou Tso-jen's lectures on the origins of the new literature *Hsin wen-hsüch ti yüan-liu*, delivered at Fu-jen University in 1932 and prepared for publication the same year, provide the only example of sustained literary analysis by him and so must form the basis for any appraisal of his ideas about literature. The theory central to this analysis is that Chinese literature can be divided into two classes according to the old antithesis between 'poetry expressing the heart's wishes'[1] (*shih yen chih*) and 'literature as a vehicle for the Way' (*wen i tsai tao*). Both theses, despite their originally limited field of application, the first to lyrical poetry and the second, less obviously, principally to formal prose, are taken by Chou in the usual manner to refer to literature in general, so the distinction is between literature simply as an uttering of feeling, free from any direction or control and oblivious of its putative effect, and literature written in the service of a philosophy of life. The one belongs to expressive theory, the other largely to pragmatic theory, but their lines do cross and there is obviously ground for conflict between them. Chou Tso-jen thought them absolute alternatives, and that only one of them, the expressive theory, was valid; literature which sought to be a 'vehicle for the Way' (hereafter designated as *tsai tao*) was not literature.

The reasoning which justifies such a decided distinction, as set out in *Yüan-liu*, is heavy with the weight of the cultural anthropology which Chou Tso-jen generally relied on to explain the world to himself. His basic premise is that literature originated in religion. With the proven example of Greek tragedy in mind, he produces a Chinese counterpart in the ancient rite of welcoming spring by enacting the drama of the slaying and subsequent rebirth of the spirit of the season, in order to confirm the premise. The implication is that literature could only establish its own identity when this symbiotic relationship was

[1] The translation is adopted from James J. Y. Liu, *The Art of Chinese Poetry*, pt. 2.

dissolved. This was done when it ceased to share the same aims as religion, in fact ceased to have any aims at all.[2]

Chou had put the point rather better ten years earlier when he had explained that the arts of primitive societies, while being irrepressible (artistic expression amounting to a kind of 'physiological satisfaction'), had had the extra dimension of attempting to communicate with the supernatural. True art was born when the poet (the maker) ceased to expect that the execution of his works would call forth any response or that they would have any efficacy, and when the audience began to look on rituals as entertainments.[3]

History itself, therefore, had settled that the distinguishing characteristic of literature should be that it should have no aim or object. Unfortunately, in China the *tsai tao* school of thought had inherited and embodied the attitude which still lingered from primitive times that literature should be put to serious use. The *yen chih* school, on the other hand, apprehended the true nature of art as expression.

To vindicate his assertion of the one theory being right and the other wrong, Chou proceeds in *Yüan-liu* to test it against the record of Chinese literary history. To make this manageable he classes different periods as *yen chih* or *tsai tao*, according to which outlook prevailed at the time. The ascendancy of *tsai tao* is linked with effective government control of the empire; conversely, the *yen chih* thesis comes to the fore when the central government cannot enforce conformity. So in the periodization of Chinese history, from the Spring and Autumn to the Warring States periods, literature was guided by the *yen chih* principle, and was therefore good, in Han by the *tsai tao* principle, and therefore poor. In the Wei-Chin-Liu-ch'ao period it was 'interesting', in T'ang there was a downturn (the huge volume of poetry produced, encouraged by the state examinations, inevitably threw up many good works, but the situation was different from the creative Six Dynasties period). From the Five Dynasties to early Sung, when the *tz'u* came into its own, literature was good again, but after Sung was firmly established only things tossed off carelessly were written well. In Yüan the shackles were thrown off again, and the *ch'ü* resulted. In Ming imitation of the ancients was the accepted dogma (bad), whereas at the turn of the sixteenth–seventeenth centuries the Kung-an and Ching-ling schools supported the right line with the slogan 'if you trust to the wrist and trust to the mouth, all will form melodic numbers' (*hsin wan hsin k'ou, chieh ch'eng lü tu*). From 1700 to 1900 literature again took the opposite direction, the representative school being the T'ung-ch'eng p'ai, advocates of the 'ancient prose' style.

[2] Lecture 1, section 5.

[3] 'Sheng-shu yü Chung-kuo wen-hsüeh' (The Bible and Chinese Literature), 1920, *I-shu yü sheng-huo*, pp. 64–5.

It will be seen from the above outline that the *yen chih/tsai tao* antithesis is not a very delicate analytical instrument. The T'ang dynasty presents an obstacle that cannot so easily be wished away, but an even more important deficiency is the fact, noted by Chou with regard to the Sung dynasty, that many writers had a dual attitude to literature, certain forms being written in the approved fashion and others allowing a free rein, which indicates that the problem lies in personal attitudes, not periods. Furthermore, taking as it does external circumstances as the determining factor, it leaves out of account autonomous developments in literature, such as the exhaustion of genres. The latter is probably the most common explanation for the changes of tack that have occurred over the centuries; it ascribes the high-points in literary history to the creative phases following the 'discovery' of genres when authors drew freely and fully on their powers to fill out the form, and the troughs to their awareness in the later stages that wherever they went someone had been there before.[4] It also ignores the more sophisticated theory put forward by Yüan Hung-tao of swing and counter-swing, according to which the style dominant in any particular period is explainable by the attempt to correct the excesses of the previous period by taking an opposite line. Chou did quote, and commend, Yüan's exposition of this idea in *Yüan-liu*[5], but the mechanism of change it postulates is quite different from what Chou proposes.

The most that can be said for Chou's key to literary history is that the average writer might have been deterred from allowing his talents full scope by restrictive conventions, which exerted more influence at some times than at others. Chou appears to have been aware that he was pressing these concepts into service, for in Lecture Three he puts forward the alternatives of 'extempore' (*chi-hsing*) and 'prescribed' (*fu-te*). Using these terms he is confident enough to state that all outstanding works of literature have been extempore (p. 70). The main weakness of 'prescribed' literature, he says, quoting Liu Hsi-tsai (1813–81), is: 'Before the opening theme is done, the composition is subservient to me; once the opening theme is there, I am subservient to the composition' (p. 71).

Despite its academic deficiencies, the *yen chih/tsai tao* opposition crystallized an issue of real concern for Chou Tso-jen. The question of its importance to him will later be discussed at length, but already the interpreter of Chou Tso-jen's views runs into difficulties. Such a bald explanation as that offered so far can convey no more than an inkling of what the argument could ever have been about. All along the line it

[4] Argued by Fu Keng-sheng, *Chung-kuo wen-hsüeh p'i-p'ing t'ung-lun* (Comprehensive Discussion of Chinese Literary Criticism), p. 98.
[5] The relevant passage is translated in Appendix B, pp. 160.

will be necessary, if one is to say how *a* Chinese looked at literature, to explain also how *the* Chinese traditionally looked at literature. In this case, since the terminology is only barely comprehensible, except to a few specialists, it would be wise to find out first the connotations of *shih yen chih* and *wen i tsai tao* from their history before going any further. While I in no way pretend to be writing (or to be able to write) a general history of the subject, these two contending views do represent opposite poles in Chinese literary theory, and a summary of them will provide a framework for much of the ensuing discussion. So, disconcerting as it may be before having been properly introduced to Chou Tso-jen, we are already to meet the ancients.

Shih yen chih *historically*

The phrase *shih yen chih* is of very early origin and in its time has been interpreted in different ways, initially in a sense quite other than Chou's.[6] The character *chih* is by its radical *hsin* clearly connected with the heart. The other element is thought by most scholars to be *chih* 'go', giving the interpretation for the whole character of 'where the heart goes'. Wen I-to on the other hand reads it as *chih* 'to stop', and interprets the character as 'what rests in the heart'.[7] Whether based on such etymological grounds or not, the later differences of interpretation of the slogan *shih yen chih* are summed up in these two readings, for the first implies something the heart attaches itself to, hence would mean 'intentions', 'purpose', 'will', 'aspirations', 'ideal', or some such, while the second would mean 'feelings' or 'ideas' of a both more generalized and more private nature.

One of the earliest occurrences of the phrase *shih yen chih* was in the *Book of History*, 'Canons of Yao' (*Shu ching*, 'Yao tien'). For a translation I quote Legge, who renders *chih* as 'earnest thought': 'Poetry is the expression of earnest thought; singing is the prolonged utterance of that expression. The notes accompany that utterance, and they are harmonized themselves by the pitch pipes.' (*The Shoo King*, p. 48.) Seminal though it is in Chinese thinking, by itself this passage does not much help to define the meaning of *chih*. The use of this word in the *Tso chuan* in the phrase 'six *chih*',[8] to refer to love, hate, joy, anger, sorrow and pleasure, would encourage us to think of it in a broad

[6] In this section I draw heavily on Chu Tzu-ch'ing's *Shih yen chih pien* (Analysis of *shih yen chih*)

[7] For a summary of possible interpretations of the word *chih*, see Chow Tse-tsung, 'The early History of the word *shih*', in *Wen-lin*, pp. 160–6.

[8] 'Chao Kung', Year 25.

sense, since these six are the 'six feelings' (*liu ch'ing*) of the *Li chi* (Book of Rites). The T'ang scholar K'ung Ying-ta,[9] remarking on this, deduces that *chih* and *ch'ing* (feelings) are basically one, that *ch'ing* refers to feelings in repose, *chih* to feelings when aroused. If this were correct, *shih yen chih* would represent the same cognition as Byron's 'Poetry is the expression of excited passion'.[10] More prosaically, it is still quite likely that originally it meant nothing more specific than 'poetry speaks the mind'. Poetry, however, was not left to its own devices in the Spring and Autumn and Warring States periods from which these works derive. It was customarily used as a means of communication, a kind of diplomatic code, among political advisers. Furthermore, 'presenting a poem' (*hsien shih*) was the gentleman's way of making a comment; according to Chu Tzu-ch'ing[11] the purpose was to express one's own *chih* (i.e. ideals), but not to tell of private preoccupations. The *Tso chuan* also relates how nobles were invited to quote from one of the *Odes* as a token of their loyalty or a test of their political feelings (*fu shih yen chih*).[12]

Given the nature of the canonical works, having to do with affairs of state or the art of statesmanship, it is natural that the colouring which both *shih* and *chih* took on from their contexts should have been a political one, and equally natural that *chih* should have been used principally in a moral sense in the Four Books. The result is that modern scholars have been unable to discover in these early times any unambiguous appreciation of *chih* as a motive for composing poetry other than the political and moral ones.[13] Ch'ien Mu puts it that the *chih* poetry of that period needed an object of address, unlike later times when the poet could use the words *yen chih* to describe talking to himself. And yet it was the Great Preface to the *Odes* (*Shih* 'Ta hsü'), composed probably in the Ch'in or early Han dynasty, which elaborated most fulsomely the political interpretation of poetry, that contained the statement of principle that Chou Tso-jen identified with the lyrical springs of poetry and all literary creation. The passage he was most fond of quoting (e.g. *Yüan-liu* p. 27) runs:

> The feelings are stirred within and take form in words. When words are not enough they are sung. When song is not enough unwittingly the hands and feet take up the rhythm.

[9] Quoted Chu Tzu-ch'ing, p. 3.

[10] Letter to Tom Moore, 1821, quoted M. H. Abrams, *The Mirror and the Lamp*, p. 49.

[11] op. cit., p. 26.

[12] 'Hsiang Kung', Years 16 and 27.

[13] Chu Tzu-ch'ing, p. 11, and Ch'ien Mu, *Chung-kuo wen-hsüeh chiang-yen chi* (Lectures on Chinese Literature), p. 92.

This is associated with the *shih yen chih* idea because of the preceding words: 'poetry is where the *chih* go. In the heart it is *chih*, when given voice it is poetry.' Chou's comment on this passage is: 'Literature has only feelings, no aim. If you have to state an aim, then its only aim is to give voice.' (*Yüan-liu*, pp. 27–8.)

It is true that in isolation the Great Preface passage gives the impression of regarding poetry as simply expressing feelings (*ch'ing*) – of seemingly diverse sorts – which are inwardly and most powerfully felt. But the relationship between these feelings and the *chih* mentioned in parallel is by no means clear. Chu Tzu-ch'ing[14] thinks the author is in fact thinking of poetry in two different ways. Firstly it had to do with government (the *chih* aspect); this is clear from the rest of the Preface: through poetry, we are given to understand, the 'former kings'

> regulated the duties of husband and wife, effectually inculcated filial obedience and reverence, secured attention to all the relations of society, adorned the transforming influence of instruction, and transformed manners and customs. (Legge, *The She King*, p. 34.)

Secondly the author had to recognize the spontaneous nature of the act of making poetry – 'the emotions are stirred within.'

These two ways of understanding the nature of poetry are different but not inherently contradictory. Any body of spontaneous occasional poetry would yield a fair incidence of positive attitudes which could qualify as *chih* in the then accepted sense. However the Preface, once launched on its Confucian way, acknowledges no exceptions; the emotions that the *Odes* express, however unaffected, are always politically sound: 'That [the *pien-feng* ('deviant airs')] should be produced by the feelings was in the nature of the people; that they should not go beyond the rules of propriety and righteousness was from the beneficent influence of the former kings.' (Legge, op. cit., p. 36.) Again, the Preface says that the Historiographers 'sang of their feelings' (*yin-yung ch'ing-hsing*) but only to deplore bad government. So Chou Tso-jen was right to quote from the Preface because it has the classic statement of the principle of spontaneity, of genuine, uncalculating feeling as the source of poetry, but right also not to quote any more from it, to illustrate his own conception of *shih yen chih*, for taken as a whole it represents an alien standpoint, that of literature participating in the political processes of the state.

The Preface recognizes that a certain type of poem or song has its roots in a man's personal circumstances: 'Thus when the affairs of a particular state reach down to a particular person, it is called 'air' [*feng*].' So too does the later work, the *Han shu*, but it continues the

[14] op. cit., p. 36.

tradition of seeing its value in acting as a gauge to the state of society. Thus the 'Shih huo chih' chapter notes how the people 'each sing of their affliction' when displaced by the winter ingress; these songs were then collected before the spring dispersal and processed by the official verse gatherers for the information of the emperor. Similarly the 'I wen chih' chapter harks back to the famous phrase from the *Book of History* and gives it a more modern gloss: 'The *Book* says: 'Poetry expresses *chih*, song gives melody to words.' Thus susceptibilities to sorrow and pleasure are moved and the sound of song comes forth.'[15]

This certainly seems to *equate chih* with ordinary human feelings. But again this proposition is not taken up for its aesthetic implications but for its political significance: 'The ruler by this means observes the people's *mores*, knows his successes and failures,' and so on.

Despite these limitations the concept of *chih* had been expanded in these Han dynasty writings, including the Great Preface. Chu argues (pp. 27–30) that a crucial new factor had been the rise of the individual poet. The first and most outstanding of them, Ch'ü Yüan, claimed to express his *chih* in the *Ch'u Tz'u*[16], yet he wrote very clearly of his personal predicament. His epic could still be regarded as basically admonitory in character, but in order to accommodate its personal aspect, poetic theory leaned more towards stressing the way an individual is worked on, how a poem is produced in response to stimuli, rather than as an act of commitment.

In Chu Tzu-ch'ing's opinion (p. 32), poetry only escaped from 'politics', which term is meant to include moral and ethical considerations, under the influence of the *yüeh-fu*,[17] but the decisive change in poetic *theory* came still later, in the Six Dynasties period. This period is generally regarded as an age of individualism. When states were so impermanent the 'object of address' must have been difficult to ascertain, and the individual cathartic function of literature should conversely have assumed greater importance. According to Shen Yüeh, it was only in the Chien-an period (A.D. 196–220) that self-conscious literature, that is, the deliberate framing of personal feelings in an aesthetically satisfying form, came into being: 'only then was literature woven with the fabric of the emotions, and substance clothed in literary guise.'[18]

[15] Both quoted by Chu, p. 24.

[16] 'Pei hui feng p'ien', quoted Chu, p. 28.

[17] 'Music Bureau' poems, the Han folksongs recorded by officials of the Music Bureau.

[18] From *Sung shu*, 'Hsieh Ling-yün chuan lun' (Biography of Hsieh Ling-yün), quoted Lo Ken-tse, *Chung-kuo wen-hsüeh p'i-p'ing shih*, I, p. 123.

Such a refinement in poetic practice inevitably gave rise to a refinement in theory. During the Han dynasty there had been noted further functions of poetry to supplement the basic *yen chih*, such as the *Han Shih*'s 'singing of food' ('the hungry sing of food') and 'singing of work' ('the toilers sing of work'), as well as the *Han shu*'s 'singing of afflictions',[19] – these were perhaps formulated to avoid the words *yen chih* because of their high-minded connotations – but it was Lu Chi, in about A.D. 300, who first coined the term which, if it did not replace *yen chih*, at least satisfactorily complemented it; it was 'poetry derives from the feelings' (*shih yüan-ch'ing*). The whole line from the *Wen fu* reads: 'Poetry deriving from the feelings is subtle and intricate,' or, in Chen Shih-hsiang's rather more ambitious translation: 'The lyric [*shih*], born of pure emotion, is gossamer fibre woven into the finest fabric.'[20] Li Shan of the T'ang dynasty, interpreting this passage in the *Wen Hsüan*[21] remarked that 'poetry is the means to *yen chih*, hence the expression "poetry deriving from the feelings",' but that does not, I think, mean that there is no difference between the two concepts, only that they are associated. The word *ch'i-mi* which forms the predicate of Lu Chi's formula, would be a poor epithet for verse of much gravity; on the contrary, it suggests something light and elegant. In the light of this, it would have been historically more apt if Chou had chosen the term *yüan ch'ing* rather than *yen chih* to set against *tsai tao*. But as time went on the distinction between them became blurred.

After Lu Chi critics showed a much more sophisticated awareness of the mechanisms of poetic creation. Even when writing in the dynastic history, which fosters a moralizing tone, Shen Yüeh provided a fairly broad definition of the origins of poetry: 'The people inherit the spirit of Heaven and Earth, are invested with the virtue of the Five Constants;[22] 'hard' and 'soft' come into play alternately, joy and anger possess the feelings separately. When the *chih* moves inwardly, song comes forth externally.'[23] We might note in passing that Shen seems to share Kung Ying-ta's conception of *chih* as activated feelings, but what his definition mainly reveals is a cognizance that poetry brings into play all the faculties of man, spiritual and moral, and involves the inconstants of temper and mood. His words can be seen as an elaboration of the 'sing of feelings' (*yin-yung ch'ing-hsing*) of the Great Preface, with the political proviso left out.

[19] All quoted Chu, pp. 24–5.
[20] *Anthology of Chinese Literature*, ed. Cyril Birch, p. 208.
[21] Shang-wu edition, I, p. 352.
[22] i.e. *jen* 'benevolence', *i* 'righteousness', *li* 'propriety', *chih* 'knowledge', and *hsin* 'trustworthiness'.
[23] 'Hsieh Ling-yün chuan lun', quoted Chu, p. 34.

The major critical work of the period of disunity, the *Wen-hsin tiao-lung* (*c.* A.D. 500), insists that poetry should not only embody but also sustain proper feelings, but this statement of principle is accompanied by the idea of a natural response to surroundings: 'Man is endowed with seven emotions. When stimulated by external objects, these emotions rise in response. In responding to objects one sings to express one's sentiment [*chih*]. All this is perfectly spontaneous.'[24] Again it looks as if the author, Liu Hsieh, identifies *chih* with *ch'ing* (the 'seven emotions'), the only distinction being that *chih* are in active state. Chu Tzu-ch'ing suggests that both Shen and Liu use the word *chih* inappositely out of respect for tradition.

Chung Jung, the author of *Shih P'in*, another important critical work of the early sixth century, shows the same sensitivity in other ways with regard to the tradition, but he does not confront the question of *shih yen chih* directly. When he might have used *chih* had he been writing in the old idiom he uses *i* (purport, meaning or idea) – or *ch'ing*, as when, after giving examples of changes in Nature and human affairs, he writes: 'All these various things agitate the human spirit; if not set out in poems how could [these poets'] purport [*i*] become clear? If not given prolonged utterance in song, how could their feelings [*ch'ing*] be displayed?'[25]

Further variations on the *chih* theme in the Six Dynasties period are not hard to find. Fan Yeh favoured the term *ch'ing-chih*, a simple way of resolving any difference between the two by joining them. In *Hou Han shu*[26] he says: 'Once the *ch'ing-chih* are moved, literary form assumes priority.' Rather more instructively, he says in a letter, with reference to literature: 'It is often said to be the repository for *ch'ing-chih*, hence the main thing should be sense, and the sense should be rendered in literary form.'[27] The conclusion seems inescapable that Fan Yeh understood *ch'ing-chih* to be the thought content of a work.

This progressive blurring of the historical meaning of *chih* did not pass unnoticed. P'ei Tzu-ye (A.D. 467–528) protested against it, bemoaning the decay of ancient poetic ideals. In the old days, he wrote in his 'Tiao ch'ung lun,'[28] poetry 'both embodied the prevailing

[24] 'Ming shih' chapter, trans. Vincent Shih, *The Literary Mind and the Carving of Dragons*, p. 32.

[25] *Shih p'in chu* (Annotated 'Categorization of Poetry'), Hong Kong, 1959, p. 5.

[26] *Hou Han shu*, 'Wen yüan chuan tsan', quoted Lo, I, 122.

[27] Lo, I, 24.

[28] 'On Petty Skills', quoted Chu, p. 35; also in Wang Huan-piao, *Chung-kuo wen-hsüeh p'i-p'ing lun wen chi* (Collected Essays in Chinese Literary Criticism), p. 39.

atmosphere in all parts of the empire, and emblazoned the ideals [*chih*] of the civilized man, encouraging the admirable and reprimanding the vile. Kingly education was rooted in it.' Nowadays, he went on, the practice was to 'sing of feelings' and of this he was highly contemptuous, for, ignoring the irreproachable origin of the phrase, he seemed to identify it with *yüan ch'ing*. Despite his attempt to restore the purity of the word *chih*, Chu Tzu-ch'ing shows how P'ei himself tended to use it interchangeably with *ch'ing* (p. 35), which demonstrates how common the confusion had become.

During the Six Dynasties then, *shih yen chih* was interpreted in two senses: one continued to be the narrow sense of aspirations, purpose, ideals; the other was the wide sense which embraced all kinds of feelings, including the purely personal and ephemeral.[29] Not historically as apt as the former, the latter usage represented deference to the Great Preface as defining *in toto* the function of poetry, though the theoretical horizons of literature had been greatly extended. Both usages persisted in later ages. For instance, Po Chü-i used *chih* to symbolize a positive attitude towards the common weal. In a letter to Yüan Chen he wrote: 'My ideal [*chih*] is the common weal, my practice is self-gratification . . . My poems classed as "remonstrative" belong to the ideal of the common weal; those classed as "idle" refer to self-gratification.'[30] And Shao Yung (1011–77), the Neo-Confucian philosopher, redefined *yen chih* as referring necessarily to the state of the times.[31] On the other hand, when Chang Chien (early twelfth century) in his *Sui han t'ang shih-hua*[32] drew a distinction between *yen chih* poetry and descriptive (*yung-wu*) poetry, it turned on the issue of whether the portrayal was charged with *feeling*; clearly he belonged in the second camp. The outstanding representative of this more comphrehensive school of thought was however Yüan Mei. With him we leave the field of academic accounting and enter that of popular knowledge.

Chu Tzu-ch'ing quotes two enlightening parallel passages from two different works of Yüan Mei on the subject (p. 39). The first is: '*Shih yen chih*: the working man thinking of his wife can *yen chih*; the '300 Poems' [i.e. the *Odes*] are not all the work of scholars.' The second is: 'The "300 Poems" are partly about working men thinking of their wives and expressing their feelings [*ch'ing*] at will.' These examples

[29] For further evidence, see Chu, pp. 33–4.

[30] 'Yü Yüan Chiu shu' (Letter to Yüan Chen), quoted Chu, p. 37. 'Remonstrative' and 'idle' are both section headings in his collection *Po shih ch'ang ch'ing chi*.

[31] Discussed by Kuo Shao-yü, '*History*', pp. 194–5.

[32] (Talks on Poetry from Sui han t'ang), in *Hsü li-tai shih hua* (Poetry Talks over the Ages, continuation).

show that Yüan used the terms *chih* and *ch'ing* synonymously. Elsewhere he explained the multiple aspects of *chih*: 'The poet has life-long *chih*, and *chih* of a day, has *chih* beyond the poem and *chih* beyond the matter, has *chih* which arise haphazardly, or when lingering among beautiful scenery, or on the spur of an event. The word *chih* cannot be pinned down.' Yüan's illustrations show that any kind of genuine emotional response, and not only the 'life-long' ambition, qualifies as *chih* in his book.

Famous though he was, Yüan Mei would not have had much personal influence on the broad mass of the literati of strictly Confucian persuasion, which still supported the demand for the kind of 'serious' poetry that would elevate and inspire the reader. The confident tone of his remarks does however seem justified, for my impression is that by his time his side had captured the slogan *shih yen chih* from the moralists, who seldom appealed to it again for authority.

Chu Tzu-ch'ing thinks Chou Tso-jen was influenced in his choice of terms by Yüan Mei's example (p. 40). Certainly they both seem to mean the same thing by '*shih yen chih*', though Chou extends the jurisdiction of the dictum to all literature. To him *yen chih* appears to be synonymous with the modern expression *shu ch'ing*, which is normally translated as 'lyrical' but does not necessarily have the intense personal and even rhapsodic connotations of the English word. The equation in his mind between the two is demonstrated by the opening sentence of his essay 'On the short poem': 'Actually poetry is something which expresses the feelings [*yen chih*]. Though it can also be used to relate or to reason, by its nature it is primarily lyrical [*shu ch'ing*].'[33] In preferring *yen chih* over its modern counterpart as a signpost to his preferences Chou was asserting his sense of continuity with the tradition, but not necessarily with Yüan Mei in particular. He was of course aware of Yüan's existence, but was not very taken with him.[34] He did acknowledge Chin Sheng-t'an as an early mentor,[35] though, and Chin's approach was very similar to Yüan's. Chin proposed the simple definition, 'what moves the heart and is uttered from the mouth is called poetry'[36] in order to explain the Great Preface passage on *shih* and *chih*. It may well have been Chin Sheng-t'an's influence which caused Chou to write in his diary in 1904: 'No matter on earth

33 'Lun hsiao shih', *Tzu-chi ti yüan-ti*, p. 53.

34 See 'Li-weng yü Sui-yüan' (Li Yü and Yüan Mei), *K'u chu tsa chi*, p. 83.

35 'Chiu jih-chi ch'ao' (Excerpts from my old diary), *Feng yü t'an*, p. 213. On Chin Sheng-t'an (1610? –61) see John Ching-yu Wang, *Chin Sheng-t'an*, New York, 1972.

36 Trans. James Liu, *The Art of Chinese Poetry*, p. 74.

can be divorced from the word 'feelings' [*ch'ing*]; this is the case with literature: feelingless works, though backed by strong reasoning, in the end cast a pall.'[37]

Chou Tso-jen, then, chose *shih yen chih* to stand for an attitude to literature to which the parallel in the West would be Wordsworth's premium on the 'spontaneous overflow of powerful feelings'. Such a view could be thought incomplete, but hardly in itself a matter of dispute. Its real significance lay in its use as a rallying point for those opposed to the contending view of 'literature as a vehicle for the Way.' In fact the two are not in principle mutually exclusive. To the Confucianist the Way was natural to man, hence spontaneous feelings conformed to the Way. Furthermore, the two dicta both could be and were taken to apply to different provinces; some writers consciously distinguished certain forms of literature where *tsai tao* pertained, others where *yen chih* was proper, including the arch-advocate of *yen chih*, Yüan Mei, whose attitude Kuo Shao-yü sums up as 'in poetry [*shih*] stressing native sensibility [*hsing-ling*],[38] in prose [*wen*] emphasizing soundness [*yu-pen*]' (op. cit., p. 485). However, in the first case to advocate *wen i tsai tao* was not only to expect writing to conform to the Way (in the Confucian phrase, to have 'no evil thoughts' [*ssu wu hsieh*]), but also to uphold and impart the dogma; and in the second case, as we have indicated, *wen* was commonly taken not simply as the alternative to *shih*, but as a blanket term for literature in general. So if the terms *shih yen chih* and *wen i tsai tao* themselves could be seen as a formula for coexistence on the basis of division of territory, in fact they represented more often than not monistic ways of thought which contended for absolute supremacy. The nature of the conflict will I hope emerge more clearly from the summary of the *tsai tao* position that follows.

The idea of an association between *wen* and *tao* has a long history, and as with *yen chih* views diverged on its nature. One problem which immediately arises is, as mentioned above, what particular *tao* is meant where such a connection is made. Every school of thought in China had its own *tao*, so with this background *tao* might simply mean truth, philosophy or morality. Some association between literature and truth or moral values is common in theories of literature formulated all over the world, in ancient and modern times. Aristotle stated that poetry expressed universal truths. Horace matched 'pleasure' with 'instruction.' Dante, Boccaccio, and Petrarch all regarded themselves as more or less subtle revealers of the truth. Sydney's *Defence of Poesie* asserted that

[37] As n. 35, p. 219.

[38] 'Native sensibility' is a term coined by James Liu, *The Art* . . ., p. 74.

poetry had a good moral influence. Romantics such as Shelley, Schiller and Hugo all believed in the moral purpose of literature, and today the teaching of English Literature has been defended as producing a civilized (and virtuous) man. So too have Chinese literary theorists used *tao* without a trademark. T'u Kung-sui believes[39] that Liu Hsieh conceived of it as 'the best that is known and thought in the world' when he wrote: 'The *tao* has been given lasting expression in writing through the agency of the sages, the sages throw light on the *tao* through their writing.'[40] T'u is not very fastidious in fathering Arnold's sentiment on Liu Hsieh, but he is not the only one to think that Liu's meaning is at least non-particular, that he is thinking along the general lines indicated in the first words of the *Chung Yung* (Doctrine of the Mean) – which Ch'ien Mu regards as synthesizing Confucianism and Taoism:[41] 'What is ordained by Heaven is called [human] nature, what conforms to nature is called the Way.' Chu Hsi's interpretation of this passage is: '*Tao* is like a path. If people and things all follow their natural bent, then all of the normal business of life has its path to follow: this is what *tao* is.'[42] *Tao* here appears to be close to natural law. Huang K'an too thinks that *tao* in the *Wen-hsin tiao-lung* is simply the reason why things are as they are.[43] It was certainly along these lines that Liu Hsieh framed his definition of *wen*. Drawing on the word's basic meaning of pattern, grain, markings, he compared *wen* in man to the configurations described in the sky by the heavenly bodies and those marked on the face of the earth by mountains and rivers: on the human level *wen* reflects, so to speak, the natural contours of the mind. The fact remains, however, that Liu Hsieh saw the *tao* exemplified in the Confucian classics, and it is this view, more narrowly interpreted, which is the bone of contention in the Chinese historical context.

Wen i tsai tao *historically*

As Chou Tso-jen sas in *Yüan-liu* (p. 39), the slogan 'literature as a vehicle for the Way' was coined by a 'Sung man'. The man in question was Chou Tun-i, the Neo-Confucian philosopher. But Chou laid the main responsibility (and the blame) for this Confucian doctrine at the

39 *Wen-hsüeh kai-lun*, (General Discussion of Literature), p. 82.
40 'Yüan tao' chapter.
41 *Chung-kuo wen-hsüeh chiang-yen chi*, p. 115.
42 Quoted Su Hsüeh-lin, *Chiu ke chung jen shen lien-ai wen-t'i* (The Problem of Love between Man and God in the Nine Songs), p. 147.
43 *Wen hsin tiao lung cha chi* (Notes on the *Wen hsin tiao lung*), quoted Kuo, p. 106.

door of Han Yü, of the T'ang dynasty, to whom we will come in due course. Han Yü himself stood in a long line of Confucian literary dogmatists, and we had best look first at some of his predecessors.

We have already caught a glimpse of Confucian teachings being applied to literature in the Han exegesis of the *Odes*. There are indications in the *Lun yü* itself that the *Odes* can be of service in practical politics and moral education.[44] Mencius too seems to include the *Odes* in the category of political writing by bracketing it with the Ch'un-ch'iu (thought to combine crhonicle and criticism) in his statement: 'After the *Odes* waned the *Spring and Autumn Annals* were written.'[45] But as is usually the case the hard doctrine came from those who interpreted the word. Thus it is stated in the commentary to *Shih p'u hsü*, by Cheng Hsüan (A.D. 127–200), the famous classical scholar: 'The *Odes* have three exegeses: receiving, aspiring and upholding. The author, receptive to the rights and wrongs of the government of his prince, composes songs to set out his own aspirations. The making of the songs is the means to uphold people's conduct, and prevent lapses.'[46] This emphasis on the social function and ethical contribution of the *Odes* is typical of Cheng's *Shih p'u hsü*.[47] As influential as Cheng Hsüan was Yang Hsiung, who not only insisted on a severe attitude to writing, exemplified in the proposition 'If writing is not based on the Classics, it is non-writing; if words are not based on the Classics they are non-words,'[48] but according to both Chu Kuang-ch'ien and Su Hsüeh-lin[49] was primarily responsible for restricting *tao* to Confucianism. That this was his intention is clear enough from the above quotation; it is made doubly clear in his unequivocal assertion: 'What approximates to the teachings of Yao, Shun and King Wen is the proper *tao*. What conflicts with the teachings of Yao, Shun and King Wen is a heretical way.'[50] This attitude did not die with the

[44] For instance, a passage in Book 13, 'Tzu lu', reads: 'Even if the Odes can be recited by heart, if they are applied without good results in governing, and if they cannot be individually turned to [allusive] use in diplomacy, however much [they are recited] it is all in vain.' This implies that the *Odes* when properly exploited *can* be of use in governing and diplomacy. I follow the interpretation of Aoki Masaru, *Chung-kuo wen-hsueh ssu-hsiang shih kang* (Outline History of Chinese Literary Thought), p. 18.

[45] Book 4, pt. 2, section 21.

[46] Quoted Wang Meng-ou, *Wen-hsüeh kai-lun*, p. 227.

[47] Lo, I, 78–80.

[48] *Yang-tzu fa yen*, 'Wen shen' chapter, *Chu tzu chi ch'eng*, VII, 14; quoted Chu Kuang-ch'ien, *Wen-i hsin-li hsüeh* (The Psychology of Literature), p. 99.

[49] *Chiu ke . . .*, p. 149.

[50] In 'Wen tao' chapter, *Chu tzu chi ch'eng*, VII, 9.

Han, the great age of classical exegesis. In the relatively open-minded Wei-Chin period Huan Fan was clearly referring to Confucianism when he wrote: 'Creative works and dissertations should open up the great *tao*, expound the saintly teachings, extend the known principles of things, go to the bottom of feelings, note rights and criticize wrongs, so as to provide a standard.'[51]

The succeeding age of the Six Dynasties is always associated in literary history with concentration on form at the expense of content, with frivolous themes and playful attitudes. To the Confucian such writing betokened political decay (*wang kuo chih yin*). It was natural that with the restoration of political unity and order there should have gone a campaign to restore a sound and disciplined literature. So one finds in the Sui dynasty such tracts as Li E's 'Letter requesting the rectification of the mode of literature' ('Ch'ing cheng wen-t'i shu'):

> I have heard that the way of the ancient philosopher kings in educating the people was to alter their perceptions, guard against their addictions, stifle their wicked thoughts, and show them the simple and moderate way. *The Odes, History, Book of Rites* and the *Changes* were the gateway to right and reason . . . Memorials and prose-poems, funeral orations and epitaphs, in praising virtue and grading worth brought merit to light and testified to the fitness of things . . . But in later ages morals and education fell into decline, and the rulers of Wei (the three Ts'aos) prized the art of words and neglected the great Way of prince and subject for the petty techniques of ornamental composition. Their example was followed throughout society . . . In the southern states of Ch'i and Liang the rot spread wider. All conditions of men devoted themselves to minstrelsy. Consequently they put aside what was right and preserved what was unusual; they sought after the empty and trivial, competed to find exotic rhymes and striking phrases. All their writings were filled with 'moon and dew', 'wind and clouds'. Reputations and appointments were made on this basis, material rewards encouraged such pursuits . . . and no-one cared about or gave ear to [the scriptures] . . . But when the great Sui dynasty received the mandate the saintly way was restored, shallow rhetoric and dressed-up pretentiousness were done away with.
> (From *Ch'üan Sui wen*, reproduced in Yang Chia-lo, *Wen-hsüeh p'i-p'ing wen hsüan* vol. I.)

As this epistle was presented to the Sui emperor it is not surprising that the author should have described the achievement of the dynasty in glowing terms. By common consent however the empire had to wait for Han Yü two hundred years later to raise it from the decadence that Li E so energetically deplores.

[51] In *Shih yao lun*, 'Hsü tso' chapter, quoted Chu Kuang-ch'ien, *Wen-i hsin-li hsüeh*, p. 100.

In the phrase of Su Shih, Han Yü's 'writing lifted the debility of eight ages'. This tribute is matched by 'his Way relieved the depravity of the empire.'[52] The association of Han Yü with the Way is natural, for he rarely left the subject, but he himself created no slogans connecting *wen* and *tao*. This was left to his student, Li Han, who ascribed to him, in the first words of his preface to Han's collected works *Han Ch'ang-li chi*, the view that 'literature is the means of holding together the *tao*.' The identical words had been used before, by Wang T'ung of the Sui dynasty: 'Is scholarship just extensive reading? It must also hold together the *Tao*. Is literature just writing? it must also serve righteousness.'[53] But Han Yü had the prestige and therefore was given credit for the doctrine. His views on the relationship between *wen* and *tao* are hard to pin down with apt quotation, but the following are often picked out:

> How could my appreciation for 'ancient prose' [*ku-wen*] be in the words and phrases being different from today's? You may think of the men of old, but they are not before you. To emulate the ancient *tao* you should at the same time be versed in their language; the desire to become versed in their language is the outcome of one's mind being set on their *tao*. ('T'i Ou-yang Sheng ai tz'u hou.')
> You say that in my conduct I do not contravene the teachings of Confucius, and do not direct my art to trivial ornamentation, and that you would follow me in these respects. How would I dare be jealous of my *tao* and abdicate my responsibilities [by refusing my help]? But in devoting my thought to antiquity it is not simply that I love the language, it is that I love the *tao* in it. (Ta Li Hsiu ts'ai shu')[54]

Though the burden of these statements is on doctrinal purity, Han Yü did not ignore the part which language played. So much is evident from this analogy: 'If a man does not possess all his limbs he is not a whole man; if your command of language is inadequate you cannot write.'[55] One had to be aware of the subtleties of language both to understand the meaning of the sages and to be able to convey one's own meaning. Hence his insistence that in *wen* there is neither easy nor hard, only right.[56] His attitude was summed up in the statement: 'As

[52] From 'Ch'ao-chou Han Wen-kung miao pei', reproduced in Yang Chia-lo, *Wen-hsüeh p'i-p'ing wen hsüan* (Anthology of Literary Criticism), II.
[53] *Chung shuo*, 'T'ien ti' chapter, quoted Su Hsüeh-lin, *Chiu ke . . .*, p. 150.
[54] Both these passages are quoted by Su Hsüeh-lin, pp. 150–1.
[55] ibid., 'Ta Wei Ch'ih sheng shu'.
[56] 'Ta Liu Cheng-fu shu', quoted Fu Keng-sheng, *Chung-kuo wen-hsüeh p'i-p'ing t'ung lun*, p. 103.

to the *tao* of the sages, if letters [*wen*] are not used then that is that; if letters are used then competence must be valued.'[57]

Han's friend and contemporary Liu Tsung-yüan was, according to Kuo Shao-yü (op. cit., pp. 117–118), even more intent on *wen* than he, but this opinion is based on inference. In his considered pronouncements Liu definitely fixed *tao* as the goal, warning that *wen* pursued for its own sake was a dangerous distraction. The light had apparently dawned only gradually though;

> At first when I was young and immature, I regarded diction as the skill to cultivate in writing. But when I grew older I realized that *wen* exists to make clear the *tao* . . . Everything I set out [on paper] I myself think of as approximating to the *tao*, but I do not know if the *tao* is actually near or far. Since you love the *tao* and approve of my writing, perhaps it is not far from the *tao* ('Ta Wei Chung-li lun shih tao shu', quoted Lo, II, p. 148.)

Representing the part that *wen* played was his argument that it was a fault both to have 'outer veneer' but 'nothing inside', and to have 'something inside' but no outer veneer:[58] and his recognition, expressed elsewhere, that for knowledge of *tao* to spread it had to be transmitted through the written word, so a mutual dependence was created.[59]

The latter attitude, shared by both Liu and Han, derives authority from Confucius, who is reported in the *Tso chuan*[60] as saying: 'Without elegant composition of the words, they will not go far.' It is this prominence they gave to form as well as content which distinguishes them from others of like persuasion: 'literati' they were, well and truly. But the duality was not an equal one: the art of letters was important, but only as a means. For *wen* to have lasting worth it must embody the *tao*. As a final qualification it must be remarked that the last consideration was cardinal to their discussion; they seemed to be thinking of *wen* as the kind of writing that was to be disseminated among their contemporaries and handed down to later generations – their contribution to the literary heritage. Their strictures did not necessarily apply to all kinds of writing. As Kuo Shao-yü points out (p. 119), *wen* in Han Yü's book refers only to prose, whereas, in some places at least, Liu Tsung-yüan includes poetry as well, but these are still very broad categories and may include sub-types which are not judged so rigorously; Han Yü himself has some famous prose pieces that

[57] Same letter, this time quoted Lo, II, 142.
[58] 'Ta Tou Lu-yen hsiu ts'ai nan yu hsü', quoted Fu Keng-sheng, *T'ung lun*, p. 116.
[59] 'Pao Ts'ui An hsiu-ts'ai shu', quoted Lo, II, 147.
[60] 'Hsiang Kung', Year 25; Legge, *The Chinese Classics*, V, 512.

only a very fertile imagination would link with any *tao* whatsoever, and Liu is famous for his landscape essays. Still, in their doctrinal pronouncements they did not care to note these exceptions, so it was presumably in the uncompromising form that *tao* must have absolute priority that their views exerted influence.

Doctrinally Han and Liu were both more severe than some of their outstanding T'ang predecessors and more lenient than their Sung successors who wrote on the role of *tao* in literature. Liu Mien is an example of the former. He 'flourished' only one generation before Han Yü, but while being also very concerned about the moral influence of literature, his view was more broadly based, most notably in seeing *tao* and *ch'ing* (feelings) as one. The absence of *ch'ing* would, he wrote[61], sound the death-knell for benevolence, probity, kindness and integrity, virtues which embody the *tao* in the sphere of human relationships. More human than Han Yü, he inclines more towards practical influence than moral rectitude, so his emphasis is on edification or 'enculturation' (*chiao-hua*) rather than on an abstract *tao*. But given this difference his allegiance to the traditional culture is still absolute: 'If the philosophy of literature is not rooted in edification, it is just a technique'[62] and 'Literature is rooted in edification and evinces itself in the affections [*ch'ing-hsing*]. Being rooted in edification is true of the *tao* of Yao and Shun, evincing itself in the affections is true of the words of the sages.'[63]

Liu Mien saw the perfect and complete literature of the classical period as reflecting the perfectly integrated ideal polity of the time. *Wen* summed up the practice and was the mark of the culture of the gentleman (*chün-tzu*) in all that he did, and 'not to be able to make his words *wen* was the ignominy of the gentleman.'[64]

When this harmonious society deteriorated, literature and the Teaching became divided. Such a situation Liu of course could not approve:

> Confucians of superior quality must have their *tao*. For there to be *tao* there must be *wen*. If *tao* does not link up with *wen* then the moral intent will be overpowering; if *wen* does not acquaint itself with *tao* then the impetus is weak. If *wen* is in plentiful supply and *tao* is scarce, then the result is trivialism. The *Analects* say: 'When the art and substance are in due proportion, then we have the gentleman.' Excellence lies in combining the two. (*Ch'in ting ch'üan T'ang wen*, 537/14, quoted Lo, II, 131.)

61 In 'Ta Ching-nan P'ei shang shu lun wen shu', quoted Lo, II, 130.
62 'Hsieh Tu hsiang kung lun fang Tu erh hsiang kung shu', quoted Kuo, p. 108.
63 'Ta Hsü-chou Chang shang shu lun wen shu', quoted Kuo, pp. 108–9.
64 As n. 61, Lo, II, 131.

Liu's broad definition of *wen* is an indication of what might be called his culturalism: it was a manifestation of civilization, and indispensable to all forms of expression in that it conferred order and elegance. Though it was nothing by itself, it was not a snare and delusion. The sentiment that *wen* was positively a snare and delusion, Han Yü and Liu Tsung-yüan sometimes aired, but the Sung Neo-Confucians took it as their by-word.

The formula of Chou Tun-i (1017–73) that literature was a 'vehicle' for the Way may be taken as an index of the attitude of the Neo-Confucians. It was not an empty metaphor. He indeed thought of *wen* as a cart; moreover, the 'cart' should be as plain as could be: 'To decorate the wheels and shafts, and then for people not to use it, is empty decoration – even more so when the cart is empty.'[65] This clearly imputes a lowly role to the art of letters, and though he goes on to acknowledge the contribution of this art in facilitating the transmission of the *tao*, his view is more holistic than that of the T'ang writers we have been discussing: he is intent, that is to say, solely and soberly – and one feels more genuinely than Han Yü – on the *tao*. The same can be said of Ch'eng I (1032–1107), but he goes further than Chou Tun-i, and states what surely must be the most extreme position that the moralists could hold. His most famous comment on the relationship between *wen* and *tao* is this:

> Someone asked: does literary art [*wen*] harm the *tao*? Master Ch'eng replied: 'It does. All literary art which does not absorb the attention is not well done. If the attention is absorbed then the will is confined to this. Then how can [the man] share the greatness of Heaven and Earth? The 'Book of History' says: 'Amusements dissipate the will.' Literary art is also an amusement . . . The scholars of old only devoted themselves to cultivating their human nature: other things they did not apply themselves to. Those who write nowadays devote themselves solely to the art of composition, to please people's senses. Since they are intent on pleasing people, if they are not jesters, what are they? (*Ho-nan Ch'eng Shih i-shu*, quoted Lo, III, 74–5.)

The great figure in Neo-Confucianism, Chu Hsi (1130–1200), makes explicit this implied rejection of Han Yü's dualistic attitude in the following dialogue recorded in his *Yü lei* (Colloquies) no. 139. Chu's disciple has expressed interest in Li Han's phrase about Han Yü's work, '*wen* is the means of holding together the *tao*'; the master reproves him:

> *Chu*: You commend [the expression], but in my opinion there is something wrong with it.
> *Disciple*: '*Wen* is the means of holding together the *tao*.' The Six

[65] *T'ung shu*, 'Wen tz'u' chapter, quoted Kuo, p. 156, and Lo, III, 73.

> Classics for example are all literature [*wen*]. All it speaks of is this principle; where is the fault?
> *Chu*: Not so. *Wen* all flows from the *tao*, how can you say that *wen* holds together the *tao*? *Wen* is *wen* and *tao* is *tao*: *wen* is just what makes the diet palatable. If you regard *wen* as holding together the *tao* you are reversing the order of things. Later writers have all made this mistake. (Taiwan Cheng-chung shu chü ed., vol. VIII, p. 5309, quoted Kuo, p. 202.)

It is clear from this that Chu Hsi objects to the idea of *wen* and *tao* as two entities working in parallel, but it is not absolutely clear whether the two are separable. It was his normal view that they were not. As he explains in a letter to Lü Po-kung:

> Are *wen* and *tao* actually the same or different? If there are things which exist outside the *tao*, then the writer may talk nonsense just as he pleases without harming the *tao*. It is because there is nothing outside the *tao* that if there should be one word at odds with the *tao*, the only difference in the harm is between gradual and immediate, superficial and profound, (Ta Lü Po-kung, *Chu Wen-kung wen chi* p. 33, quoted Lo, III, 191.)

Another passage explains what Chu Hsi meant by '*wen* flows from the *tao*'. It comes from 'Colloquies', no. 139:

> *Tao* is the root and trunk of *wen*, *wen* is the leaves and branches of *tao*: because it is rooted in *tao*, what is put forth in *wen* is all *tao*.[66] The sages of the Three Dynasties all produced their works in this state of mind, so their *wen* was *tao*. In the present age, [Su] Tung-p'o says: 'What I call *wen* must go hand in hand with *tao*,' which is to see *wen* and *tao* as independent. When he goes to compose *wen* he hunts for a *tao* to put into it, and this is his great fault. (Quoted Lo, III, p. 191.)

Given this organic relationship, then, with *wen* being just the visible part of *tao*, it follows that the quality of *wen* depends on comprehension of *tao*, not on studying the art of letters.

> Nowadays those who study letters [*wen*] have never been able to produce a [good] piece; they have simply wasted a lot of effort. Those who have devoted themselves to learning in order to understand the true nature of things write good prose as a matter of course. The same applies to poetry. (ibid., quoted Lo, III, 192.)

[66] This is not of course the first use of this metaphor. Hsü Kan wrote at the end of the Han: 'Art is the branches and leaves of virtue, virtue is the root and trunk of man. These two things are not equally weighted, nor are they independent. If a man is without art he cannot perfectly complement his virtue, hence he is called "uncouth". If one were to be a gentleman should one not unite them? ' (Quoted Takeda Sakae, *Chung-kuo wen-i ssu-hsiang* (Chinese Literary Thought, p. 9.)

Chu Hsi has many other passages in the same vein, all insisting that if a man has *tao* in his heart his writing cannot but have classical grace and substance (*tien shih*), and conversely if the writing has not this quality then the reason is that the man has not a firm grasp of the Truth. Given the premise that there are no amoral topics which would permit the individual to express himself as he pleased ('nothing exists outside the *tao*'), but on the contrary that there is a revealed truth which embraces all aspects of life, what place is there for wayward idiosyncracies licensed in the name of *wen*, that most potent gift of the gods? The conscientious custodian of that truth like Chu Hsi could not believe otherwise. Within the framework of that belief Chu Hsi's views are probably the most sensible. He was also, though this is not the place to demonstrate it, a very perceptive critic.

In the literary field it was the leaders of the *ku-wen* movement, and in the philosophical field the Sung Neo-Confucians, who defined the tradition that came down to Chou Tso-jen. As Neo-Confucianism remained the intellectual orthodoxy for the duration of the Chinese empire, the extent of the authority of their literary doctrine is obvious, though as these Sung and later exponents of the view that the Confucian philosophy should dominate literature always complained about their contemporaries not following their guiding light, it is questionable how far the creative artist was bound by their ruling. There was of course available the alternative theory – perhaps it is better described simply as an attitude – of artistic creation that belongs to Taoism, and presumably in any case genius will always out. Nevertheless, as we have already suggested, the *ex cathedra* pronouncements of Confucian authorities could be expected to have had a considerable influence on the broad mass of writing. Their influence seems to have been most widely felt – and most pernicious, in Chou's view – in the Ch'ing dynasty into which he was born.

There had according to Chou been a glimmer of light on the horizon with the emergence of the Kung-an and Ching-ling schools at the end of the Ming, but it was soon clouded over in the succeeding Ch'ing dynasty. Chou Tso-jen (in *Yüan-liu*, p. 88) attributes the final discrediting of the advocacy for a spontaneous literature that these schools supported to Chang Hsüeh-ch'eng (Shih-chai), the outstanding Ch'ing historian. Chang was indeed firmly opposed to 'belles lettres' and all that implies, and was in favour of a 'literature of knowledge', to use De Quincey's phrase. His *tao* was not the Confucian revealed truth, rather was it the historian's kind of truth, the significance in events: '*Tao* is the reason why things are, not how they ought to be.'[67] His own formula was; 'Literature [*wen*] is indeed the means of conveying the

[67] *Wen shih t'ung i*, 'Yüan tao' chapter, Hong Kong, 1964, p. 34.

principle of things.'[68] However broadly this might be interpreted it is still opposed to *shih yen chih.*[69]

It is true that Chang was a master of vituperation, and he contributed greatly to the reputation of his locality K'uai-chi (present-day Shao-hsing) for producing acid-tongued scribes (*shih-ye*), a tradition carried on in modern times by Lu Hsün, but Chou credits him with this particular demolition job on the Kung-an succession in order to suit his own temporary purposes. These literary rebels were in any case in the process of being smothered by the T'ung-ch'eng school, the most influential school of thought in the Ch'ing dynasty, to which Chou gave due attention and by which he gives the impression of having been personally menaced. Chou thought them worse than the Eight (*ku-wen*) Masters of T'ang and Sung whose style they followed because they tried to be holier than they: what they aimed for, he says, was to write as well as the Eight Masters, and at the same time to be as ideologically correct as the Sung philosophers (*Yüan-liu*, p. 78). Because Chou and other leaders of the literary revolution grew up in the last years of the Ch'ing empire, when the prestige of the T'ung-ch'eng school was still high, a rather full exposition of its literary doctrine is called for (and is given in Appendix A), but for now a few quotations will suffice to show how fully the school was committed to the doctrine of *wen i tsai tao*. Thus Fang Pao (1668–1749), the progenitor of the school:

> What does not expound the *tao* and assist the Teaching, what is not concerned with proper human relationships and public morals, should not be carelessly undertaken. ('Lei Hung Ts'ui t'ing pu shu', quoted Chiang Shu-ke, *T'ung-ch'eng wen-p'ai p'ing shu* p. 23.)

and Yao Nai (1732–1815), the main prop of the school:

> Do not lightly set anything on paper unless your words serve to elucidate the meaning of the Classics which eluded previous scholars. ('Fu Ts'ao Yün-lu shu', quoted Chiang, p. 39.)
> How could one think that the writing of the ancients only consists of *wen*? To explain ethical principles, to uphold public morals, to be a guide to society, this is the calling of the civilized man [*chün-tzu*]. And the form of words adequate fully to express his calling is the *wen* of the civilized man. ('Fu Wang chin-shih Hui-tsu shu', ibid.)

To judge by these words the basic theory of the T'ung-ch'eng school was the same as before, only more so. The effect, combined with the ideological control exercised by the Manchus, must indeed have been stultifying.

[68] *Wen shih t'ung i*, 'Pien ssu' chapter, p. 75.
[69] For Chang's theory of literature see David Nivison, *The Life and Thought of Chang Hsüeh-ch'eng*, esp. pp. 134–138.

The doctrine of *wen i tsai tao* has now been followed chronologically, but a word must still be said about literary anthologies. What was the message for the person who sought not uplifting discourses from the pundits but a selection of the great literature of the past? It depends on who the editors were (for a great many anthologies were put together), but the prefaces to some of the later important ones offered them no different theoretical fare. Fang Hsiao-yüeh, in his book *Chung-kuo wen-hsüeh p'i-p'ing* (Chinese Literary Criticism), is the only person I know who has singled out anthologies for special attention. I now borrow some of his examples.

In his preface to his collection *Wen-chang cheng-tsung*, which gathers prose and verse from Pre-Ch'in times down to Sung, Chen Te-hsiu (1178–1235) erects 'grasping the ultimate truths and putting them to use' (*ch'iung li erh chih yung*) as his principle. He explains:

> The main consideration in selecting these pieces from past and present is their elucidation of ethical principles and their being of direct service to society. Only those whose form is basically ancient and whose purport is similar to the Classics have been chosen. Other pieces, even where the diction is accomplished, have been excluded. (Quoted Fang, p. 152.)

That these were not empty words is attested to by Liu K'e-chuang, to whom Chen Te-hsiu entrusted the task of selecting the poetry. In his *Hou-ts'un shih-hua* he tells how severe Chen had been in pruning his selection on moral grounds.[70] Chen, incidentally, was the first man to link Han Yü, Liu Tsung-yüan, Ou-yang Hsiu, Su Hsün, Su Shih, Su Ch'e, Tseng Kung and Wang An-shih as the Eight Masters of T'ang and Sung (*T'ang Sung pa ta chia*).[71]

Hsieh Fang-te (1226–89), though he did not identify the 'Eight Masters' as such, was clearly predisposed to favour them in his *Wen-chang kui fan*. Out of sixty-nine examples, fifty-nine belong to them. One is not surprised to learn from his disciple Wang Yüan-chi in his postscript to the collection that Hsieh's intention was to 'make manifest the right way and [Confucian] integrity'.

The person who made the grouping of the Eight Masters famous was Mao K'un (1512–1601), through his well-known anthology *T'ang Sung*

[70] Quoted Fang Hsiao-yüeh, *Chung-kuo wen-hsüeh p'i-p'ing*, p. 152. Ku Yen-wu also criticized Chen for overlooking individual merit in dismissing wholesale periods like the Six Dynasties, though he approved of the general intention to uphold moral standards (the relevant passage from his *Jih chih lu* is quoted in Fu Keng-sheng, *T'ung lun*, pp. 112–13).

[71] According to the *Chung-wen ta tz'u-tien* (Encyclopaedic Dictionary of the Chinese Language), VI, 351.

pa ta chia wen ch'ao. In his preface Mao says he regards them all as following the principles that Confucius observed in editing the Classics. More interestingly, Mao rejects the broader cultural theory which ties literature to the quality of the age in which it is written in favour of the more puritanical view of relating literature to faith in the *tao*: '*Wen* only thrives or declines in accordance with *tao*; the times do not come into the question.' (Quoted Fang, p. 222.)

In the Ch'ing dynasty the particular byword was *ch'ing chen ya cheng*, as untranslatable a phrase as could be found, but meaning something like 'immaculate, refined, and correct'. It came appropriately from an edict of the tenth year of the Yung-cheng period (1733), and was widely cited by compilers of prose anthologies. It was also employed by Fang Pao in his preface to his collection of examination essays put together at imperial behest called *Ch'in ting ssu shu wen*, in the variant form *ch'ing cheng ku ya*. It was meant to apply beyond examination essays to literature in general (Fang, p. 264).

The impression should not be given that the Chinese under the empire were limited to such anthologies as these for their reading matter. Doubtless the mature reader could find a satisfactory amount of heretical material also, though censorship might have made it difficult to maintain a proper balance. But in education and particularly in preparing for the state examinations both the philosophy of literature to be imbibed and the models to be followed were as described above.

Having now learned something of the substance behind the slogans *shih yen chih* and *wen i tsai tao* we know better what Chou Tso-jen was for and what he was against. To ask what subtle refinements he himself introduced to the argument would be unproductive: the answer would be none. The interest lies, rather, in his reasons for taking up so uncompromising a stance on the subject. It was not merely with him a judicious preference for the one theory as against the other, the issue had the character of a personal vendetta.

To provide a standard of comparison, the contemporary literary critic Chu Kuang-ch'ien when appraising the two concepts did not baulk at the idea of *wen i tsai tao*. Though he could not admit the proposition in its narrow sense of moral teaching, he attempted to reconcile *tao* and *chih* by interpreting the former as the nature of human life and society, in which case *chih*, being the truthful expression of what lies in the human heart, fits into the framework of *tao*, and there is no conflict.[72] This is to take a detached and relative view of the question, and betokens a willingness to make allowances for the literary theorists of the past being limited by their cultural assumptions and to extract their general principles from their Con-

[72] *T'an wen-hsüeh* (On Literature), pp. 8–9.

fucian background. But Chu Kuang-ch'ien is a younger man and a scholar of modern education. Chou Tso-jen grew up when China was still the old China, when *tao* was still *the tao*, when what was lacking in public was the honest expression of honest feelings, while cant was plentiful. Chou remarked in later years[73] that the old Reformists are sometimes more radical than post-revolutionary youth, 'giving not an inch to the old forces and the old ways of thought, because they know better the suffering they cause'. The point is pertinent here: to Chou the term *wen i tsai tao* symbolized the worst thing about Chinese literary culture, the closed mind and the dead hand. So for him as for the other leaders of the May Fourth movement, the response to this aspect of their Chinese tradition as well as others was in absolute terms. He does not pause to reason what *tao* might mean; his purpose is not to consider but to condemn.

In the first instance, Chou's opposition to the *tsai tao* idea is on the grounds of the harm it did to Chinese intellectual and cultural life, judged by the record. As a young man he personally, like all aspiring intellectuals under the empire, had practised the 'eight-legged essay' (*pa-ku-wen*). This was the supreme embodiment (or *reductio ad absurdum*) of the *tsai tao* precept. Originally designed for the state examinations, and composed in eight prescribed steps to a given theme, it was meant to test the candidate's grasp of Confucian doctrine. Chou had already described it as the quintessence of a literary culture which had the idea of 'speaking on behalf of the sages'.[74] Now in *Yüan-liu* he explains that what the essay taught, since the content could arouse no interest, was ingenious word-play and the all-importance of sound patterns (*sheng-tiao*): it did not matter what the thing meant as long as the rhythm was right. To get the spirit of the eight-legged essay you needed to wag your head as you read, as Lu Hsün described their own teacher doing in 'Morning flowers gathered at dusk'.[75] The same principle applied, Chou found, far beyond the scope of the eight-legged essay, affecting for example the attitude to the theatre, where attention was paid only to the sound. The frame of mind that this bias reflects was clearly not the best suited to produce a healthy culture or practical new ideas.

But in *Yüan-liu* Chou is not merely working off a grudge against the Chinese tradition, he is writing a tract for his times. For though the eight-legged essay was dead, it lived on, in fact its kind was multiplied. In its extended sense the name denoted anything written in

[73] 'Tzu-chi so neng tso ti' (What I can do), *Ping chu hou t'an*, p. 5.
[74] 'Lun pa-ku-wen' (On the Eight-legged Essay), 1930, *K'an yün chi*.
[75] *Yüan-liu*, Lecture 3. Lu Hsün's remark is in 'San wei shu wu' (Three-taste Studio), *Lu Hsün ch'üan chi* (Complete Works), II, 256.

an approved convention and expressing the currently required sentiments; one was not required to show knowledge of the subject one was dealing with. Chou quotes Wu Chih-hui as saying that the 'native' eight-legged essay had been succeeded by the 'foreign' eight-legged essay, and now they had the 'Party' eight-legged essay.[76] For his own part Chou added, in 1936,[77] another species, 'new native' eight-legged essay, to eke out his description of the contemporary literary product. The effect of being drawn into the maw of this machine was the debasement of the currency of thought, so that even the best imported ideas were given the kiss of death.[78]

If Chou's description of the contemporary literary scene is rather too bleak, it is quite true both that foreign models were imitated indiscriminately and that in the '30s the pressure for 'Party' literature from the Communists, through the League of Left-wing Writers, set up in 1930, and, mostly as a countermeasure, from the Nationalists too – their campaign for a 'nationalist' literature gathered momentum after 1932 – was strong and increasing. From a third source there were repeated calls for a 'return to ancient ways' (*fu ku*), which were sometimes put into practice in schools in the provinces under warlord direction. Chou was therefore warning his contemporaries that the *wen i tsai tao* mentality was still prevalent, and was asking them to recognize it for what it was. Perhaps he had some hope that dire warnings might help put off the evil day of a return to another age of *tsai tao* monopoly of the writer's world, but it was his prediction, later to be over-fulfilled by events, that literature, after having enjoyed comparative freedom since the May Fourth movement, would again be required to be of benefit to life and society.[79]

If the past and the present were, then, not absent from Chou's thoughts, a third setting for his argument was in eternity, for he was also discussing the true nature of literature. The point at issue was whether good literature could be written in the service of an ideology or whether it must be entirely personal; alternatively, could literature aim at 'usefulness' and still be literature? Judged against Chou's definition it could not. That definition runs:

> Literature is something which has aesthetic form, which conveys the author's unique feelings and thoughts, and enables the reader to feel pleasure thereby. (*Yüan-liu*, p. 10.)

[76] *Yüan-liu*, pp. 71–2.
[77] Introduction to Vol. VI of *Chung-kuo hsin wen-hsüeh ta-hsi* (Compendium of New Chinese Literature), p. 12.
[78] 'Wen-i fu-hsing chih meng' (Dream of Literary Renaissance), *K'u k'ou kan k'ou*, p. 16.
[79] *Yüan-liu*, p. 103.

Not an exhaustive statement, perhaps, but some things can be gleaned from it. The first is that the feelings and thoughts expressed must be the author's own (he should not be the spokesman for anyone else), and the second is that the effect is to give the reader 'pleasure', not instruction: in fact it is the *dolce* half of Horace's formula without the *utile*. The most he concedes in respect of the function of literature is that this 'pleasure' could include relief from pain, as when a boil is lanced.

Another attempt of Chou's at a definition, from the year 1925, apparently quite different, leads in the same direction:

> Literature is not a true record, it is a dream. Dreams are not the true replica of waking life, but if removed from waking life their material is gone, no matter whether the dreams are in the nature of a response [to the stimulus of actual events], or wish-fulfilment. ('Chu-lin ti ku-shih hsü' [Preface to 'Stories of the Bamboo Forest'], *K'u yü chai hsü pa wen*, p. 127.)

The key thing here is that dreams do not go beyond the mental activity of one person, having to do with psychological adjustment to the environment; they cannot be transferred to the waking world, so they cannot be ordered to serve any particular end.[80] Such a view is typical of European Romantic theory, which stresses the transformation of the raw material in the mind of the artist, as opposed to Classical theory which tends to maintain that literature holds a mirror up to reality.

Chou's essay on 'Obscene songs'[81] provides an example of practical criticism which shows his definitions at work. In it he dismisses the idea that the incidence of lewd songs is an index of the moral depravity present in society, for the reason that: 'Though poetry expresses the author's feelings, mostly it is as a reflection, not truly a confession of them.' The folksongs, he continues, which laud illicit sex are the means of satisfying the desire for free love on the part of those who cannot realize it; it is a case of sex in the mind. 'These songs are their dreams, their "*ekstasia*" '; and the same is true of all love poetry. Chou's thoughts on the subject are summed up in the line he quotes, 'The mouth sings only when it cannot kiss.'

[80] Feng Fei-ming, Chou's disciple, also talked about art being a dream: 'In the process of creation there should be "rumination"; only then can art become a dream. Being a dream there is a zone of haziness between it and the real life where it originated.' ('Shuo meng', *Yü Ssu*, no. 133, 28 May 1927.)

[81] 'Wei-hsieh ti ke-yao', in *T'an lung chi*, pp. 123–5.

Both this psychological theory and the conception of 'physiological satisfaction', referred to earlier, see artistic creation as outgoing – the relief of pressure built up inside – not as the faithful copy of external reality, still less the deliberate plan to employ cognitive powers to encourage social trends or hold up models to follow.

Yet even though for the author the work of literature may have no purpose beyond itself, it cannot avoid affecting the reader in some way. Chou has said, as a reader, that he expects literature to give him pleasure, but it is more often the relief it affords that he talks about in his middle period. One could produce many examples of Chou arguing that both writing and reading are ways of purging evil humours, are comfort to those who need comfort, and nothing else. For now we will see how he expounds the theme in *Yüan-liu*:

> In [literature] there is not much energizing force, there is no teaching; it can only afford pleasure to people. But affording pleasure can be thought of as a kind of use. By giving expression to it it can assuage the author's sense of grievance, and though the reader gets no instruction he does get some benefit.
>
> As to the benefit the reader can derive, it can be elaborated – but this was argued long ago by Aristotle in his *Ars Poetica* – as a kind of purging function. The *Shui-hu chuan* used always to be described as teaching banditry, but in our opinion the contrary is true; it not only does not teach banditry, in fact it might well reduce many dangers to society. Everyone who has been humiliated or harmed wants to take revenge, but on reading *Shui-hu* he feels relieved, as if his spleen had been vented, as if the person hated had been laid low by the heroes of Liang-shan-po and his own indignation thereby dissipated. The *Hung-lou meng* can give rise to the same kind of effect in the reader. A still living English thinker regards literature as a kind of spiritual exercise.[82] When we are busy with our work and over a long period do not engage in any muscular activities, then the muscles get flabby and we need to take some exercise to work off surplus energy; only then do we feel relaxed. This seems to be the function of literature. (pp. 29–30.)

He goes on to explain how frustrations have an easy outlet in primitive societies, but in civilized societies the involved processes of the law prevent this. Similarly the old custom of the 'cursing day', when ordinary citizens were licensed to let off steam in any direction, has died away. Literature now fills the same kind of role. Thus 'there are no real works of literature which are not of benefit to people; positively they have no use, but negatively they do have use.' (pp. 30–1.)

[82] I do not know who this Englishman is. De Quincey did describe poetry as a kind of emotional gymnastics, but only in that it keeps active human sensibilities – 'The Poetry of Pope', quoted Abrams, p. 331.

These are general propositions about the nature and function of literature and so would apply to all ages, but from the way Chou continues it is obvious that they are slanted to meet a present challenge. He goes on to commend the argument that if youth expends its energies on exposing its discontents on paper it will have no initiative to take action. It would be a mistake to think that literature could be of positive use; that which tries to be is 'perverted'. Chairs and ink-boxes have been used in Parliament as weapons before, but that is not what they were meant for. His concluding paragraph reads:

> It seems as if only the weaklings defeated in society need literature. For those who are well placed and quite satisfied, and can do what they will when they will, literature is naturally unnecessary. But the weak, when they are discontented, or when face to face with questions of life and death beyond the power of man to influence, mostly use literature to give play to the emotions provoked. Those who have a positive way open to them, assuming that action is not made impossible by, for instance, political corruption, can of course go and join some political reform movement. They do not need to make use of literature to proclaim their woes. (*Yüan-liu*, p. 32.)

This view of literature as a safety-valve or a means of venting grievances is hardly one which Chou, a writer himself, all things being equal, would have been eager to espouse. In the event he speaks of his art in such disparaging terms that one is reminded of Hamlet's 'like a whore, unpack my heart with words, / And fall a-cursing, like a very drab, / A scullion! ' Though as a frequently disgruntled essayist the subject of venting grievances was near to his heart, his concentration on this aspect in his theoretical writings seems to be due to trying to refute on their own ground the arguments of an opposition which wanted to capture literature as a platform for protest, and through protest effect social change.

It has now become possible to make out three separate facets to the *tsai tao* thesis which Chou objected to: the political – in particular, the revolutionary political; the religious, or quasi-religious; and the utilitarian. These can be further explored with the aid of Chou's other writings.

Literature and Revolutionary Politics

It was in the second half of the 1920s that the movement for revolutionary literature grew too vociferous to be ignored. The main journals to uphold the cause were those run by the Creation Society, namely *Ch'uang-tsao yüeh-kan* (Creation Monthly), 1927, *Hung shui* (Flood), 1925, and *Wen-hua p'i-p'an* (Cultural Critic), 1928, and that of the Sun Society *T'ai-yang yüeh-k'an* (Sun Monthly), 1928. Another magazine called *Ta-chung wen-i* (Art of the Masses) was started in 1929, and of course many more similar ones followed the setting up of the League of Left-Wing Writers in 1930. There is no need to go into their arguments; their main lines are predictable, and few or none of their ideas are original, the theory and much of the example being imported from the U.S.S.R. The several essays that Chou wrote from the late 1920s up to the Japanese war in 1937 that deal with the subject of literature and revolution were clearly prompted by this new 'tide', but typically do not confront it head on. He did grapple with the question of the class nature of literature in 'On literature'[83] (1927), in which he freely admitted that certain attitudes pertain to capitalist or feudal society, but denied the possibility of anyone writing from class consciousness – in any case all classes in China tended to share the same ideals; and in 1930[84] he questioned whether the folksong, the study of which he had until then energetically supported, could truly be said to be the creation of the 'people', and whether it had much literary value. He also, while greatly respecting socialist martyrs, declined to believe in the masses.[85] But the central question he discussed in those years was what constitutes literature and what does not. Writing which has a revolutionary purpose does not. An important statement of his position is contained in 'Preface to Stories of Big Black Wolves'[86] (1928); the question arises in this unlikely place because the collector of the stories, Ku Wan-ch'uan, had rightly given up literature to go south to practise revolution:

> If revolution is opium, then could we compare literature to *ya-chih-nai*?[87] Just as the rich and powerful openly smoke opium, when red-blooded youths feel discontented with the present age they stand up, risk danger, and reckless of their lives go out and put revolution into practice. They do not sit at home and sigh and curse to dispel the pent-up air inside them. It is only the debilitated, whose bones are like matchsticks, who have not the strength to truss a chicken, who sit as if paralysed in front of a desk and pour out the foul humours inside them on to lined paper, lest they swell up with them. It is rather like the poor addicted fellows who can only

[83] 'Wen-hsüeh t'an', in *T'an lung chi*.

[84] 'Ch'ung k'an *Ni shang hsü p'u hsü*' (Preface to the reprint of *Ni shang hsü p'u*), in *K'an yün chi*.

[85] See postscript to *T'an hu chi*, 1927, p. 622; and 'Pei kou yen t'ung hsin' (Letter to Pei kou yen), *Chou Tso-jen shu-hsin*, p. 142.

[86] 'Ta hei lang ti ku-shih hsü', *Yung jih chi*, pp. 192–4.

[87] I have been unable to discover what this substance is. From the context it would appear to be the brand name of some medicine for settling the stomach, like Milk of Magnesia.

swallow a little *ya-chih-nai* at mealtimes – hardly anything to be proud of, yet there is nothing to be done about it . . . someone rightly said that all those who issue anonymous announcements, advertisements, or pamphlets, saying how so-and-so has done the dirty on them, are in general people who have taken a knock and have no power to fight back or take revenge; though unwillingly, they can in the end only put up with it . . . The dog which bites does not make a sound; those which bark are frightened themselves. In these troubled times youth has only two courses: the strong press on and become martyrs to human progress; the weak draw back and curse, live out their allotted span and propagate their kind – apart from their other course of becoming an official and making a fortune, but there are already very many taking this road, and there is no need for anyone else to guide the way . . .

Although I hear that nowadays there is a very clever ploy, that of using literature as a substitute for revolution, like in the old days the camp-following recorder with the red ink getting promotion on the strength of his 'martial merit', I cannot but feel it to be a little too opportunistic, and not too good a thing. True, Byron and Petöfi deserve the name of revolutionary poets, and had the power to put spirit into the people, but Byron died at the battle of Missolonghi, Petöfi in the field at Segesvar – they, rather, are revolutionary heroes; their literature only arose spontaneously from the trenches, and is unlike the shaking of the thin fists of the literati.

This passage should be read in conjunction with another statement that appeared the same year. From the fact that Chou repeated it in his introduction to volume VI of the 'Compendium' (p. 9) seven years later, it can be taken as definitive:

I often think that literature is the reverse of revolution. If one is able to engage in revolution, one has no need for literature and the various other arts, or religion, because one already has one's world. The mouth that is kissing no longer wants to sing, for the same reason. But if the political world has been conquered and there remain longings in other respects, then there are times of course when one would venture into the world of art: Napoleon carrying *Die Leiden des Jungen Werther* on his campaigns can serve as an example. So though literature is non-revolutionary it still has its right and need to exist. ('Yen chih ts'ao pa' [Postscript to *Yen chih ts'ao*], *Yung jih chi*, p. 181.)

Apart from impugning the motives of 'revolutionary' writers, the substance of these two statements is the same as that put forward in *Yüan-liu*, that literature and revolution are separate and normally alternative activities. He concedes that the genuine man of action may seek diversion in literature after his labours, and that literature may arise as a by-product of the revolutionary struggle, but it may not be a *substitute* for revolution. Since perhaps the majority of those who pretended to write revolutionary literature were indeed only making revolution on paper, the point is well made.[88] Again he may be right that only the weak and ineffectual actually *need* literature because they have no positive way of righting wrongs done, or felt to be done, to them. But many questions arise that he leaves unanswered. What flows from the pens of the weak and debilitated bent on venting their grievances must necessarily be a literature of protest of some kind, and this Chou recognizes as proper. As a Chinese, whether or not schooled in general literary theory, he would have had to, for the doctrine that literature arises in dissidence has a long history in China. It is represented by the phrase *fa fen* 'giving vent to indignation' or 'wrath'. The inspiration and example was provided by the martyred Ch'ü Yüan, who used the words 'vent my wrath and give release to my feelings'.[89]

Such motivation was, according to Lo Ken-tse (vol. I, p. 90), common to the *Ch'u Tz'u* school of writers. Lo also points out that Ssu-ma Ch'ien once ascribed the source of all the great works to indignation (p. 92). Even Han Yü joined in the chorus: 'Things give sound when their equilibrium is disturbed.'[90] Those very words were repeated by Chang Hsüeh-ch'eng,[91] who then went on to deal with the idea that 'wise men are prevented by their age from achieving their aspirations, and in their dudgeon write books to vindicate themselves.' Now such writings could well be socially disruptive, so where is the line to be drawn between them and 'revolutionary' literature? Chou does not say directly. The only clue in his statements is that Byron and Petöfi's work is exempted from criticism because it was 'spontaneous', which implies that the other 'revolutionary' writing he has been talking about is not spontaneous, is in fact written to propound a given ideology, to *tsai tao*. I would not agree with the accusation that Chou's erection of the abhorrent *tsai tao* principle was prompted by antipathy to left-wing literature as such.[92] His natural sympathies had always lain with the left wing in its opposition both to capitalism and traditionalism. His

[88] A case in point was the career of Chiang Kuang-tz'u, described unkindly but not unjustly by T. A. Hsia in *The Gate of Darkness*, 'The phenomenon of Chiang Kuang-tz'u'. On the other hand Hu Yeh-p'in, another 'revolutionary' writer, seems to have eventually followed the logic of Chou's argument, and died for his beliefs in 1931; see Hsia, ibid., 'The enigma of the five martyrs', esp. p. 188.

[89] In 'Chiu chang', *Ch'u tz'u*.

[90] 'Sung Meng Tung-yeh shu', quoted Lo, II, 146.

[91] *Wen Shih t'ung i*, 'Chih hsing' chapter, p. 87.

[92] According to Pa Jen, *Lun Lu Hsün ti tsa-wen* (On Lu Hsün's Essays), p. 118, Lu Hsün regarded Chou's repudiation of *tsai tao* as a veiled

target was quite straightforwardly that class of left-wing writing which was injurious to the cause of literature. Work written in the service of an ideology could not accommodate certain literary values that Chou consistently held – they were not brought out specially to deny validity to revolutionary literature. One of these was the private character of literature – person talking to person. That this was the true nature of literature was an arbitrary and subjective view, as all views on literature ultimately are: it defined literature according to the standard of what he liked to read and write. Chou's personal preferences in this direction will be examined in detail later, but his objection to the validity of literature that seeks to appeal to a mass audience is relevant to the present context. He appears to think that the medium of the written word precludes any kind of mass response:

> I think that the trend of literature is in the end towards individualization. In this 'individual' there naturally subsists still quite a large number of national elements, but the work is still *national* and cannot be collective. Sometimes there may be an honest reaction in favour of the revival of collective art, and, especially when literature is sought as an ally for politics, there can be a dishonest movement to use art to create collectiveness, but neither works out. This is not surprising, because collective art, if it is not visual, has to be aural, otherwise it is hard to take in.

The epics of Homer, he continues, the Greek tragedies, the plays of Shakespeare, lost their 'popular' character when transmitted in written form. For the present:

> If a writer wants to undertake collective service he can run to the market place, suppress his own private obsessions, accept traditional methods and the mass mentality, and probably succeed. But this type of art has the misfortune of dying with its creator, his fame can only last a lifetime, and even if the draft is preserved, be it as good as the *San kuo chih yen-i* or the *Shui-hu chuan*, once it has become literature it takes leave of the collective, ends up in a quiet corner of the library, and is attentively perused not by a special group but still by a small number of readers. I believe reading is in fact quite aristocratic, and is very far from being natural. ('Wen-hsüeh ti wei-lai' [The Future of Literature], 1936, *Feng yü t'an*, pp. 151–2.)

One might think from this that Chou has failed to take into account the prospect of mass literacy, but it is clear from other remarks in the

---

attack on the left wing. The target of the essay in question ('T'ing shuo meng' [Listening to People Talking of their Dreams], *Lu Hsün ch'üan chi*, IV, p. 357) is actually not Chou Tso-jen. Clearly Lu Hsün did regard Chou's theory as a red herring, but probably no more than that.

essay that by reading he means close and discriminating reading, followed by reflection. As the habit of reading in this sense is determined by cast of mind rather than the mere ability to read, the number of readers will always be small, an intellectual 'aristocracy'. If the reader of literature has to be able to quietly reflect on what he has read, it follows that literature for its part must provide food for thought, must have some depth. Writing done for a mass audience would not normally have that quality. But the main point I want to bring out here is that if books are to be enjoyed in seclusion, this does emphasize the private nature of the act. And if the reader is a private person, the writer should be even more so. The effect on literature of making the act *public* Chou elaborates elsewhere, in 'The art of composition' (*T'an wen-chang*), 1945:

> In composing a work of literature one of the easiest faults to commit is to attitudinize. When it is committed the work is spoiled. In my view, some compositions could have been quite all right: they have something to say, have a vocabulary up to saying it, and in fact could have been written without any trouble. But here we come to the difficulty. A work of literature is written by an individual, but the other party is a plurality. So in this it is close to speechmaking, and speechmaking in turn is not far removed from playacting. The speaker has something in mind that he wants to persuade the audience of, but he is quite liable instead to fall under the control of the audience. If a phrase or gesture is appreciated by the audience, he is frequently unable to avoid repeating it; if for example he bangs on the table and says everybody should charge forward into battle, and gets clapped and cheered, the next time he will roar that everyone *has* to charge forward, *cannot but* charge forward, and bang the table fair to make the glasses jump. In this way speeches made to guide the audience and playacting meant to amuse the audience really have become difficult to distinguish. I do not understand plays, but I have heard that good actors do not perform in this manner. They have their own rules, and are not willing lightly to bend themselves to the will of others. When I was young I heard the old people telling a story about a local actor. When he had taught his pupils enough about acting and was sending them onto the stage to perform, he used to tell them: 'It is your own acting that is important. Don't on any account pay any attention to those fellows with nostrils like chimneys below stage.' For a country actor to have so much sense shows that he has confidence in his own craft, and is wiser than the average politician or writer. Reading the literature of past and present I often detect the flaw of speaking like speechmakers. I seem to hear the author contorting his vocal cords to yell, banging the table, baring his teeth in awful rage: all sorts of strange grimaces disclose themselves behind the text . . . The writer is writing in his study, but his eyes are all on the reader, with the

> result that though the finished work may be accomplished, it just lacks its core. (*Chih-t'ang i yu wen pien*, pp. 125–7.)

So if a writer abandons his integrity, 'attitudinizes', ceases to be true to himself, then his work is invalidated. When an author writes about an area of experience the he has not lived through, or speaks on behalf of a class or group to which he does not belong, or parrots slogans, all of which was generally true of 'revolutionary' literature, as Mao Tse-tung agreed,[93] then this stricture applies even more.

It is easy to see why Chou should want to decry 'literature' which suffers from such faults, but the interesting question is whether he would want to debar writing which suffers from none of these faults, which is written from knowledge and fron the heart, and yet the effect of which is likely to be revolutionary.

Since the saying of Upton Sinclair that 'all literature is propaganda' might well be used to justify such writing, one could have hoped that when Chou turned to that famous quotation in 'Propaganda' ('Hsüan-ch'uan') – undated, but written between 1940 and 1943 – he might have faced the question, but in fact he does not go into the subject deeply. He only says that he dislikes propaganda because it is unreliable, in the same way as commercial advertisements are, and because it cannot be well expressed: 'If there is any falseness in the matter, it cannot be presented entirely satisfactorily. Though we have never studied the art of detection of Judge Pao,[94] if only we have read a fair number of books and seen a fair number of things, we can still spot [the falseness] at a glance.'[95] This goes no way to answering our question.

Something Chou says in the essay 'The tradition of Chinese Literature' (1940) cuts nearer the bone, however. He has been arguing that the outlook inherent in most of Chinese literature had in the past been a kind of Confucian humanism, and has expressed the hope that it will again become the mainstream of literary ideology in his own lifetime; then he adds:

> But I have not the least intention of promoting it, because I am profoundly convinced that anything, no matter what, that tries to force the growth of anything whatever is harmful. If 'literature for life' is misinterpreted, it might easily turn into the vocabulary of gangsters or the attitude of charitable old ladies. ('Han wen-hsüeh ti ch'uan-t'ung', *Yao-t'ang tsa-wen*, p. 5.)

[93] *Mao Tse-tung on Art and Literature*, Peking Foreign Languages Press, pp. 80, 90.
[94] Judge Pao (Pao Cheng) was a Sung dynasty official later accredited with supernatural powers of detection. His cases were written up in the late Ch'ing *Lung-t'u kung-an*.
[95] *Yao-t'ang tsa-wen*, p. 91.

Though this remark was made in special circumstances, and may have been directed against the cultural policy of his new Japanese masters, it is consistent with his pre-war attitudes. If he sees even the comparatively liberal and broadly-based campaign for 'art for life's sake', to which he had once lent his own weight, as misconceived, then the movement for revolutionary literature would be even more so. However, since his argument is that when an idea is taken up as a campaign it is either killed or transformed into something different, we are dealing here with practicalities, with what the world does with men's thoughts, and still not with whether those thoughts were sincerely conceived and sincerely expressed.

We have been trying to find a direct statement on the issue of whether Chou's condemnation – or rather denial – of revolutionary literature necessarily included the hypothetical work sincerely written which has a revolutionary effect. What we have found have been criticisms only of literary campaigns and causes. I think it legitimate to conclude that these were indeed the things he objected to. His concern as stated was not that literature might incite revolution, but that the *intention* to incite revolution would result in bad literature. To take a case in point, Chou did say, a propos of Yamamoto Yūzō, that a man whose heart was imbued with hatred of imperialism could write good literature,[96] but to relate that to his general proposition he would have had to have argued that if that man wrote with the *aim* of fostering anti-imperialism then what he wrote would be unworthy of the name of literature.

Chou was quite happy to state that literature is rebellious (*fan-k'ang-ti*),[97] that is, it is in opposition to the existing state of affairs. But revolution requires a plan of action, and concerted action at that; a writer, who speaks for himself, cannot therefore propound revolution. He may however express his discontent, and put forward his ideas about what should be, in which case the distinction between *yen chih* and *tsai tao* disappears: hence Chou's own corollary to his thesis: 'To express other people's *chih* is to *tsai tao*; to convey your own *tao* is to *yen chih*.' ('Compendium', VI, p. 11.)

Literature and Religion

We have seen that in Chou Tso-jen's view writing which has an aim is quite definitely not literature. As he said: 'If you want to use literature

[96] In his introduction to his translation of Yamamoto's *Eiji-goroshi*, *Yü Ssu*, IV, no. 38, 1928.
[97] In 'Yen chih ts'ao pa' (Postlude to *Yen chih ts'ao*), 1928, *Yung jih chi*, p. 181.

to further your aims, that is the business of the priest.'[98] Let us now see what the business of the priest is. In *Yüan-liu* (pp. 27-8) Chou writes:

> The difference in the nature of literature and religion is in whether they have an aim or not. All religious rites have an aim, but literature has not. To give an example: in summer when it is going to rain we often feel irritable because of the closeness of the weather and can't help ejaculating, 'Hurry up and rain! '; this is the attitude of art. Taoists priests have all sorts of ceremonies for bringing on the rain, like striking a drum to represent thunder, waving a black flag to represent wind, sprinkling water to represent rain, and so on. Their idea is to use these various ceremonies with the aim of hastening a downpour.
>
> The Preface to the *Odes* says, 'When the feelings are moved within they take shape in words. If words are inadequate the feelings are expressed in sighs; if sighs are inadequate they are given prolonged utterance in song; if song is inadequate unwittingly the hands and feet take up the rhythm.' My view actually does not differ from this. Literature has only feelings; it has no aim. If there has to be an aim, then it is only to 'give voice'. In everyday conversation in winter we often say: 'It's really cold today.' The intention is not of course to borrow money or clothes from the other person, it is purely and simply to give voice to one's own feelings.
>
> Writings that we regard as literature the religionists always want to use as tools to promote goodness. When we read the poem 'Kuan chü'[99] we just think it is a good nuptial poem; for the country tutor it contains principles of a kind that the universe is based on. Again, on our desks the psalms are literature; when chanted in church they are religion. These are points of difference between literature and religion. Supposing these differences did not exist of course we would not separate them.

We should note in passing how closely this description of the attitude of the priest corresponds with the notions of Andrew Lang, one of Chou's favourite Western savants. In his *Custom and Myth* Lang said of Ruskin: 'His disparagement of Coleridge as 'useless' is a survival of the belief that art should be 'useful'. This is the savage's view of art. He imitates nature, in dance, song or in plastic art, for a definite practical purpose. His dances are magical dances, his images are made for a practical purpose, his songs are incantations.'[100]

Another discourse of Chou's on the difference between religion and

[98] 'Chieh yüan tou' (Beans for forming Affinities), 1936, *Kua tou chi*, p. 255.

[99] This is the first poem in the *Book of Odes*. It was interpreted as exemplifying the virtue of the queen and setting the pattern for the relationship between husband and wife.

[100] London, 1901, p. 91.

literature, set in his own culture and owing nothing to Western thinkers, reveals more of his real concern:

> I feel that literature is like an incense burner. On either side of it there is a pair of candlesticks, belonging to the left and the right. It does not matter which is left or right, it is enough that there are two places, occupied by Zen and Mantra, if you allow me to borrow two Buddhist terms. Literature has no use, but these two on left and right have use and potency. The man who follows the Zen way does not leave a body of writing, knowing it is useless, but looks for another means. He gives a shout like a peal of thunder, or lashes out with a stick, or comes out with 'latrine stick! ',[101] in order by direct and immediate means to make people come to a sudden awakening. Admittedly this requires a fair degree of receptivity on the other person's part, and cannot easily produce an effect, but in essence this method is absolutely right. You can almost say it is the highest form of art, but in fact art has aspired to but cannot realize this ideal – or perhaps only music can be thought of in this way.[102] Literature which is caught up in the entanglement of the written and spoken word, though it is trying to fight its way out with the aid of symbols and what not, still lags behind.
>
> Adherents of the Mantra sects simply plight their troth to the sect and recite incantations, mouthing some mumbo-jumbo which seems to be quite meaningless but actually can have tremendous power. By singing out '*Amitabha Buddha*' the old woman can have peace and security, feeling she has her place in paradise. And the member of the gentry who regularly shouts and yells at his cook might one of these days become a petty official in the Imperial Commissariat, and then he will think himself a very fine bird indeed. This is the kind of thing I am talking about. To take the example of the numerous cases brought at imperial behest of ancient and modern times, which killed off people like flies, if you enquired into the charges you would find they were just a few words like '*lèse-majesté*' or 'treasonable turpitude' – quite empty and hollow, but in days gone by lots of people, living and dead, were sentenced to various forms of the extreme penalty for them. It strikes one now as a great injustice, but in those times probably none apart from the person concerned thought it was not deserved. Just names! That the power of words is so great is really something to be respected and feared too.
>
> As to literature, it can neither give nor receive orders. It can not be so untrammelled as to be able to use a unique form of expression

[101] *Kan shih chüeh*: This was an answer once given to the question: 'What is the Buddha's nature? '; see *Chung-wen ta tz'u-tien*, II, 76.

[102] Compare the theory of German aestheticians in the 1790s, who regarded music, in M. H. Abrams' words, as 'the art most immediately expressive of spirit and emotion, constituting the very pulse and quiddity of passion made public' – *The Mirror*. . . , p. 50.

to give direct utterance, neither has it the boldness to choke someone with holy writ. The result is that subjects may be discussed at interminable length, and books may run to hundreds and thousands of chapters, only for the unoccupied to skim through. ('Ts'ao mu ch'ung yü hsiao yin' [Short introduction to 'Plants, insects, fishes'], 1930, *K'an yün chi*, pp. 25–6.)

To summarize, the reason why literature cannot emulate Zen is that it cannot plumb the depths of experience or explain the mysteries of life (these inherent limitations will be discussed later). Neither may it, since it only exists to express feelings and ideas, capitalize on the potency of words to comfort oneself or to terrorize others. The analogies are introduced in order to define the limits of literature proper and to demonstrate its ineffectiveness. In the first passage, while he is similarly arguing that literature cannot have a use, he does appear also to be warning of a threat to literature from the outside. The Buddhist monk is unlikely to make depradations against literature (the Buddhists were inventive enough in producing their own propaganda), but the Confucianist is apparently both willing and eager to take a work of pure literature under his wing. We have already seen that historically this was indeed the case, but one might reasonably think that in the 1930s it was no longer a real issue. Was Chou then talking about 'old, unhappy, far-off things / and battles long ago'? As before we have to remember Chou's own statement made in 1936[103] that when he is abusing Han Yü or talking about ghosts he is attacking their living counterparts, when he rants about *pa-ku* or traditional opera, it is not so much for their own sake as for the power they exercised. In this instance it would be impossible to quantify the survival of Confucianism. C. K. Yang, in his book *Religion in Chinese Society*, dismisses Confucianism as institutionally too diffuse and conceptually too irrelevant ever to have had any chance of regeneration in republican China.[104] This was true of Confucianism as a 'religion', but it had more power behind it as the way of thought underlying the true Chinese way of life. Chou was able to cite many instances of support for it in this regard. In 1927, to give one example among many, he named three universities where attempts were being made to restore the classical language and instil the idea of 'saving the nation through studying the Classics'[105]. Looking back in 1966, even, he still wrote in some awe of the weight of opinion in favour of Confucianist restoration.[106]

[103] 'T'i chi' (Inscription), *Kua tou chi*.
[104] pp. 355–8.
[105] 'Nan pei chih li-chiao yün-tung' (The Religious Movement in North and South), *Yü Ssu*, no. 151, 1 October 1927.
[106] *Chih-t'ang hui-hsiang lu* (Memoirs of Chih-t'ang), p. 508.

It is in any case enough for our purposes to know from the many essays Chou wrote deploring its contemporary manifestations that for him Confucianism was still an active force, and still determined to distort the due processes of literature. Otherwise he would hardly have devoted the greater part of his preface to Sun Hsi-chen's *Hsien-tai san-wen hsüan* (Selection of Modern Prose), in 1934, to an attack on the current movement to revive *ku-wen*, which was based essentially on ethical, behavioural and political motives, and incidentally on *pai-hua* literature subject to the same directions.

Though Chou thought religion still a force to be reckoned with, his description of the methods of the priest obviously applies beyond the bounds of religion proper. Using literature to further one's aims belongs also to the sphere of politics, so too does the terrible practice of name branding. So religion and revolution can be seen as two wings extending from the same centre. In calling attention to the contrast between literature on the one hand and religion and revolution on the other Chou was seeking to define and pass on his own understanding of the nature of true literature, but his insistence on the difference was such as to demand other explanations. In my view he had a more immediate and practical aim than stating eternal verities, and that was, by differentiating between the three, to establish a different identity for each one, so that each could get on with its own business. Particularly he wanted to distinguish between literature and revolution, so that in the midst of the political turmoil literature could remain inviolate, could be free from pressures and prohibitions, both from the point of view of what could be read and what could be written. Apart from disagreeing in principle with revolutionary literature, he did not want the whole tree to fall for the sake of that branch. Hidden away at the end of the essay 'The future of literature' we can indeed find Chou declaring this interest. He says there:

> If people everywhere are willing . . . to use visual and aural things for propaganda, and leave alone written things, this could have one advantage, namely that we could enjoy a little literary freedom, even if freedom of speech is beyond our reach. If literature is neither used as a tool nor interfered with any more, with this degree of freedom its life should be more secure. ('Wen-hsüeh ti wei-lai', 1936, *Feng yü t'an*, pp. 152–3.)

Utilitarianism

The assumption that underlies all *tsai tao* theories, whether religious or revolutionary, is that literature is or can be useful. It is therefore one that Chou has to deny. But its relevance goes beyond these two specific uses, and Chou does deal with it as a general proposition. Naturally, if he wanted to deny that literature was useful he would have to say the same thing about his own writing. That he does, and repeatedly. For instance, in an essay in letter form entitled 'Bitter rain', dated 17 July 1924, he anticipates the objection that he is only talking about personal matters of no benefit to the public, saying that that was precisely his intention.[107] Typical of the '30s is the lament that he had expended his spirit wastefully in writing 'positive' essays, when he had known all the time they could have no effect.[108] He thinks it is just a habit, a hang-over from the May Fourth period, but also something inherited from his native place, East Chekiang, which is famous for its disputatious intellectuals.[109] What he is willing to say about the possible positive influence of his own essays (disregarding the theoretical one of catharsis) can be seen in 'Chieh yüantou' (1936). The practice referred to in the title is the distribution of 'beans for forming affinities' by Buddhist priests, in the hope that the connection thus made will initiate the recipient on a course leading to eventual salvation. Chou says here that he writes essays for himself, but he wants a reader to talk to – 'perhaps writing is not being reconciled to loneliness.' He does not want a reward from the reader:

> I just wish for some small degree of affinity, so that when we meet we may treat each other with consideration, not just obliviously come and go. The great men of old have passed on, their fame after death was not worth taking into account, but if they have left two or three masterpieces which give the modern reader the delight of recognition, this is enough. What modern man can bequeath to those who follow is the same and nothing more, and both are 'beans'. Just a few beans; there is no objection to forgetting you have eaten them, but if you can vaguely remember, no matter what form [the memories] have assumed, it is all to the good. I think this is perhaps the little bit of effect that literature has – it just forms links. (*Kua tou chi*, p. 255.)

This is a very modest ambition, and certainly disclaims any pretension to influence the course of history or even the undramatic conduct of people's lives.

The furthest Chou is willing to go in the '30s towards recognizing the element of utility is in conceding that since in his work he 'conveys' his own 'way', that way has to be passable; but whether anyone takes it

[107] 'K'u yü', *Yü t'ien ti shu*, p. 6.

[108] 'Kuan-yü hsieh wen-chang chih erh' (About writing Essays, no. 2), 1935, *K'u ch'a sui-pi*.

[109] On this subject see 'Tzu heü erh' (Second preface), 1925, *Yü t'ien ti shu*.

is up to them.[110] Likewise he admits that to be of benefit to society is a good thing, but doubts whether society sees things as he does.

Whether Chou secretly cherished higher hopes than these one does not know, but he had to talk of his own work in this way in order to be consistent with his reiterated attacks on the fallacy, as he saw it, that literature could be useful. His conviction that it was a fallacy stemmed from three sources, his own frustrated efforts to enlighten through literature, his acquaintance with writing that attempts to put the principle into practice, and his reading of other people's discussion of the subject. The first belongs to his 'May Fourth' period, and so falls outside the scope of this study (but my essay 'Chou Tso-jen and cultivating one's Garden' deals with it). The second can now be taken up.

A large proportion of Chou's essays in the '30s were about Chinese books he had read, mostly of the *pi-chi* (notes and comments) variety, and in his comments he frequently deplores the tendency of the literati, encouraged by the belief that literature is useful, to write about practical matters and affairs of state of which they are basically ignorant. Typical is his comment on such a book of *pi-chi* in 1935, where poor Han Yü gets the blame again: 'I have long suspected that the reason why the Chinese believe that literature is useful and yet can only say hackneyed or unhelpful things is to be found in Han Yü, and the other Seven Masters rounded the thing off.'[111] In the same essay he adds: 'We mostly know the 'eight-legged essay' is a fitting target for abuse, but we really ought to add to it the 'treatise' (*lun*), because while the eight-legged essay teaches people to talk glibly about principles, the treatise teaches people to talk nonsensically about affairs. The eight-legged essay makes one stupid, the treatise corrupts people.'

Since in this essay Chou is retailing criticism of Sung scholars, it would be appropriate to recapitulate the point of view of one of them. Wang An-shih, the eminent scholar-statesman (and incidentally one of the Eight Masters), controversial figure though he was, in this represented his breed. He put forward his view in 'Shang jen shu'. [112] Not surprisingly, in view of the responsibility he bore for the wellbeing of the people, his main point is that literature is concerned with *mores*. He does assert, following in Confucius's footsteps, that cultivated diction is indispensable, but maintains it was not the prime object of the sages: writing must be of benefit to society. As decoration is proper

[110] 'Tzu-chi so neng tso ti', *Ping chu hou t'an*, p. 6.
[111] '*Tun yin tsa lu*', 1935, *Feng yü t'an*, pp. 43 and 45.
[112] From *Wang Ching-kung chi*, reproduced Yang Chia-lo, op. cit., Vol. III.

to a vessel or utensil, so cultivated diction is appropriate to writing, but in both cases the thing has first and foremost to be of practical use.

This is not a very extreme statement, but Chou would doubtless have seen in it the kind of utilitarianism that not only sanctioned the filling of thousands of books with tiresome nonsense, but deluded the Chinese into thinking that they accomplished something by it.

In attributing the main blame for this utilitarian attitude to Han Yü, Chou introduced a historical element into the argument. If the rot started with Han Yü, then pre-T'ang literature should have been relatively healthy. Such was indeed the view that Chou expressed. In the essay just quoted, he says: 'Reading Six Dynasties literature is better than reading the Eight Masters, and the harm is less serious.' (pp. 43–4.) Now the literary philosophy of the Six Dynasties means to most people the Preface to the *Wen hsüan*, which set up purely literary criteria in selecting the best that had been written,[113] and the kind of statement made by Hsiao Tzu-hsien (489–437), a member of the house of Ch'i:

> Literature is the outward mark of the personality, is the musical scale of the divine intelligence. As one ponders one moistens the brush; one lets one's thoughts wander and forces are set in motion inside one. When the words come out and fall onto the paper, the impetus and harmony come without effort. Nothing is not endowed with life, or moved by the affections. (From *Nan Ch'i shu*, quoted Lo, I, p. 122.)

In the words of Lu Hsün, the age of Ts'ao P'i, which begins this period, was ' "an age of literary self-awareness", or, as we say nowadays, was of the "art for art's sake" persuasion'.[114]

Chou Tso-jen would doubtless have found Hsiao Tzu-hsien's sentiments too high-flown, but he did more or less agree with the second view, at least if 'self-aware' means independent in thought and feeling, which Lu Hsün's elaboration does in fact bear out. It was not, though, the works of 'pure' literature that Chou particularly singled out from the period. In both *Yüan-liu* and '*Yen Shih chia hsün*'[115] the works he commends belong to the historical (*shih*) or philosophical (*tzu*)

[113] See J. R. Hightower, 'The *Wen hsüan* and genre theory', *HJAS* 20, 1957.

[114] *Lu Hsün ch'üan chi*, III, 382, cited Wang Yao, *Lu Hsün yü Chung-kuo wen-hsüeh.* p. 32. Note, however, that Lu Hsün appreciated most the defiant essays of Hsi K'ang: see Wang Yao, *Kuan-yü Chung-kuo ku-tien wen-hsüeh ti wen-t'i* (On Questions in Chinese Classical Literature), p. 31.

[115] *Yeh tu ch'ao*, p. 168.

categories, rather than the literary (*chi*). This has interesting implications, which will be explored in a later chapter; for now we need only note that as regards *periods* of literature Chou was at least consistent in showing preference for that of Wei-Chin-Six Dynasties, in view of the later success of Han Yü and others in spreading the word that literature should be useful. Chou would most likely not have claimed that that word was heard universally, in fact we have already seen the strength of the school of writers who deliberately stopped their ears to it, but there was also always an important 'third force'. Their standpoint was an intermediate one between the 'pure' and 'utilitarian' camps. The outstanding creative writers were less wedded to the utilitarian idea than even Wang An-shih's statement of faith described above would indicate. There he pointed out that due regard had to be paid to elegance of form – and the popularity of the slogans *wen chih pin pin* 'form and content on equal footing'[116] and '*hua shih ping mao*' 'flower and fruit flourishing together' back up this view – but the majority of better writers went beyond this. As Wang Meng-ou points out[117], after the Wei-Chin period, when 'pure' literature established its position, attention was usually paid to its claims as well as to those of 'useful' literature, and critics generally saw literature as giving play to both the reasoning and emotional sides of man's nature. Another modern critic, T'u Kung-sui, thinks Po Chü-i, who upheld such a dualistic view, fairly represents the typical outlook of the enlightened literati from T'ang times. T'u quotes this key passage from Po Chü-i's 'Yü Yüan Chiu shu'.

> *Wen* is supreme. Heaven, Earth and Man all have it. Of Heaven's *wen*, the sun, moon and stars stand out; of Earth's *wen*, the Five Elements are to the fore; of Man's *wen* the Six Classics predominate. And of the Six Classics the Odes are supreme. Why? The world is at peace when the sages affect men's hearts. In affecting men's hearts nothing taks precedence over feeling, nothing is more basic than words, nothing is more immediate than sound, nothing is more profound than truth. Poetry's roots are feeling, its shoots are words, its blossom sound, and its fruit truth. Ranging from sages to imbeciles, at the lowliest, pigs and fishes, at the most rarified, spiritual beings, the host is divided but the basic matter is the same, the outward appearances differ but the feelings are one. There is always a response when the sound penetrates, there is always a response where there is *rapport*. Being aware of this the sages went back to the root of words and arranged the songs according to the Six Genres (i.e. Air, Ode, Psalm, Description, Simile, Metaphor), looked at the basis of sounds and distributed them according to the pentatonic scale, so that the sounds had consonance and the genres

[116] from *Lun yü*, 'Yung yeh' chapter.
[117] In his *Wen-hsüeh kai lun*, p. 219.

> classification. The consonance being harmonious, words flow smoothly; when words flow smoothly the sound enters easily. The classifications being observed, feelings are brought out; when feelings are brought out, emotions are easily engaged. When this happens it harbours greatness and depth and reaches down to the subtle and minute; high and low are joined, and unity happily prevails; sorrow and happiness are shared, and all men's hearts are gratified.' (*Wen-hsüeh kai lun*, pp. 37–8.)

As Po Chü-i sees it then *wen* is an ordered manifestation of the human personality, the lines for which were drawn by the sages, hence it tends to exert beneficent influence. He highlights the importance of affecting people's feelings through its agency – the utilitarian idea – but does not insist on the inculcation of any saintly way: in this he is reflecting the proposition in the Great Preface, 'originating in feeling and ending in propriety'. On the other hand he describes the literary process from an aesthetic point of view, and has in view the perfect work of art, not the most effective sermon. In practice, if any aspiring young writer were to take Po Chü-i as his guide, he would find nothing in these words to lead him into pernicious habits. (One has to add that Po Chü-i goes on to deplore the lack of serious, remonstrative poems on current affairs and social injustices, but perhaps that can be ascribed to a special interest).

It would appear that the predominant theory of literature among practising poets, at least, tended in effect more towards the expressive than the didactic. We must also make allowances for the fact that it is rare for apologists for art anywhere not to mention the good it does people.

It was however against prose writing that Chou's complaint about 'useful' literature was principally directed. Here one has to distinguish from the general a specifically Chinese element. On the one hand he deprecates authors pronouncing on subjects in which they were not competent. Apart from the fact that logically this leaves open the possibility that if someone were to write on a subject in which he *was* competent the result would indeed be 'useful' literature, one does not normally think of writing on practical matters as literature at all. This is where the Chinese traditionally differed: *wen* was *wen* whatever the subject. In their word-bound culture writing had an efficacy that could stand for the deed: persuasive exposition of a theory absolved the author from checking his facts and testing his findings. In this regard Chou was really deploring the failure to take responsibility for one's own words and the pretension to be able to discourse on matters best left to the expert.[118] On the other hand his criticism applies also to the

[118] This was the burden of Chou's complaint in several essays, e.g., 'Tse-jen' ('Responsibility') in *K'u chu tsa chi*.

general class of speculative and philosophical literature; that too is 'useless'. Chou's case in this respect is based ultimately on his understanding of human history, largely interpreted by others.

Chou's first major statement on the historical theme is contained in 'The Uselessness of Instruction".[119] His authorities in that essay, written in 1924, are Havelock Ellis and Herbert Spencer. He quotes Ellis as saying that no book, whether intended to be moral or immoral, can have any measurable effect on the great mass of the people, while Spencer's contribution is to the effect that after 2000 years of preaching a religion of love in Europe, it is a religion of hate that prevails. Chou concurs in their judgement with a like assessment of the fate of Confucius and Lao-tzu – it is as if 'they had never existed'.

In 1944 his tune is the same, only he has added another verse, that of T'o-sheng (Christopher Dawson?), whose work on Greek religion asserts that ordinary Greeks clung to their ancestral beliefs quite impervious to the great philosophers.[120]

Another quotation in the same piece, this time from his own essay 'Reading behind closed doors' (1928) illustrates his belief that history teaches us that nothing really changes, with the inference that attempts to reform mankind are doomed to failure.

If you take a sample from Chou's essays midway between these two dates you hear the same voice. In 1935,[121] for instance, he repeats the same words that 'literature is useless', but here, possibly to relieve the monotony, offers a description for works that are meant to be useful. Assuming that those works which are realized to have a negative effect are 'little ornaments'[122] then the other kind might be called 'sacrificial vessels'. But he hastens to add, in case anyone might rashly assume that sacrificial vessels have some tenuous connection with efficaciousness, that though they may impress the worshipper in fact they are just another sort of ornament, as their acceptability as antiques bears out.

An attempt to explain Chou's negative attitude follows in the next section.

[119] 'Chiao-hsün chih wu-yung', *Yü t'ien ti shu*, pp. 171–2.

[120] 'Teng hsia tu shu lun' ('On Reading by Lamplight'), *K'u k'ou kan k'ou*, p. 31.

[121] 'Kuan-yü hsieh wen-chang' (On the Subject of Composition), *K'u ch'a sui pi*.

[122] The term 'little ornaments' (*hsiao pai-she*) was used by Lu Hsün in 1933 to denote and deride the artistic kind of essay currently in vogue (*Ch'üan chi*, IV, 440).

Summing up

By now a very depressing picture of Chou Tso-jen's attitude to literature must have been built up. He must be emerging as a querulous, cantankerous man busying himself with denying as fast as they are suggested the contributions that literature can make in the fields of politics, morality and religion, the things that matter in a community. The picture is depressing because Chou was truly depressed. The confident, vigorous, and often frivolous tone of his early essays gave way at the end of the '20s to increasing soberness, sombreness, and more bitter irony, and his lamentations tended to tail off in a gesture of impotence. But we must be clear that he was not saying that the things which matter in life should not be written about, only that to do so would not have any positive effect. He himself of course continued to both read and write, and thought reading, at least, one of life's most pleasurable pastimes.[123]

We have suggested some immediate reasons for his stand on specific issues, but beyond these there was an underlying conception of the role of literature which arose naturally from his background. It was not something that made epochs, nor the particular province of the exceptionally gifted man, but a normal activity for an educated man. As a result he tended to regard literature as both very broad in scope and ordinary in quality. So when he writes about the capabilities of literature it is not, as is common in the West, with the work of the genius who might appear once in a century in mind, rather is it the vast majority of literate men who have committed their thoughts to paper, and that includes himself. The genius appears in his discussions only as the (possible) exception to the rule.

The Chinese of course have been as fond as any people of geniuses – perhaps fonder – but they did not exalt them as high as the Romantics to whom we in the West are still the heirs. In their turn the Romantics inherited the ideas of ancient Greece and Renaissance Italy. In the ancient world Plotinus saw how the artist could bypass the phenomenal world and imitate at first hand the Platonic Ideas. To the Italians, in the words of M. H. Abrams,[124] 'here was an argument to elevate art from the realm of flux and shadows to an eminence over all human pursuits, in close connection to the Ideas and God himself. The artist, from being a craftsman, became a . . . creator, for it was sometimes said that of all men the poet was likest God because he

[123] He said so in 'Ssu chih mo hsiang' (Silent Thoughts on Death), *Yü t'ien ti shu*, 1924.

[124] *The Mirror and the Lamp*, pp. 42–3.

creates according to the patterns on which God himself has modelled the universe. In this way, the theory of Ideas . . . became – and has to this day remained – the resource by which the critic reaches the stratosphere of panegyric for the arts.'

Though there are coincidental correspondences with the Chinese understanding of *wen*, I do not think there is any really comparable idea in Chinese literary thought. *Wen* too parallels the cosmic order, but its role is essentially to maintain standards rather than create new forms. So as a Chinese Chou would probably have felt no compulsion to launch into the 'stratosphere of panegyric for the arts'. On the contrary, there was a strong strain in Chinese thought which depreciated the power of words to describe and communicate. This leads us to examine in further detail Chou's ideas on the inherent limitations of literature.

The Limitations of Literature

Early in his career as a critic Chou Tso-jen had made a passing reference to the grand design in literature in 'On the short poem' (1922).[125] He said then: 'The more ardent and profound of emotions, like the bitterness or sweetness of love, the tragedies and joys of parting and reunion, life and death, can give rise to all sorts of grand works,' but went on immediately to recommend more everyday feelings to the attention of poets. His phrasing alone indicates only a very wan enthusiasm for such ambitious projects. His true position was revealed in the introduction to a series of articles on creatures and plants, in 1930[126] – and this statement he thought important enough to repeat in his introduction to Volume VI of the 'Compendium of Modern Chinese Literature', 1935 – where he tells us that the sorrow of death and the happiness of loving, the deepest griefs and joys 'absolutely cannot be described in speech, let alone the written word'. He makes the gesture in the direction of the genius – if he exists – who would be an exception, but 'for us ordinary mortals, what we can express in writing is only a certain category of sentiments, admittedly not very crude or shallow, but also not very vital – something in other words of little account, that can be taken or left, the expression of which serves only to console or divert one.' So he is forced to agree with the recluse who said there was nothing in the world that could be spoken of, and acknowledges that he himself is incapable of producing 'true literature',

[125] 'Lun hsiao shih', *Tzu-chi ti yüan-ti*, p. 53.
[126] 'Ts'ao mu ch'ung yü hsiao yin', *K'an yün chi*, p. 24.

but nevertheless thinks there is nothing wrong with continuing to write essays.

No doubt there is an element of irony in all this, as he is contending also that there are few subjects that it is politically safe to write about, but he goes on too long not to be taken seriously. His strictures on the scope of literature would be quite clear and categorical if he had not referred to the 'true literature' that he is incapable of.

Let us see if we can learn anything further from an essay prompted by the death of Hsü Chih-mo, which solemn circumstance would rule out any facetiousness. It turns out that he says the same as before. He confesses indeed that the very thing that made him reluctant to write an obituary was this thought that 'compositions that are capable of being written are mostly of no consequence.'[127] He goes on to state that tone of voice, facial expressions and gestures can express perhaps ten or twenty per cent of a really profound feeling; in putting the feeling into words there is something dubious, even more so in writing. Our most intimate experiences, he says, are shared by Heaven alone; set down they are only run-of-the-mill 'laments' or 'nuptial poems', and such like. Once again, however, we find the saving clause: 'Apart from saints and geniuses none can escape this dilemma.' Unfortunately we are not told who these favoured gentlemen might be, and in fact we never do learn their identity; they remain entirely hypothetical. This is an interesting point, because when discussing the potentialities of a medium one would normally concentrate on its highest exemplars. The fact that Chou has his sights on the ordinary practitioners suggests that at times when Chou wrote 'literature' he meant 'my kind of literature'; it also supports my contention that he took the view that literature was both a normal function and fare for man. A long time before Liu Hsieh had put that feeling into words: 'The civilized man finds his way of life in proving his worth and publishing his thoughts. Do not think that I am fond of argument; it is simply that I cannot do otherwise [than write]! '[128]

We can still discover something more about, if not what prompted, at least what reinforced Chou's low opinion of literature. In 'On literature again' (1935) he finds parallels for his contention in the past. He writes:

> 'The feelings are moved within and take form in words.' This is indeed the established principle, but the words are very often inadequate to convey the feelings, and there is a sense of 'the words

[127] 'Chih-mo chi-nien' (In memory of Chih-mo), 1931, *K'an yün chi*, p. 126.

[128] *Wen hsin tiao lung*, 'Hsü chih' chapter.

brief but the feelings long'. In Buddhism the Ch'an school does not put things in writing; even among Confucians there is a similar idea. Ch'ü Weng-shan,[129] for example, in his account of the school of Pai Sha[130] in *Kuang tung hsin yü* says: 'Master Pai Sha also said: "The subtlety of this truth cannot be expressed. Sometimes I have an apprehension of it, but though I conceive and hold it in my mind, my mouth is unable to put it into words. When I attempt to speak of it, it is no longer what I had in my mind. Hence all conceptions that can be put into words are not worth conceiving and enunciating." ' This is actually to do with the nature of the mind, but the same applies to literature. Ssu-k'ung Tu's *Piao-sheng Wen chi* refers to the dimension of 'achieving the fullest poetic effect without writing a word', which is admittedly rather too mystical, but T'ao Yüan-ming also has a poem which says; 'Herein lies the true meaning, but when I go to explain I have already forgotten the words,'[131] which proves that this phenomenon really exists, only we ordinary mortals rarely experience it. If you have not experienced it you do not know the marvel and mystery of this state; when you do know it you are frustrated at not being able to put it into words. So it is after all very difficult. ('Tsai t'an wen', *K'u chu tsa chi*, p. 292.)

In seeking a vindication of his theory about the limitations of literature Chou is right to have recourse to Buddhist thought (for even the Confucians he refers to had affinities with Buddhism), but the fact that he gives no indication of appreciating the headway Buddhist (or Buddhist-influenced) literary theorists made with the problem of the ineffable in poetry is further proof of his prosaic attitude, for they did not merely state the dilemma, they suggested a way round. Although Ssu-k'ung T'u and T'ao Yüan-ming recognized that some things cannot be directly conveyed in words, the one stated and the other implied that they can be hinted at – and so *indirectly* conveyed. The emotional temper of the artist, which is after all the essential thing,[132] can be apprehended behind and beyond the inadequate words. T'ao achieved

[129] i.e. Ch'ü Ta-chün, who lived in the first half of the seventeenth century.
[130] Courtesy name for the Ming philosopher Ch'en Hsien-chang.
[131] This comes from 'Yin chiu erh-shih shou' ('Twenty Poems on drinking Wine'), no. 5.
[132] So thought J. S. Mill, whose opinion is retailed by Abrams. *The Mirror*. . ., p. 24: ' "The poetry is not in the object itself" but "in the state of mind" in which it is contemplated. When a poet describes a lion he "is describing the lion professedly, but the state of excitement of the spectator really", and the poetry must be true not to the object, but to "the human emotion". Thus severed from the external world, the objects signified by a poem tend to be regarded as no more than a projected equivalent . . . for the poet's inner state of mind.'

this, and so, strangely enough, did Chou Tso-jen, most notably in his lament on the death of his daughter, 'The Death of Jo-tzu':[133] he could not, he said, bring himself to record more than the bare facts, but the facts are stated with an awful simplicity that brings home unmistakably that 'worst pang that sorrow ever bore'.

The reason why Buddhist theorists in particular excelled in this subject is because of the Buddhist assumption that reality is distinct from appearances; this predisposed them to look for significance beyond the words, which are just surface things. Hence their concentration on 'the intent/relish beyond the writing' (*wen wai chih chih*). Wang Meng-ou sums up the way they looked at literature thus:

> The writer tells of his feelings through the medium of things, expresses his vision by means of figures of speech. The final end of criticism is not the figure of speech, nor even the vision: it is the emotional disposition that accompanies the vision, the 'meaning/relish beyond the taste' [*wei wai chih chih*], that is the object of criticism. (*Wen-hsüeh kai lun*, p. 222.)

The 'meaning/relish beyond the taste' Wang interprets as the pleasant or unpleasant experience we get from, for instance, 'saltiness' or 'sourness', terms which Ssu-k'ung T'u was fond of using to characterize the flavour of poetry, rather than these tastes themselves. It is not a quality perceptible in the verse itself, but the disposition of the poet at the time of writing.

Wang goes on to describe how the outstanding Sung dynasty literary theorists not only placed little importance on the kind of imagery a poet should use – hence the saying, 'if a poem has to take this form and no other, one can be sure the author is no poet': they even disregarded what kind of vision it should stem from, so giving rise to such expressions as, 'the feelings on this, but the words on that'. This dislocation between words and sentiment, characteristic of runes and riddles, opened the way for Yen Yü to discuss poetry as Zen.

In this case as in many others, good principles for appreciation may be bad for prescription, but whatever practices derived from this approach to poetry, it is in essence a fruitful one,[134] and one that Chou Tso-jen should have taken into account if he were really trying

[133] 'Jo-tzu ti ssu', 1929, *Chou Tso-jen hsüan-chi.*

[134] The habit of referring the poem to the processes of the poet's mind evident in the approach of J. S. Mill just noted was characteristic of European critics of the Romantic age. Another representative was De Quincey, who once wrote: 'The fact is that no mere description, however visual or picturesque, is in any instance poetic *per se*, or except in and through the passion which presides.' (From notes to his translation of Lessing's *Laocoön*, quoted Abrams, p. 54.)

objectively to define the limits of literature in general. In fact he was not. He was generalizing only from his own experience, and the principle object of his attention was still, one feels, the prose literature that he was most familiar with.

His attitude betokens a simple man who knows that existence has its depths and mysteries but does not expect to fathom them, let alone express them. Like Confucius with his ghosts and spirits, he prefers to let them alone, and does not think anyone else will have much success in probing their secrets.

2

INDIVIDUALISM

In an important sense Chou Tso-jen was justifying his own writing in denying to true literature the attributes that his own work lacked – or perhaps more to the point, was frequently denounced for lacking. Attacks were often made on him for his 'eremitism', and as he said more than once, his friends used to urge him to write more 'constructively'. His refusal to change his ways stemmed from a determination to be himself; in intellectual terms it found justification in a positive principle that underpinned his literary philosophy, namely individualism.

Chou's belief in individualism had many ramifications. It clearly dictated his own choice of reading matter. Firstly there was his partiality for letters. He says in 'Letters of Pai huan t'ang'[1] that he bought this collection of letters by T'ao Ch'ung-tao (early seventeenth-century) because letters are 'more estimable than other writing'. The quality that makes them more estimable he had already set out ten years previously, in 1925: 'They express more freshly than other forms of writing the author's individuality. Poetry, prose, novels and plays are written with a third person in mind, so though they are more well-wrought artistically, they bear more signs of artifice. Letters are only written for a second person to read, diaries, for oneself (with the exception of those written with a view to future publication), and so obviously are more genuine (*chen-shih*), and more natural.' And 'there have always been many good letters in China, which are able to combine both style and delicacy, but the finest must be accounted those which can reveal the author's personality.'[2] Of the different kinds of letters, he says, 'private letters' (*ch'ih-tu*) are better than 'public letters' (*shu*) because they are written 'as the fancy dictates, with no artifice, and along no fixed lines: all is natural outflowing'.[3]

1 'Pai huan t'ang ch'ih tu', *K'u chu tsa chi*, p. 63.

2 'Jih-chi yü ch'ih-tu' (Diaries and Letters), 1925, *Yü-t'ien ti shu*, pp. 11, 12.

3 'Wu lao hsiao chien' (Missives of Wu lao), 1934, *Yeh tu ch'ao*, p. 144.

Also tied to individualism, on a somewhat broader plane than letters, is Chou's support for the essay as an art form – *hsiao-p'in-wen* – which he was himself famous for writing as well as sponsoring. As he says in his 'Compendium' introduction, quoting his own words written in 1930,[4] '*Hsiao-p'in-wen* is the culmination of the development of literature' (p. 6), and '*Hsiao-p'in-wen* is at the head of individual literature' (p. 7), individual literature in turn being the most advanced stage in literary evolution, and *hsiao-p'in-wen* being described as *yen chih* prose.

It can be seen from the above that other values lie behind the paramountcy of individuality. Those mentioned are *yen chih*, genuineness, naturalness, revelation of personality, and natural outflowing. While 'individualism' as a concept did not exist in traditional China, and is therefore not amenable to analysis, we can investigate these secondary values that it embraced.

'Genuineness' is something that must pertain to the sentiments expressed in a work of art. *Yen chih*, as we have seen, meant no more to Chou than giving play to the feelings. The other qualities in question also bear upon the feelings. So it is best to begin the examination of individuality as Chou elaborates it in these passages in the general area of the feelings (*ch'ing*).

Chou shared the dominant Chinese critical idea of creative literature as both stemming from the feelings and having the feelings as its subject matter. In the one respect he quoted with approval the assertion of Wang K'an (b. 1795–?) that 'poetry's function is to tell of feelings. [The poet] is moved by what he meets, pours out what is in his heart; the setting he takes from what is before him. What need is there for cogitation? '[5] There is no accolade given here to cerebral activity, it might be noticed. In the other respect he says the thing he values in the art of compositions is 'style and feelings flourishing together' (*wen ch'ing ping mao*), and in thought 'feelings and argument in accord' (*ch'ing li ping ho*).[6]

It seems the feelings loom large whatever angle literature is viewed from. The modern professional critic ChuKuang-ch'ien was also culturally receptive to the idea of the supremacy of the feelings. He himself wrote that the author's first purpose was to give expression to what had to be expressed in his heart. Being modern, however, he attributes the idea to Croce, whose view, according to Chu, was that art is expression, expression is intuition, intuition is the pure spiritual synthesis which is the concrete form taken by blending feelings and

[4] Preface to *Chin-tai san-wen ch'ao*.

[5] 'Chiang-chou pi-t'an', 1934, *Yeh tu ch'ao*, p. 215.

[6] 'Tzu-chi so neng tso ti', 1937, *Ping chu hou t'an*, p. 5.

images: 'Hence artistic creation is entirely conceived, nurtured and completed in the heart.'[7]

Moving back into traditional literary theory, we are particularly concerned with what was thought the nature of the feelings, whether they are general or particularized, whether they are subject at any stage to control or selection or else expressed indiscriminately; for presumably if a writer expresses his feelings freely, without regard to the prejudices of his readers, the result would be a kind of individual literature. The first question is precisely whether, provided they are genuine, the writer should have scruples about the kind of feelings he communicates to his readers.

Hsü Fu-kuan has an interesting essay on this subject called 'The problem of the individual and social character of poetry in traditional literary thought'. In it he points out that the standard Confucian approach was to deny the distance between the artist and the people. He quotes K'ung Ying-ta's comment on the passage in the Great Preface to the *Book of Odes* about the affairs of a particular state reaching down to a particular person:

> The 'one man' referred to is the writer of the poem. In writing the poem the writer is expressing one man's heart, namely his own. In essence the heart of one man so expressed is the heart of the whole country. The poet incorporates the sentiments of the whole country in his heart, hence a country's affairs devolve on this one man as spokesman . . . hence the term 'airs' [*feng*] . . . The poet encompasses the heart of the whole empire, the customs from all quarters, to form his own ideas, and sings of kingly government, hence the term 'odes' [*ya*]. (*Chung-kuo wen-hsüeh lun chi* [Collected Essays on Chinese Literature], p. 85.)

According to this the poet, though an individual, does not make his individuality the stuff of his poetry; his consciousness is a refined and aggregate social consciousness – the people's consciousness is taken by the poet into himself. As Hsü Fu-kuan says; 'On the surface the poet moves the reader, but in fact the poet gives back to countless readers the various feelings they have but cannot express.' (p. 86)

Within this framework there is a further limitation on the kinds of sentiments that the true poet expresses – they should be 'right' or 'proper' (*cheng*). This is a question no orthodox Chinese cultural theory can ignore. However, such a requirement entails no coerciveness or insincerity, since human nature was thought to be good and all men were believed to inherit the same basic characteristics. Hence the poet is only being true to his real self when the sentiments he expresses are

[7] 'Wen-hsüeh t'an', p. 147.

'right'. In this connection Cheng Hsüan stressed the need for common acceptability in *Liu i chih*:

> There is no poet who does not adopt the feelings of the masses in composing his verse . . . Supposing there were a sage ruler whose merit were known to all around, and that one man spoke ill of him . . . The universal feeling would be against him. Or in the case of an unprincipled ruler who was an affliction to the people, if there were one man who alone praised his virtue, the feeling of the whole country would be against him. Words must match the feelings of the whole society, actions must conform to the opinions of the whole nation, then works may be ranked as 'airs' and 'odes' and be set to music. (Quoted Hsü, p. 87.)

To write this kind of poetry, to be receptive to the feelings of the common man at different times and in different situations, the poet has to cultivate his sensibilities, not, clearly, his ego.

There is another kind of poetry accorded blessing which is called 'true' (*chen*). To attain to this state also involves setting aside purely personal contingencies, but the process is different. According to Hsü it requires an unconscious straining and cleaning off of impurities, which is effected mainly through adversity. War and poverty, for instance, give rise to 'truthfulness' to human nature. To compare the two, 'right' feelings are the summation of the joys and sorrows of society at large in the heart of the individual, 'true' feelings are the momentary inner realization of what it is to be human brought about by external contingencies.

If this interpretation by Hsü Fu-kuan of the Confucian view of the place of feelings in poetry is correct, then it does not take us far in our search for a theory of individual literature in the Chinese past: it is directed, typically, to their relevance to the business of living. Naturally it did not appeal to Chou Tso-jen. In fact he praised Shu Po-hsiang (of the mid-Ch'ing period) for deriding the moralists for making a division between 'right' (*cheng*) and 'idle' (*hsien*) feelings: 'idle' feelings are, they both thought, actually a necessary complement to 'right' feelings.[8]

Fortunately this Confucian view did not have a monopoly. To go into the question properly it would be advisable to take a look at the whole quesion of 'feelings' in Chinese literary thought. We might start worse than with a definition. Kao Ming has collected some relevant data in his article 'Researches into Chinese Rhetoric'.[9] He quotes Chu Hsi as saying 'nature is the law of the heart, feelings the function'. The function of the heart is in having desires – as the *Shuo wen* says,

[8] 'Ku nan yü hua', 1935, *K'u chu tsa chi*, p. 119.

[9] 'Chung-kuo hsiu-tz'u hsüeh yen-chiu', in *Chung-kuo yü wen* (Taipei), Vol. II, no. 2.

'*ch'ing* is man's passive nature conceiving desires': following *yin-yang* theory, the passive gives birth to the active, so the originally still heart passes over into activity. The catalyst is external stimuli: *ch'ing* is defined in *Lun Heng* as 'formed through the nature coming into contact with things'[10] We need not be surprised then if the theories we are to encounter tend to be mechanistic. But we are recalled first to the question of the 'rightness' of feelings as we take a look at the treatment of the topic in the classical critical texts (the subject is too diffuse to make selection from later writings possible).

Of the Great Preface to the *Odes* we need only reiterate that it gave first place to feelings, but went on to elaborate at great length the condition of correctness. The *Wen-hsin tiao-lung* also championed the primacy of *ch'ing*, and likewise accepted that feelings not exactly should be, but *are*, 'right'. Despite its sophistication and understanding of the variety and complexity of the elements that go into a work of literature, the general trend of the *Wen-hsin* is to reassert the moral potency and seriousness of literature, so it is not surprising to find Liu Hsieh ranking as the first condition of literature 'feelings deep and not specious'.[11] Elsewhere he writes: 'Feelings are the warp of literature, linguistic forms the woof of thought. Only when the warp is right (*cheng*) can the woof be perfect, only when the thought is definite can the linguistic forms be perspicuous. This is the basic principle in writing.'[12] The phrase 'when the warp is right' is ambiguous, but it is clear from Liu's amplification that the feelings which give rise to poetry (as opposed to the feelings that are 'manufactured for the sake of poetry') are exemplified in the *Book of Odes* pieces which were bred by the grievances of the people. It is also evident that Liu believed that feelings had a kind of 'negative capability', in conformity with the definition mentioned in the *Lun heng*, with no permanent existence or consistency. This one can deduce from his assertion: 'Man is endowed with seven emotions. When stimulated by external objects, these emotions rise in response. In responding to objects one sings to express one's sentiments. All this is perfectly spontaneous.'[13] There is no recognition of such a thing as 'personality' here. Emotions are a kind of sounding-board, and the poet is the 'Aeolian lyre' celebrated by Shelley in his 'Defence of Poetry'. If we refer to the *Li chi*, from which Liu's

[10] Kao Ming says this occurs in the 'Ch'u ping' chapter. Actually it is in the 'Pen hsing' chapter, and is quoted from Liu Hsiang. Wang Ch'ung criticizes it for not making feelings depend on nature (*Lun heng chiao shih*, I, 133).

[11] 'Tsung ching' chapter, *Wen hsin tiao lung chu*, p. 14.

[12] 'Ch'ing ts'ai' chapter, p. 1.

[13] 'Ming shih' chapter, Vincent Shih's translation, p. 32.

passage is derived, so much is clear: 'The people have physical powers and conscience as their nature, but there is no constancy in their grief, joy, pleasure and anger [a paradigm for the feelings in general]. Only when they are moved in response to events do the ways of the heart become apparent.'[14] To sum up, Liu's theory of *ch'ing* was bounded by the ideas of natural response, rightness, and truthfulness ('literature written for the sake of feelings is concentrated and truthful' – 'Ch'ing ts'ai' chapter), though we must acknowledge that any treatise of *Wen-hsin*'s stature that gives primacy to feelings must have given a certain stimulus to personal literature, though Liu's mind was not on purely personal feelings.[15]

In case this theorizing seems all too commonplace, it might be salutary to remind ourselves at this stage that the centrality of the feelings in poetry was fully acknowledged in Europe only with the Romantics, in whose age much of the discussion strikingly resembles what had gone on in China up to 1500 years earlier; previously Aristotle's proposition that poetry derived from the instinct to imitate had been generally accepted. In his time John Stuart Mill found it worth remarking, for instance, that 'poetry is the expression or uttering forth of feeling'.[16]

I say 1500 years because the *Wen fu*, written about A.D. 300, antedates by two centuries the *Wen-hsin tiao-lung*, but it is not an easy text to start with. It was written in an age when nature held the place in men's minds that Confucian morals had occupied in the Han, and Lu Chi lays more stress than Liu Hsieh on 'natural' creation. This is how he describes the preparatory stage in the creative process:

> His [the writer's] lament for fleeting life is in observance of the four seasons that ever revolve, His regard for the myriad growing things
> His regard for the myriad growing things inspires in him thoughts so profuse,
> As with the fallen leaves in autumn's rigour his heart sinks in grief,
> So is each tender twig in sweet spring a source of joy . . .
> Thus moved, he will spread his paper and poise his brush
> To express what he can in writing.
> (*Anthology of Chinese Literature*, trans. S. H. Chen, p. 205.)

Thus primed, writing can achieve the state where:

> The wind of thought bursts from the heart, the stream of words rushes through the lips and teeth . . . Shining and glittering, language

[14] *Ssu pu pei yao*, 5, 13B, cited in notes to *Wen hsin tiao lung chu*, II, 3.
[15] To complicate matters, Liu Hsieh does relate the poet's work to his personality (*hsing ch'ing*), and not just to stimulus, in the 'Ming shih' chapter.
[16] In 'What is Poetry? ', quoted Abrams, p. 32.

> fills your eyes, abundant and overflowing, music drowns your ears. (Bishop, *Studies in Chinese Literature*, trans. A. Fang, p. 20.)

The feelings described here are also essentially responsive (the fact that they join forces with a questing mind (lines 8–12) is not relevant to our purposes), and the act of creation described in the second passage is spontaneous to the point of obliterating self-awareness: it resembles the by-passing of conscious direction typical of calligraphy. Though Lu Chi rejects plagiarism (lines 67–71) and recommends, conversely, originality (lines 14–15), the idea is to produce a compelling work of literature, not to prove the author's individuality.

The other major critical work of the pre-T'ang period, the *Shih p'in* of Chung Jung, written in the first half of the sixth century, also embraces the idea of the feelings being activated in response to events. Its first words are these:

> The spirit sets the phenomena in motion, the phenomena influence man, hence human nature and emotions are agitated and seek expression in dancing and singing.[17] (Translated Hellmut Wilhelm, 'Chung Hung and his *Shih-p'in*, *Wen-lin*, p. 118.)

Like Liu Hsieh's formulation quoted above, this one of Chung Jung is also indebted to the *Li chi*, in which the parallel passage is: 'When men's hearts are moved, it is things which make it so. The movement is in response to things, and is embodied in sound.'[18]

Chu Hsi, as usual, gives the most explicit summary of this trend of thought:

> Man is born passive: this is his given nature. He is moved in response to phenomena: this is how his nature conceives desires. Once there are desires there must be thought; once there is thought there must be words; once there are words, then what the words cannot fully convey and is expressed by the secondary means of sighs and song must have natural resonance and rhythm and never comes to an end. (*Shih chi chuan hsü*, quoted Fu Keng-sheng, *T'ung lun*, p. 49.)

As these various formulations all deal with the *urquelle* of poetry, the emphasis is all on basic, powerful emotions which naturally overflow. The view is the same as that based on the character of primitive poetry put forward in the late eighteenth century in

[17] Compare the following definition by Hazlitt: 'The best general notion which I can give of poetry is, that it is the natural impression of any object or event, by its vividness exciting an involuntary movement of imagination and passion, and producing, by sympathy, a certain modulation of the voice, or sounds, expressing it.' (*Complete Works*, 1, quoted Abrams, p. 52.)

[18] *Ssu pu pei yao*, 5, 6B.

Europe – primitive poetry being 'rude effusions', the passion in which prompts 'a certain melody, or modulation of sound, suited to the emotions' (Abrams, p. 95), or, in a word, 'loose numbers wildly sweet' (Thomas Gray, 'The Progress of Poesy'). The German theoretician J. G. Sulzer concluded: 'The poet is put in a passion, or at least a certain mood, by his object; he cannot resist the violent desire to utter his feelings, he is transported . . . He speaks, even if no one listens to him, because his feelings do not let him be silent.' (Quoted Abrams, p. 89.) In England, Sir William Jones put forward a similar theory around the same time, in 1772, based on oriental poetry (Abrams, p. 87). In itself this analysis of the genesis of poetry does not point the way to individualist literature. Individualist literature needs to be based on natural and genuine sentiments, to be sure, and these may, perhaps in one sense must, be occasioned by external stimuli, but the sentiments are moulded and particularized by the uncommon personality of the author. This latter aspect is what these theories neglect.

The feelings we have been discussing come from the 'heart'. There is another source to which some Chinese theorists ascribed the feelings that takes us nearer what we are seeking, and that is the innards, variously 'liver', 'lungs' and 'bowels'. As Hsüeh Hsüan (1392–1464) wrote: 'All works of literature that arise from true feelings are accomplished; they are what our predecessors used to refer to as coming from the lungs and bowels [*fei fu*].'[19] This way of putting it certainly gives the impression of more immediacy and identity with a man's physical being than 'heart'. The counterpart in the West, employed by more uncouth critics, would be 'guts' or, less contemporarily, the Biblical 'bowels'. Chu Tung-jun quotes from Hsiung Chu of the Yüan dynasty:

> Ch'ü Yüan's *sao*, T'ao Ch'ien and Tu Fu's *shih*, highly indignant and profoundly sorrowing, all flow from their liver and lungs [*kan fei*], and so live on. Otherwise, though one might rack one's brains or ponder deeply, and use all possible embellishments, the effort is wasted and the work committed to oblivion. ('Outline', p. 58.)

And this from Li Ke-fei of Süng:

> Chu-ke K'ung-ming's 'Ch'u shih piao', Li Ling's 'Chiu te sung', Li Ling-po's [Li Mi's] 'Ch'i yang ch'in piao',[20] all poured out copiously as if flowing from the heart and liver; there is absolutely no trace of workmanship. These few great men of the Han-Wei-Chin period actually never sought to make a name for themselves with their

[19] Quoted T'u Kung-sui, *Wen-hsüeh kai lun*, p. 87.

[20] This probably refers to 'Ch'en ch'ing piao'; 'Yang ch'in' (Supporting Parents) sums up its plea.

> writing, yet their diction and thought so far surpassed others. From this we can conclude that in writing, 'animus' [*ch'i*][21] is the main thing, and in this animus, sincerity is the main thing. The reason why Tu Fu's poetry is superior lies simply in his genuineness. Where there is genuineness it will manifest itself. Most scholars fail to recognize this.

The problem of 'genuineness' we will discuss later; for now we only note the use of 'liver' and 'lungs'. One might have thought them the kind of terms peculiar to unorthodox thinkers, but the eminent Confucian Tseng Kuo-fan had occasion to use them too. In 'Hu-nan wen cheng hsü' he wrote:

> As to the natural literary expression which every soul possesses prior to that acquired by imitation, its two sources are sense (*li*) and sensibility (*ch'ing*). These two surely exist in everyone. To set down sense as I understand it and make it known to the world; to adduce my sensibilities of affection and repulsion, sorrow and joy, and put words together so as to convey them, is as if to dissect my lungs and liver and lay them out on bamboo slips: all this is natural literary expression, and people of genuine feelings are all capable of it. (Wang Huan-piao, p. 215, and *Tseng Wen Cheng Kung ch'üan-chi*, p. 313.)

This essay takes a considerable step further towards individualist literature. In addition to the 'dissecting of lungs and liver' we have the significant reference to 'ideas as *I* understand them' and '*my* sentiments', which indicates that literature is essentially subjective, or at least written from a personal point of view.

If I might seem to be forcing an interpretation on this passage, let us compare Tseng's *Chia hsün*:

> The work of every great and famous artist must have a kind of mien, a kind of guise, quite distinct from other people's. To take an example from calligraphers, Wang Hsi-chih [and seven others] just needed to make a dot or a stroke: their mien is entirely distinct, their guise is also quite without correspondencies. Chang Te-t'ien and Ho I-men of the present dynasty, though they are called calligraphers, have not been able to get away from the manner of the masters. It is due to the fact that Liu Shih-an's mien and guise are different [from others'] that he can be commended as a great artist. Literature is just the same. If a man has not his own mien and his own guise, and does not stand head and shoulders above the crowd, he is not worthy of the name of great artist. (Wang Huan-piao, op. cit., p. 219.)

[21] I use 'animus' in the sense of a vitalizing and creative force.

It is not so much his use of significant terminology that places Tseng in the individualist camp, it is more simply the fact that he himself was a very independent person, and what he writes about literature naturally reflects this. Of course he was not unique in this regard; other Confucian scholars before him similarly stressed the personal subjective element in literature. One such was Huang Tsung-hsi (Li-chou), 1610–95. Some of his statements on literature appear to signify complete subjectivism, e.g. 'poetry is the vessel for joy and sorrow',[22] and 'the poet exhibits for himself his weeping and rejoicing'.[23] Others include the wide world aspect: 'Poetry expresses my spirit and sentiments in relation to the whole of creation,'[24] and one that represents his outlook more fully, 'the role of poetry is extremely broad. The individual's character and feelings, the peace or disorder of the empire, are all included in it.'[25] With the last item Chou Tso-jen may have affected to disagree, since it infringes his taboo on questions of public order and morals, but all it need mean is that literature should relate to general as well as personal issues, or, put more simply, that it should be 'serious'.

If Tseng Kuo-fan and Huang Tsung-hsi did not make any contribution to aesthetic terminology, despite the fact that what they advocated was in effect individual literature, there are still other terms to be considered, ones used quite widely, which in themselves betoken a kind of literature rooted in the character and being of its author. One of these is *pen-se*, 'native hue' or 'true colours'. Its meaning is explained by T'ang Shun-chih (1507–60), who writes interestingly enough to bear quoting at length:

> Nowadays there are two types of people. One of them is of outstanding intellect, the man who is a so-called 'eye of the ages' [i.e. one who has rare independence and clarity of vision]. Even if he has not taken hold of pen and paper and painfully set himself to learn the art of writing, but instead, relying directly on his inmost feelings, writes just as it comes out, as if writing letters home, though there may be a lack of finesse [in his writing], it will never be vulgar, fusty, or hackneyed, and will result in a first-class work. The other may be said to be a mundane person. Though his heart may be set on learning the art of writing, and he may have taken all possible care to work correctly to the so-called rules of composition, yet he keeps going over the same ground and [the result] is nothing but bits of old wives' talk. If we look for his so-called 'true spirit' and

[22] *Wen ting ssu chi*, 1, 'Hsieh Hsin-yeh shih hsü', quoted Kuo, p. 412.
[23] *Wen yüeh*, 4, 'T'ien yü ch'an shih shih chi hsü', quoted Kuo, p. 412.
[24] *Wen ting ssu chi*, 1, 'Lu Chen-ssu shih hsü', Kuo, p. 411.
[25] 'Shih ching t'i tz'u', Kuo, p. 413.

'viewpoint which the ages cannot efface', there is no trace of it. So though his work may be skilled, it is unavoidably second-class. This is to do with the 'native hue' of a composition.

To take poetry as an example, T'ao Ch'ien never paid much attention to prosody or embellished his phrases, he just wrote as it came out, with the result that his poetry is the best in the world. The reason? Because his native hue was superior. Right from the beginning of poetry there has been no man who has given more attention or constructed so scrupulous a theory with regard to prosody than Shen Yüeh. He sacrificed his life's energy to it, but if one reads his poetry one finds it constrained and crabbed. In whole pages and volumes he cannot come out with a couple of good phrases. The reason? Because his native hue is inferior. If the native hue is inferior, the writing cannot be accomplished, let alone if a man disowns his native hue!

How can the reason why the writing of Han and after is not as good as of old be that in so-called technique and versatility it is not quite so skilful? Before Ch'in and Han the Confucians had their Confucian hue, as for the Taoists, they had their Taoist hue; the Politicians had their Politicians' hue, the Nominalists, the Mohists, the Yin-yang school all had their native hue. Though their approach was contradictory, all of them had a 'viewpoint which the ages cannot efface'. Hence the Taoists, inevitably, were not willing to pirate the theories of the Confucians; the Politicians, inevitably, were not willing to borrow from the Mohists' discourses: all acknowledged their native hue and their words gave voice to it. What they expressed was their native hue, hence their words were imbued with the light of their soul, and lived on down the ages. Since T'ang and Sung, all writers have talked about 'life' and discussed the way of setting the world to rights, making a great display on paper; in everything they entrusted themselves to Confucianism, but it was not something that had been cultivated to become part of themselves, they did not really have a 'viewpoint which the ages cannot efface'. On the contrary, they echoed other people's noise and stole other people's opinions, plagiarized their phrases, like a poor man stealing a rich man's coat, or a peasant decking himself out as a rich merchant. Acting a pretence to the top of their bent, their ludicrousness was in the end bound to emerge. Thus the light of their soul was misspent, and their words soon faded away like smoke. ('Yü Mao Lu-men lun wen shu', from *Ching ch'uan chi*, reproduced in Yang Chia-lo, *Wen-hsüeh p'i-p'ing wen-hsüan*, Vol. III.)

The term *pen-se* was also employed by Yen Yü in *Ts'ang-lang shih-hua*: 'Shih fa'. In his note, Kuo Shao-yü attributes its first application in literary criticism to Ch'en Shih-tao (1053–1101). He also quotes from T'ao Ming-chün on the subject, who defines *pen-se* as 'that which preserves and confirms natural predispositions', in contrast to powder and paint.[26]

From these two expositions it appears that a man first of all has to have true independence of mind for any *pen-se* to be apparent. Secondly that his writing must in mode of expression be an extension of his personality – he writes 'just as it comes out', without paying any heed to how he should write. Thirdly in content his work must be idiosyncratic, projecting his own slant on things, and conforming to his 'natural predispositions'. It is clear that the idea of *pen-se* is a very important piece in the jigsaw picture of the theory of individualism in traditional China.

T'ang Shun-chih's choice of T'ao Ch'ien to exemplify *pen-se* forms a link with Chou Tso-jen, for T'ao was one of Chou's cultural heroes. He hardly ever mentioned him without expressing his admiration for him, as for instance in *Yeh tu ch'ao*, 1934, where he calls him 'one of the free spirits in history'.[27] But the connection is less tenuous than that, for Chou himself wrote an essay on *pen-se*, dated 25 November 1935. Chou begins the essay by recommending the virtue of simplicity in writing, whence he moves on to 'ordinary talk' and then to *pen-se*. He explains why *pen-se* is a difficult thing to capture: 'To be able to bring out *pen-se*, the original temper and features must be able to bear examination. It is human nature to lack self-confidence and to rely on adornment, but *pen-se* can only be revealed if the previously applied make-up is washed away.'[28] He then proceeds to relate this desideratum to decocting herbs and medicines just to the point of eliminating unwanted elements while still preserving their essence. This essay shows that Chou Tso-jen understood *pen-se* in the same way as his predecessors. While as far as I know he made no equation between *pen-se* and individualism in literature, the fact that he was in favour of both shows that they were at least reconcilable.

With the next quality I want to discuss I can be more positive than that. The quality is *ch'eng*, variously translated as sincerity, integrity, honesty, and truthfulness. It would help to define it if we look first at what Chou Tso-jen said about it. As it was a value that Chou consistently prized throughout his life he mentioned it often. Let us take some of his pronouncements in chronological order.

In *'One's Own Garden'*, he writes of folksongs:[29] 'Their most marked and valuable characteristics are their sincerity (*chen-chih*) and good

[26] *Ts'ang-lang shih-hua chiao shih*, p. 103. The T'ao Ming-chün quotation comes from *Shih shuo tsa chi*.
[27] 'Kui ti sheng chang' (The Growing-up of Ghosts), p. 258.
[28] 'Pen-se', *Feng yü t'an*, p. 35.
[29] 'Ko yao' (Folk-songs), *Tzu-chi ti yüan-ti*, 1922, p. 43.

faith (*ch'eng-hsin*), which are *the essence of all works of art*.' These two words can be legitimately regarded as bisyllabic equivalents of *ch'eng*, as is the more colloquial '*chen-shih*', which indeed the *Han-yü Ci-dian* takes as its primary definition of *ch'eng*. *Chen-shih* (genuineness) is the quality, one recalls, that letters in particular have, and in that essay we quoted, 'Diaries and Letters', Chou regrets that it is beyond his reach: 'It is as if I can vaguely perceive the true image of myself in my heart, but if I want to write it down, even with the knowledge that nobody else will ever see it, I can never avoid a touch of artifice.'[30]

In 1931, in 'In memory of Chih-mo', where he employs another variant, 'honesty' (*ch'eng-shih*), it is contrasted with 'the great lie'. He makes the charge that practically everything in newspapers and magazines, whether about affairs of state or trivial gossip, is written either with the deliberate intention to deceive or in deceptive conventional formulae: the author 'does not himself necessarily believe it, nor does he necessarily expect others to believe it, he feels he just had to write that way.'[31] Then towards the end of his creative period he redefined the *yen chih* and *tsai tao* classification of good and bad literature as *ch'eng* and not *ch'eng*, the first being 'really and actually felt', the second just 'repeating what has been said before'.[32] And the next year he summed up that his duties are discharged if the thoughts he wants to express are honest (*ch'eng-shih*) and his words capable of conveying them.[33]

We have seen already that Chou associated *yen chih* with individual literature. By his translating *yen chih* into *ch'eng, ch'eng* also becomes associated with individual literature. Furthermore, it is evident from the above elucidations, if such they can be called, that there is a considerable overlap between *ch'eng* and the values already enumerated, since it shares with them the characteristic of trueness (*chen*). The distinguishing characteristic of *ch'eng* is indicated in its opposition to 'the great lie' and its link with 'thoughts' or opinions: with *ch'eng* the emphasis is on the truth (in a subjective sense) of the ideas the author expresses, not on naturalness, spontaneity, or immediacy, which pertain to the feelings – both of course have to be 'true' to the character of the author. *Ch'eng* would be more considered, more serious if you like, would concern belief, would not be so ephemeral as feelings might be.

[30] *Yü t'ien ti shu*, 1925, p. 11.

[31] *K'an yün chi*, p. 124.

[32] 'Han wen-hsüeh ti ch'ien-t'u' (The Future of Chinese Literature), 1943, *Yao-t'ang tsa wen*, p. 29.

[33] 'Meng-hsiang chih i' (Reveries, 1), 1944, *K'u k'ou kan k'ou*, pp. 6–7.

However loosely words might be used, however facilely interchanged with others, each has an identity of its own. *Ch'eng* is a word that has a long and prominent history in Chinese thought that must be evoked when it is used. Perhaps this singular meaning will come out as we examine its history.

Ch'eng is regarded in Chinese thought essentially as a Confucian moral virtue, and is particularly associated with Neo-Confucianism. But Chou dissociated himself from Neo-Confucianism. His source for *ch'eng* is more likely to have been the *Chung yung* (Doctrine of the Mean), which he said he read from the age of eleven.[34] In later life he frequently declared himself a follower of its general philosophy, reinterpreted to suit his taste. The most relevant comments on *ch'eng* in that work are:

> It is only he who is possessed of the most complete sincerity [*ch'eng*] that can exist under heaven, who can give its full development to his nature. *The Doctrine of the Mean*, (Trans. Legge, Chapter 22, pp. 415–16.) Sincerity is that whereby self-completion is effected, and its way is that by which man must direct himself. (ibid., Chapter 25, p. 418.)

The Sung commentary to the latter, referring back to the first chapter of *Chung yung*, says *ch'eng* is 'Heaven-conferred nature', and *tao* is 'the path which is in accordance with the nature' (quoted Legge, ibid.).

The marvellous powers that the *Chung yung* says accrue to the possessor of *ch'eng* we can ignore. The significant thing is that he has the power to express his basic nature, and that *ch'eng* is self-completion, that is, the development of one's own potential without regard to anyone else. Hence it would be appropriate to translate it as 'integrity' in this context.

In the field of literary theory, a very powerful early advocate of *ch'eng* was Wang Ch'ung (A.D. 27–?), whom Chou refers to several times in *Yao-t'ang tsa-wen* (e.g. pp. 40, 122) as one of the three enlightened men in three thousand years of Chinese history, and who came from K'uai-chi, Chou's home district, which counted a lot with him – witness the fact that for most of his life he collected the works of fellow-provincials. Wang Ch'ung's motive in writing *Lun Heng* could be (and has been) said to be summed up in one phrase, 'abhorrence of fabrication'.[35] So it is not surprising to find him expressing such sentiments as these:

[34] In 'Hsiao yin' (Short Introduction), 1928, *Yeh tu ch'ao*, p. 1.
[35] *Chi hsü wang*, from *Lun Heng*, 'I wen' chapter.

> At the base are the roots and trunk; at the top there are the flowers and leaves. At the centre there are the fruit and kernel; on the outside there are the skin and shell. Writing and words are the flowers and leaves, the skin and the shell of the scholar. Sincerity lies in the breast, while writing is put on bamboo and silk. The outside naturally matches and complements the inside. Thus when one lets one's brush flow as one's thoughts stir, the substance is revealed as the writing takes shape. Man's having art is like birds having feathers. The feathers have five colours, and they all grow from the body. If there is art without substance, this is like multi-coloured birds coming out in feathers of the wrong colour. (*Lun Heng chiao shih*, II, p. 609.)

It appears from this that literature is the direct expression of the writer's inner self – it is like a natural growth from the body of the writer.[36] 'Sincerity' or 'integrity' seems to be the commanding influence in this process of being true to the self. The value of truthfulness extends to the matter as well as to the manner, as emerges from Wang Ch'ung's parable of the archer which follows on: 'The argument's corresponding with the truth is like the arrow hitting the target' (ibid.); this incidentally is the aspect of Wang Ch'ung's thought emphasized by the contemporary critic Chiang Tsu-i.[37] It involves maintaining a critical attitude both to inherited doctrine and in forming independent judgements based on wide knowledge. Thus he praises Confucius's handling of the historical records of the state of Lu in compiling his *Spring and Autumn Annals*: in forming his critical judgements Confucius 'no longer followed the historical record; the subtle thought came from the breast [*hsiung*]'.[38] Literature might be assumed to be subject to the same principle, since it has the same source: 'Literature comes from the breast; the heart is made visible in literature.' (ibid., p. 609.)

The twin aspects of being true to oneself and serving objective truth come out in the following excerpt:

> Making up the face to impose similarity is to lose the [original] appearance; manipulating words to compel likeness is to lose the [original] feelings. The young all have different parents, are born as different types. There is no need for them to be alike. If they conform to what they are endowed with they will be beautiful by virtue of it. If literature has to conform to a certain standard to be good, this is like rating skill by not cutting one's hand while chopping wood on behalf of the master carpenter [i.e. one should

[36] Compare Buffon: 'Le style est l'homme même', *Discours*, 1753.

[37] In *Wang Ch'ung ti wen-hsüeh li-lun*, p. 42.

[38] In the 'Ch'ao ch'i' chapter, *Lun Heng chiao shih*, p. 606.

> not be deemed unskilful if awkward in the task of imitating the writings of a master].[39] Each man of letters has his calling: it may be manipulating words to give a finish to writing, or detecting falseness to put the record straight. If the thought must be consistent [with that of others] and the words must be copied, then the Five Emperors' tasks were not different, and the Three Kings' works were the same [the reverse was true]. Beauty may appear in various visages, but they are all pleasing to the sight. Plaintive tones need not share the same tunes, but they all fall sweetly on the ear. Wines may have different bouquets, but they all make you drunk. Cereals have a variety of tastes, but they all make you full. If you contend that writing should follow established practices, then this is to say that Shun's eyebrows ought to be variegated and Yü's eyes ought to have double pupils [which would be to require them to have the characteristics of their predecessors]. (*Lun Heng chiao shih*, IV, p. 1192, quoted Lo, I, p. 113.)

Suffice it to say of this passage that its theme is all of a piece with *ch'eng*, in that the message is that the writer must follow his own judgement. It is also foreshadows the *pen-se* argument in that it says that the true and unique character of the author must be reflected in what he writes. Understandably therefore Chiang Tsu-i takes it as the first proper statement of the individualist standpoint in Chinese literary criticism.[40]

While we are with Wang Ch'ung it is interesting to note that he shared Chou Tso-jen's estimation of discursive writing. Wang states that of the five forms of writing the free 'discussion' is the most worthy, because 'it gives expression to the thoughts in one's breast, treats of the affairs of the society. It is something more than commenting on the Classics, or supplementing the tradition of the ancient texts. The arguments arise from the breast, the writing is formed in the hand; it is not something an expounder of the Classics can do.'[41]

There are so many points of similarity between Chou and Wang Ch'ung that in terms of attitudes and assumptions Chou might be said to be in direct line from Wang, for though Chou stood out for the freedom to indulge personal vagaries, yet the thing he prized above all in literature, as we shall see, was sanity and independence of judgement. As with Wang Ch'ung, purely literary qualities were not the ultimate consideration with him.[42] In his chapter on Wang, Lo Ken-tse remarks

[39] From *Lao tzu*: in D. C. Lau's translation, 'In chopping wood on behalf of the master carpenter there are few who escape hurting their own hands instead', p. 136.
[40] op. cit., p. 54.
[41] 'I wen' chapter, *Lun Heng chiao shih*, III, 865.
[42] For Wang Ch'ung's position see Chiang Tsu-i, op. cit., chapter 8.

(op. cit., p. 114) that in the May Fourth period theorists generally applied the idea of 'truthfulness' (*chen-ch'eng*) only to feelings, not, like Wang, to affairs as well; in this Chou sided with Wang rather than with his contemporaries.

But to return to the matter in hand. One finds the term *ch'eng* used fairly frequently by Chinese theorists – Chang Ching (970–1018) for instance – but they do not, as far as I am aware, shed much new light on the subject, not until we come to the transitional period between Ming and Ch'ing, when we find new intellectual backing for the idea in the so-called Yen-Li philosophy. The name refers to the founder Yen Yüan (1635–1704) and Li Kung (1659–1733), his disciple. Yen Yüan, incidentally, met with Chou Tso-jen's general approval.[43] Yen's basic standpoint can be seen in this passage quoted by Watanabe Shūhō:

> In one's serious writing the only criterion should be right or wrong, not just like or unlike. If right, then the standpoint of just one or two cannot be changed; if wrong, then something may be agreed by millions of people, one does not echo them. Let alone millions of people, even if it were a conclusion shared over thousands of years, we still ought as the first to see the light instruct those who are slow in perceiving it. We cannot just tag along and parrot others. (From *I-shu*, 'Hsüeh wen' chapter, quoted in *Chung-kuo che-hsüeh kai lun*, 'Chin-shih che-hsüeh', p. 164.)

One literary theorist who is described as a follower of Yen-Li philosophy was Ch'eng Mien-chuang, 1691–1767. Ch'eng presents the following argument:

> Confucius said: 'In cultivating eloquence one establishes one's integrity [*hsiu tz'u li ch'i ch'eng*]', and 'words must simply convey [*tz'u ta erh i*]'. Integrity as the foundation, conveying as the function, in general the Sage's discussion of the art of letters only amounted to this. To demonstrate the Way through the art of letters is not integrity; to practise the art deliberately is not conveying. As a result of not going back to the root but only seeking literary accomplishment, a variety of styles have flourished, and scripts heaped up, but it has only sapped the reader's energies and is of no practical use, so what is the point of it? (*Ch'ing-hsi wen chi*, 10, 'Fu Chia Yü-men lun ku wen shu', quoted Kuo, p. 481.)

The utilitarianism of the last part is also central to Yen-Li philosophy. In present day terms it could be called 'art for life's sake'. But the important thing about the school of thought for our present discussion is its confidence in the validity of the individual point of view. It accepts no authorities apart from the ancient texts, which is

[43] 'Yen shih hsüeh chi', 1933, *Yeh tu ch'ao*.

equivalent to accepting the Bible but rejecting the theologians. In Ch'eng's literary philosophy this attitude is expressed as 'establishing one's integrity', which entails 'going back to the root' and repudiating the Han Yü doctrine of 'demonstrating the Way'. Again the idea is the same as Chou's of accepting no directions, of not writing in the service of any cause.

Let the last word on *ch'eng* be said by Chin Sheng-t'an (d. 1661). I think it can close the case for the connection between *ch'eng* and individualism. He wrote:

> In poetry one must say what the heart holds sincerely [*ch'eng-jan*], and also what the heart holds in common [*t'ung-jan*]. When you say what the heart holds sincerely, your tears may fall with the stroke of your pen; when you say what the heart holds in common, you may make the reader's tears fall as he reads aloud. ('Ta shen k'uang-lai shu', reprinted in Shen Ch'i-wu, *Chin-tai san-wen ch'ao* (Anthology of Modern Prose), p. 294.)

In this passage *ch'eng* is set against the things the leaders shares. The two are complementary but distinct. What moves the author in his own verse is the transfixing of his own unique self; what moves the reader is finding expressed the things he has in common with the author.

Ch'eng can admittedly denote something very personal, but the particular slant is typical of Chin Sheng-t'an, who is famous for his belief in unique and untrammelled genius. Two characteristic propositions of his are, on the primacy of personal style over subject matter, 'the subject matter is the affairs of Tom, Dick and Harry, but the writing is from the hand of one man'; and, on poetry as 'effusion', 'how can you limit the number of words and phrases in poetry? Poetry is the sudden cry from the heart.'[44]

I think further light can be shed on the Chinese word *ch'eng*, strangely enough, if we compare it with the English word 'sincerity'. M. H. Abrams has fortunately summarized its history and usage in *The Mirror and the Lamp*, pp. 318–20. The word sincerity 'had been popularized at the time of the Protestant Reformation to connote the genuine and unadulterated Christian doctrine, and, secondarily, a lack of pretence or corruption in him who affirms a religious and moral sentiment'. In the Chinese context we can for the Protestant Reformation substitute *Doctrine of the Mean.* To continue the story, the term 'sincerity' passed over into literary criticism, through the agency, for one, of John Keble, 'who viewed all poetry on the analogy of religion, proposed sincerity as the identifying mark of 'primary poetry', no less

[44] Quoted Ho Man-tzu, *Lun Chin Sheng-t'an p'ing kai* Shui hu chuan (On Chin Sheng-t'an Criticism and Revisions of *Shui hu chuan*), pp. 59, 69.

than of moral character . . . The first requirement is 'to thine own self be true'; this is one of the several touchstones of 'genuine and keenly felt emotion, as well as of transparently sincere poetry'. Again, as with *ch'eng*, 'sincerity', as this passage foreshadows, tended to merge with 'truth'. Thus Carlyle wrote:

> The excellence of Burns is . . . his Sincerity, his indisputable air of Truth . . .
> The passion that is traced before us has glowed in a living heart . . .
> To every poet, to every writer, we might say: Be true, if you would be believed.
> Let a man but speak forth with genuine earnestness the thought, the emotion, the actual condition of his heart.

To Walter Pater, as to Wang Ch'ung, this truth is, in Abram's words, 'Janus-faced, looking both out and in':

> In the highest as in the lowliest literature, then, the one indispensable beauty is, after all, truth: truth to bare fact in the latter, as to some personal sense of fact, diverted . . . from men's ordinary sense of it, in the former; truth there as accuracy, truth here as expression, that finest and most intimate form of truth, the *vraie vérité*.

But, once more like *ch'eng*, ' "sincere" could also be employed with the moral overtones dampened as the near equivalent of "spontaneous" and "natural", in opposition to what is artful or contrived . . . In a comment on Keats, [Leigh] Hunt appeals jointly to spontaneity and sincerity in order to condemn neo-classic artifice.'

Lastly, the Art for Art's Sake movement in Europe brought in its train an attitude reminiscent of Chin Sheng-t'an's. Henry James made sincerity 'the indispensable attribute of a specifically aesthetic conscience and integrity.' Eschewing 'the dull dispute over the "immoral" subject and the "moral",' James proposed as 'the one measure of the worth of a given subject . . . is it valid, in a word, is it genuine, is it sincere, the result of some direct impression or perception of life? '

This survey of the English scene[45] shows how closely in any language the qualities of sincerity, truth, genuineness, spontaneity, naturalness (the last two will be discussed here later) are bound up together. In making 'individual literature' the aggregate of these things, Chou drew upon aesthetic concepts long familiar in China and at least as old as the Romantic movement in Europe, without contributing anything of his own, but in a pre-Existentialist age they seem to me to sum up fairly what individualism in literature means.

[45] More recently than James, F. L. Lucas tried to banish the word 'sincerity' from the critic's vocabulary (in *Style*), but Henri Peyre's book, *Literature and Sincerity*, shows how commonly it has been used.

3

'TASTE' AND TASTES

The things we have been discussing in regard to individualism in literature refer mainly to principles the writer should observe, and issue from the attempt to identify the factors that should be in at the birth of a work of literature. The term *ch'ü-wei*, while similarly embracing the personal idiom, idiosyncratic element, singular character, and particular flavour, refers more to qualities in a work that the reader can appreciate, qualities which are often less serious and sententious.

Ch'ü-wei loomed large as a literary value both in Chou Tso-jen's mind and in other people's conceptions of him. Ho K'ai[1] was only one of the many who criticized him for 'getting his priorities wrong' in this way. It was also a factor in Chou's being associated with the school of Lin Yutang, which might be described as the cult of quirky personality.

Ch'ü-wei is such a vague term that we had best look for definitions. The *Tz'u-hai* defines it as a portmanteau word combining *hsing-ch'ü* 'interest' and *i-wei*, 'evocativeness' or 'implications'. The example cited is by Yeh Shih (1150–1223): 'Strangeness and greatness lie under an unremarkable surface, *ch'ü-wei* is on the other side of the words.' From this we gather that *ch'ü-wei* has nothing to do with formal aesthetics, but with qualities in the work that the words only hint at. The example, however, serves only to whet the appetite; we need to follow other tracks.

Of course, as commonly used nowadays, *ch'ü-wei* has the sense of 'interest', 'piquancy' or 'appeal', and Chou often uses it so. Here the only things of significance are what he finds of interest, and the frequency with which he uses the term, not the term itself. It is often linked with the more elusive qualities, like humour, irony and satire, things which do lie below the surface. For instance, Chou's judgement on Yü Cheng-hsieh (1775–1840) is that 'his criticism is fair and his style has much comical *ch'ü-wei*';[2] and he commends the Japanese

[1] In his essay 'Chou Tso-jen ti ch'ü-wei wen hsüeh' (Chou Tso-jen's 'Literature of Taste'), reprinted in T'ao Ming-chih's *Chou Tso-jen lun*, 1934.

[2] 'Yü Li-ch'u ti hui-hsieh' (The Humour of Yü Li-ch'u), *Ping chu hou t'an*, p. 47.

haibun (prose pieces related to the *haiku*) for their 'pregnant and oddly humorous *ch'ü-wei*'.[3]

More technically, Chou employs *ch'ü-wei* as a rather contrived equivalent of the English word 'taste', that is, a set of aesthetic preferences which is subject to variations from age to age: he picks out Keats, for example, as a victim of the adverse 'taste' of his times. Chou recognized 'taste' as the basis of all literary appreciation, and by so doing stressed the relativity of critical judgement[4] (thus making himself unpopular with the Left) and the great variety of works that can appeal to different people because of their diverse cultural backgrounds. Though rather unusual in emphasizing these things in his own age, he had of course predecessors in China in accepting the simple fact that individual predilections vary. Ts'ao Chih (A.D. 192–232) was an early one. He wrote:

> Everyone has his own preferences. Everyone likes the fragrance of orchids and irises, yet there is also the case of the man who had to leave home because his smell was so offensive yet was much appreciated at the sea-side. All enjoy the sound of the music of the Yellow Emperor and Chuan Hsü, yet Mo-tzu wrote a diatribe against it. How can there be unanimity? ('Yü Yang Te-tsu shu' [Letter to Yang Te-tsu], reprinted Wang Huan-piao, p. 20.)

And Tseng Kuo-fan was a later one. In his introduction to his *Sheng-che hua-hsiang chi* (Portraits of Great Men) he wrote:

> In this anthology of poems ancient and modern, from Wei and Chin down to the present dynasty, I have drawn on nineteen authors. Now the scope of poetry is wide, and one's preferences and proclivities are attuned to what is close to one's own nature. By way of analogy, if all possible varieties of succulent food were laid out on stands and dishes, I would just eat my fill of those which suited my palate. If I must scour the empire for all its delicacies, judge their flavours and finally present only one dish, that would be a great humbug; if I must compel all the tongues in the empire to like what I want, that would be a great stupidity. (Reprinted in Yang Chia-lo, vol. III.)

Chou's *ch'ü-wei* also means 'taste' in the sense of discernment. His essay 'The question of whether old books should be read or not' provides a clear example:

> Reading works of literature is like drinking wine: it requires the reader to distinguish alternative flavours. This responsibility lies

[3] 'T'an p'ai wen' (On *Haibun*), 1937, *Yao wei chi*, p. 195.

[4] A case he explicitly argued in 'Wen-i p'i-p'ing tsa-hua' (Miscellaneous Remarks on Literary Criticism), 1923, *T'an lung chi*. The reference to Keats is also in this essay.

> wholly with oneself, not with the other thing. If someone has not the ability to distinguish the flavours, to the extent of even confusing them, the fault is in himself, that is, he is lacking in *ch'ü-wei*. ('Ku shu k'e tu fou ti wen-t'i', *T'an hu chi*, p. 159).

So far, so straightforward. New subtleties emerge, however, when he eventually comes to discuss the concept directly. This was in 1935, in an essay comparing Li Yü and Yüan Mei. For convenience I shall continue to translate *ch'ü-wei* as 'taste'. Chou remarks that Yüan Mei was 'vulgar, or you could say, tasteless (*mei ch'ü-wei*)', and this gives him his cue:

> I have to confess here that I think 'taste' is very important; it is both beautiful and good, and tastelessness is a disaster. There are quite a lot of things included in what I call taste, such as refinement [*ya*], unsophisticatedness [*cho*], straightforwardness [*p'u*], perspicuity [*ch'ing-lang*], enlightenment [*t'ung-ta*], moderation [*chung-yung*], discrimination [*yu pie-tse*], and so on. All things contrary to these qualities are tasteless. There is a phrase 'low-class taste' current which I might as well borrow to elucidate, though it looks as if it has been loaned from Japan, and in my opinion there are semantic objections to it: it is probably more intelligible than 'tasteless'. Tastelessness is by no means the same as having no taste [*wu ch'ü-wei*]. Unless he is beyond the reach of human aid, there is normally no one who does not take a particular attitude to life. It may be mild, as if from indifference, or it may be niggling and fastidious, but though tendencies may vary, each and every attitude amounts to a kind of taste. It is like people having different faces: if they preserve their original features, regardless of their beauty or lack of it, they still have a vitality of their own. The worst thing is the spurious kind of tastelessness, or if you prefer it, false taste, bad taste, or low-class taste. To imitate the phrase 'great wisdom in the guise of foolishness', this is 'great vulgarity in the guise of refinement'. ('Li-weng yü Sui-yüan' [Li Yü and Yüan-mei], *Ku-chu tsa chi*, p. 84.)

By contrasting *ch'ü-wei* with vulgarity he gives the word the sense of 'tastefulness': Yüan Mei's offence was lack of good taste in expressing a liking for a certain kind of type-face Chou thought showy. But his reluctance to accept the word 'low-class' as a modifier for *ch'ü-wei* indicates that it does not correspond with 'taste' all along the line: *ch'ü-wei* can only be properly described pejoratively as false or lacking. This is because the exercise of any genuinely held personal values in accepting some things and rejecting others is a legitimate assertion of *ch'ü-wei*. In other words *ch'ü-wei* is an extension of the personality. It is significant that in his amplification of what he himself regards as *ch'ü-wei* Chou picks on qualities consistent with the bent or bias of an individual which would manifest themselves in and through a writer's work. It seems that the word covers the dual aspects of what the reader brings to his reading and what the writer brings to his writing. This is borne out by Chou's description of his attitude towards poetry: 'I am not concerned with the poetical merits or demerits; actually I just try to make out the author's character and *ch'ü-wei* as revealed in the poetry.'[5]

Ch'ü-wei is in fact commonly linked with character or personality in Chou's critical comments. Of the Japanese monk Kenkō Hōshi (1282–1350) he says that the greatest value of his work *Tsurezure gusa* (The Harvest of Leisure) is in its '*ch'ü-wei hsing*' (being characterized by *ch'ü-wei*): 'Although there is logical dissertation in the book it is not dry or inhuman, as is usual with dogmatists. It has at its root a kind of warmth and kindness; at every turn he observes society and the world from the point of view of *ch'ü-wei*, so even in his sermons there is a rich strain of poetry.'[6] This is not the only place where Chou says what is good abut Kenkō Hōshi; in an aside during a discussion of Yen Chih-t'ui, he writes: 'Yen is not narrow, which is where his *jen-ch'ing-wei* [humanity, literally, 'taste of human feelings'] lies. I feel that one also likes Kenkō Hōshi for this.'[7] These parallel assertions suggest that the degree to which a work has *ch'ü-wei* corresponds to the reader's sense of the author's personality perceived through it.

Such a bias is understandable when one takes into account Chou's agreement with Anatole France that the literary remains of anyone, distinguished or commonplace, are valuable 'as long as they had something they loved, believed, hoped for, as long as they left part of themselves at the tip of their pen',[8] and Chou's own unsolicited confession that whereas he had previously believed in humanist literature for the sake of the ideas behind it, now (1926) his liking was for the thing itself.[9] The Chinese reader in particular would have been prepared for this bias. Chang Hsüeh-ch'eng was not unique in feeling, in Nivison's words, that 'the content of *wen* is not the burden of the message communicated by it, but the quality of the writer's emotional temper or moral insight manifested in it.'[10]

[5] 'Erh-t'ung shih' (Children's Poetry), 1937, *Ping chu hou t'an*, p. 62.
[6] 'T'u-jan ts'ao ch'ao' (Excerpts from *Tsurezure gusa*), *Yü Ssu*, II, 2, 1925.
[7] 'Yen shih chia hsün', *Yeh tu ch'ao*, p. 169.
[8] 'Tzu-chi ti yüan-ti chiu hsü' (Original preface to 'One's Own Garden'), *T'an lung chi*, pp. 51–2.
[9] Preface to *I-shu yü sheng-huo*, 1926, p. 3.
[10] *The Life and Thought of Chang Hsüeh-ch'eng*, p. 138.

I have kept to the Chinese word '*ch'ü-wei*' because I cannot think of an English word to translate it: 'taste' lacks the extra dimension we have been discussing. But there is a German word, coined by Friedrich Schlegel, which seems to represent the same critical approach, though it too inevitably misses some of its connotations. It does however bring us back to *ch'ü-wei*'s common meaning of 'interest'. It is *das Interessante*, used by Schlegel as an antonym to 'objectivity'. M. H. Abrams explains:

> This term he uses in an old sense, close to its Latin etymon: it signifies a lack of *dis*interestedness, and the intervention in a work of the attitudes and proclivities of the author himself. The work of such a poet . . . is also said to show 'manner' or 'an individual turn of mind, and an individual turn of sensibility', as opposed to 'style', which signifies an impersonal mode of expression according to the uniform laws of beauty. (*The Mirror and the Lamp*, p. 237.)

Both component parts of *ch'ü-wei, ch'ü* and *wei* have lives of their own, and both figure in Chou Tso-jen's critical vocabulary in other combinations. Proceeding from the simpler to the more complex, we continue with the second element, *wei*, which is immediately intelligible as 'taste' in the gustatory sense, or 'flavour'.

By itself *wei* has no special interest, but in certain combinations it has. We had best begin with the gloss the *Tz'u-hai* provides for *ch'ü-wei*, namely *i-wei*, 'evocativeness'. Chou applied this term in distinguishing between two approaches to trite subjects:

> One is the customary 'the weather today . . . ha-ha-ha'; the other is to say 'the weather today is good' or 'is cold', only then to make some further observations about the cold, to the effect that one saw frost in the morning, or that it is depressingly chilly, so appealing to physical principles or human feelings: then one feels there would be a little evocativeness. ('*Ch'un tsai t'ang tsa wen*', 1939, *Yao wei chi*, p. 107.)

If I might make an unpardonable intrusion myself, Chou is right to say 'a little' evocativeness, for it is only a little, so fearful was he of appearing sentimental. Let me provide a better example to bring out the meaning of *i-wei*; it is in English, and it comes from the pen of Alexander Smith:

> 'My son Absalom' is an expression of precisely similar import to 'my brother Dick' or 'my uncle Toby' . . . It would be difficult to say that 'O Absalom, my son, my son' is not poetry; yet the grammatical and verbal import of the words is exactly the same in both cases. The interjection 'O', and the repetition of the words 'my son', add nothing whatever to the meaning; but they have the effect of making words which are otherwise but the intimation of a fact, the

expression of an *emotion* of exceeding depth and interest. (Written in 1835, quoted Abrams, op. cit., p. 153.)

Another key term on this side is *hui-wei*, literally 'returning' flavour or after-taste. The importance it had in Chou's mind is illustrated in an excerpt from a preface he wrote in 1926. Chou has stated that the most interesting technique for poetry is *hsing*, which in modern terminology would be 'symbol', and recalled that *hsing* style had been common in China from the earliest times. The example of it he chooses is the *Book of Odes* poem 'T'ao chih yao yao', the first verse of which, translated by Waley, runs:

Buxom is the peach-tree;
How its flowers blaze!
Our lady going home
Brings good to family and house.
(*Book of Songs*, no. 113, Mao 6.)

This poem 'does not necessarily compare the peach to the bride, neither does it lay down that at the time when the peach blossoms, or in some peach planter's family, there is a daughter getting married; in fact, simply because there is something in common between the peach blossom's fullness and fairness and marriage, so it is used to start a train of thought. Yet this creating atmosphere has nothing to do with adumbration, but with expressing the central idea, only in another way.'[11] Chou goes on: 'The Chinese literary revolution is under the influence of classicism (not neo-classicism): all works are like a crystal ball, gleaming and transparent to an excessive degree, without a trace of shadowiness. Therefore they seem to lack a kind of lingering fragrance [*yü-hsiang*] and after-taste [*hui-wei*].' (pp. 68–9.)

It is clear from the conclusion that the *hsing* form is only meant to represent the values of 'lingering fragrance' and 'after-taste': such a connotation had been given long ago by Chung Jung's *Shih p'in*, where he defined *hsing* as 'the words already finished, but the sense carrying

[11] *'Yang pien chi* hsü' (Preface to [Yü P'ing-po's] *Yang pien chi*), *T'an lung chi*. The notion of *hsing* seems to me exactly described by J. S. Mill, when he talked of 'the power of *creating* scenery, in keeping with some state of human feeling; so fitted to it as to be the embodied symbol of it, and to summon up the state of feeling itself, with a force not to be surpassed by anything but reality'. T. S. Eliot also seems to mean the same thing by his 'objective correlative', which is 'a set of objects, a situation, a chain of events which shall be the formula of that particular emotion; such that when the external facts, which must terminate in sensory experience, are given, the emotion is immediately evoked.' (Both quoted Abrams, p. 25.)

on'. Now these terms *yü-hsiang* and *hui-wei* are particularly Chinese. Indeed, just previous to this passage Chou admitted that 'there are some traditions in Chinese art and thought that possess my heart' (pp. 67–8). In common use there are phrases that describe the lingering effect, such as 'reverberating round the rafters for three days', which refers to music, and other critical terms, such as *yü-ch'ing* and *yü-yün* – the latter being the lasting effect caused by the means of expression being in perfect harmony with the state of feelings of the author.[12] As to the first, which means a kind of radiation of feeling beyond the bounds of the words, or simply, emotional overtones, Chou himself thought it had to be present before a piece of (in this case) prose could claim any literary merit. In his 'Compendium' introduction he quotes from an early essay of his, 'Ancestor Worship' (1919), and comments:

> No matter what tender regard a person might have for his own compositions, I still cannot say that the two passages quoted above are well written. They just pig-headedly put forward one's own opinion. At the most they argue convincingly, but they have no emotional overtones [*yü-ch'ing*]. (p. 5.)

Again, Chou brings out the importance of the lingering effect, though in this case he gives no name to it, when he discusses some poems of Ho I-sun (early seventeenth-century):

> These ten poems are all doggerel [*ta-yu-shih*] and by rights should be beneath notice in literary circles; orthodoxy on the one side objects to their lack of refinement and inability to convey the Way, and orthodoxy on the other side detests them for being too humorous and unable to spread revolution. Actually, to my mind, they are most powerful, at least something is left in the mind after reading them, the effect of which is not necessarily to provoke burning tears, but to make one think. To exhaust one's energies and strain one's voice in thumping the table, leaping about and hurling abuse, is to thoroughly unburden oneself; but unburdening oneself is satisfying. It is like getting a heat-rash in summer, if you squirm about . . . your affliction will be eased. The most unhappy time is when you feel oppressed, and the comic reporting of tragic events does indeed make one oppressed, make one unhappy. If the power of literature is in fanning the flames, then I feel this kind of thing must count as very powerful. ('Shui t'ien chü ts'un shih', 1937. *Ping chu hou t'an* p. 42.)

Here Chou is of course discussing a particular kind of lingering effect, but the general point is that it is contrasted with forthright expression, which gives relief, is soon over and done with, and can be forgotten

[12] See Kao Ming, 'Chung-kuo hsiu-tz'u hsüeh yen-chiu', *Chung-kuo yü-wen*, II, 2.

about. Ho I-sun's manner, which Chou describes as 'oddly humorous', is more subtle and ultimately has a more powerful effect because 'it leaves something behind'.

I have said that the various terms connected with 'taste' and 'after-taste', 'overtones' and so on, have long been part of the vocabulary of criticism in China, but they tend to occur in isolated appreciative comments (by far the greater part of Chinese literary criticism is indeed impressionistic – formulating verbal equivalents for aesthetic effects – rather than analytic). The only seminal critic who comes to mind for giving high place to 'taste' in his theory is again Chung Jung. In his *Shih-p'in* preface he asserts the primacy of 'flavour' (*tzu-wei*):

> Five-word poetry is at the heart of the verbal art: it is of all forms the one with the most flavour. (*Shih p'in chu*, p. 4.)

It is also in Chung's book the kind best suited to the full expression of feeling. Conversely, as one would expect, lack of flavour is a mark of inferiority: so in the poetry of the Yung-chia period (A.D. 307–13), 'the reasoning overpowers the words; it is insipid and short of flavour.' (ibid., p. 3.)

The first half of the combination, *ch'ü*, is more difficult to understand, as its use in criticism is far removed from the original meaning of 'to hasten to' or 'tendency' (in everyday use it means 'entertaining' or 'interesting' – *yu ch'ü*). Wang Meng-ou explains it as 'state of "spiritual life",' and 'direction taken by the thoughts' (op. cit., p. 224). I would prefer to describe it generally as a kind of inner logic, through that would not account for all the senses in which it is used. A frequently quoted example of its use comes from the biography of T'ao Ch'ien: 'If only you get the *ch'ü* in the lute itself, why bother about the sound of the strings?'[13] At least it is clear that *ch'ü* is not what the senses directly perceive – 'the sound of the strings'; it would appear on the strength of this example to be the said inner logic or inner harmony. Alternatively it might be viewed (dare one suggest it?) as the counterpart in art to *tao* in Lao-Chuang philosophy. A more stringent test of its denotations is provided by the following passage. The author is Yüan Hung-tao (Chung-lang);

> What men find difficult to attain to is *ch'ü*. *Ch'ü* is like colour on mountains, taste in water, bloom in flowers, posture in women. Even the most articulate person cannot begin to describe it, only someone who feels it intuitively knows what it is. People nowadays admire the idea of *ch'ü*, and strive after its semblance. So they indulge in debates about calligraphy and painting, browse among antiques,

[13] In the *Chin shu* (History of the Chin Dynasty).

thinking it 'rarified'; or they cast their thoughts on Taoist profundities, flee from the mundane, thinking it 'aloof'. Then on a lower level there are those fellows in Suchow who burn incense and brew tea. This kind of thing is just the shell and skin of *ch'ü* – it has nothing to do with the expressions of vitality [we have mentioned].

Ch'ü owes much to nature, little to learning. As a child one has not heard of *ch'ü*, yet there is nothing a child does which has not *ch'ü*. Life has no greater pleasures than at this time when the facial expression is never composed, the eyes are always roving, the mouth is ever on the point of muttering something, trying to speak, and the feet dance and will not be still. No doubt this is what Mencius was referring to when he spoke of 'staying like a new-born babe', and Lao-tzu too when he asked: 'Can you be as a babe?' This is the ultimate attainment of *ch'ü* and is of the highest order.

The men of the hills and forests, being free and unconstrained, answer only to themselves, so though they do not seek *ch'ü*, *ch'ü* comes near to them. The reason why the naïve and the outcasts get close to *ch'ü* is because of their lack of standing: the humbler the station the humbler the demands. Whether in their taking meat and drink or in their rendition of a song, they follow their inclinations, without inhibitions. Since they have given up expecting anything from the world, they pay no attention to the disapproval and mockery of the world. This is another kind of *ch'ü*.

When one grows heavy in years, receives promotion, achieves higher status, the body becomes like a fetter, the heart like brambles, and the hair-roots and body-joints are constringed by experience and knowledge. One might penetrate ever deeper into the principle of things, but one gets ever more remote from *ch'ü*. ('Hsü Ch'en Cheng-fu Hui-hsin chi', reprinted in *Wan Ming hsiao-p'in hsüan-chu* [Annotated Selections from Late Ming Essays], pp. 39–40.)

Ch'ü, we gather from the analogy with sensible objects ('colour on mountains', etc.), is an intangible quality inherent in, typical of, and unique to a class of things, being particularly evident in the finer specimens. In this sense it is not far from 'glamour'; perhaps 'tone' would suit. In people it is related to behaviour which is natural, apt, unreflecting, unselfconscious, unforced and free; it comes from following the inner promptings of one's nature, or from being as one is. One might suggest, again tentatively, 'flair' as a translation. Both are of a kind that the spectator would find charming or exhilarating.

In the field of aesthetics, Wang Meng-ou has criticized Yüan Hung-tao's formulation as inferior to Yen Yü's in *Ts'ang-lang shih hua*, 'Shih pien' (Kuo Shao-yü edition, p. 24), where his examples are 'the sound in the air', 'colour in the appearance', 'the moon in the water', 'the image in the mirror'. Yüan refers to intrinsic qualities that are apprehended by the senses, while to Yen Yü the *ch'ü* lies in giving rise to associations, so that (again) 'the words are finished, but the idea is never exhausted'. Wang contends that 'colour on mountains', 'taste in water', etc. are only the 'saltiness of salt', the 'sourness of plums' (i.e. qualities inherent in and indissociable from particular objects) that Ssu-k'ung T'u belittled (Wang, op. cit., p. 222). What Ssu-k'ung T'u and Yen Yü prized was 'the sense beyond the words' and 'the relish beyond the flavour'. They tended, as we have already seen, to denigrate the importance of imagery, and went directly for, in Wang's words, 'the aggregate of feelings and perceptions induced by the imagery' (p. 225). The distinction is an interesting one, but as far as Chou Tso-jen is concerned, we already know that he thought Ssu-k'ung T'u's kind of reasoning too abstruse, so there is no point in pursuing it, though with regard to Yüan Chung-lang's exposition, it is worth noting that the attributes Chou called *ch'ü-wei* would fit the 'men of hills and forests' he described.

It may have by now emerged that *ch'ü* is the element in *ch'ü-wei* that provides the lift or exhilaration. Such a tendency is increased when *ch'ü* is combined with *feng* 'wind', to form *feng-ch'ü*. Chou used this term more than once, but possibly because it would have been familiar to his Chinese readership, he did not explain it. As they do not tell us much, two examples from his works will suffice; both are taken from essays we have already quoted. In the essay on diaries and letters in *Yü t'ien ti shu*, he writes:

> All along there have been a large number of good Chinese letters which have been successful in combining literary art and *feng-ch'ü*, but the most outstanding would be those that bring out the author's personality. (p. 12.)

And in '*Ch'un tsai t'ang tsa wen*', following the passage on 'evocativeness', he sums up:

> Ch'ü-yüan [Yü Yüeh]'s prefaces always have thoughts on this kind of thing, expressed in a heartfelt and *feng-ch'ü* manner which gives the reader something. (*Yao wei chi*, p. 108.)

All we can deduce from these examples is that *feng-ch'ü* has no direct reference to the personality of the author, but appears instead to be something in the way a point is put over.

We are fortunate in having a definition of *feng-ch'ü* ready-made for us. The modern scholar Chou Chen-fu discusses it in his study of classical literary devices. He is pleased to quote Lin Shu on the subject:

> Writing which has *feng-ch'ü* does not solely depend on comic phrasing. *Feng-ch'ü* is measured by the ingenuousness of the writing: *feng-ch'ü* is sometimes present in the utmost solemnness. So too when the perception is high and the spirit full, enough to fill and overfill

the scope of the written word, then without deliberation *ch'ü* can be created from the flow of the pen. (From *Ch'un chüeh lou lun wen*, quoted *Shih tz'u li hua*, p. 259.)

Lin Shu then, advisedly, gives some illustrations, the first from *Shih chi*, Tou Huang-hou chuan:

> When Empress Tou and her [long-lost] brother Kuang-kuo met, she was grief-stricken [at the memory of their tragic separation]. Then unexpectedly we read: 'Her ladies-in-waiting all sank to the ground, and helped the empress to grieve.' How can grief be 'helped'? But if you dispense with the word 'helped', there seems to be no other word to substitute for it. If Empress Tou herself were to have seen it, when the marvellous aptness of the word 'helped' struck her, her tears would also have dissolved into laughter. Those who look for *feng-ch'ü* will only find its true image if they set their sights on this.

Chou Chen-fu's comment on this is: 'The word "help" not only brings out the funniness of the feigned weeping, it also counterpoints the sincerity [on the part of the brother and sister] at that point. The meeting of brother and sister was a joyful occasion, they wept only from an excess of joy on recalling the past; there was absolutely nothing distressing to make bystanders weep, so they could only "help" and not really grieve.' (p. 260.)

The second illustration is based on *Han shu*, Ch'en Wan-nien chuan:

> Wan-nien fell ill, and summoned his son Hsien to give him parental advice at his bedside. The lecture continued into the night. Hsien dozed off, and bumped his head on a screen. Wan-nien was furious, and prepared to beat him, saying: 'Your father is giving you the benefit of his advice, but you fall asleep, of all things, and do not listen to my words. What is your explanation?' Hsien kowtowed and excused himself: 'I knew all you wanted to say. In essence you wanted to instruct me in the art of flattery.' At first sight it seems that Wan-nien is giving right and proper counsel, and that Hsien is a disobedient son. But to follow 'instruction' with 'flattery' would have made even the man on the sickbed, let alone the reader, burst out laughing. This is a case of one word creating *ch'ü*. (pp. 259–60.)

The third example is from 'Wang Tsun chuan', and is a comment on Wang Tsun's subordinate Chang Fu illegally enriching himself at the expense of the community. Wang Tsun says the latter has collected all the money of the locality in his house, 'enough to bury him'. Chou Chen-fu explains:

> This word 'bury' has *feng-ch'ü*: it denotes the large amount of money he has got his hands on, large enough for his burial; at the same time it is stern in that it implies that he is ripe for the executioner. A witty and *feng-ch'ü* tone like this produces the effect

> of severity not levity, and has rich implications. Therefore it is a good example. (p. 261.)

It appears from all the foregoing that *feng-ch'ü* stands for delicacy or subtlety in giving a revealing twist to phrasing in order to bring to the surface undercurrents in a situation and point up factors that might otherwise be neglected. The effect is often humorous or satirical, but a serious point can be made. The touch needs to be light.

As *feng-ch'ü* is again a portmanteau word, we ought to take at least a brief look at the 'wind' element in it. It does not give us very much trouble. Kao Ming explains that the essence of *feng* is movement and the power to move.[14] He quotes from the 'Little Preface' to the *Odes*: 'For lessons of manners [i.e. *feng*-style songs] the term "wind" is used, denoting the influence of instruction. Wind moves [things] and instruction transforms the people.' (Trans. Legge, *The She King*, p. 37.) Also from the 'Great Preface': 'Superiors, by the *feng*, transformed their inferiors, and inferiors by them satirized their superiors.' (Legge, p. 35.) Kao's elucidation is that *feng* therefore is 'a general state of motion caused by the movement of the spirit'.

If we look at Liu Hsieh's exegesis of this part of the preface to the *Odes*, we find rather fuller comment:

> The Odes are made up of six classes, and *feng* is the foremost of these. It is the source of influencing feelings and the counterpart of will. He who in a melancholy mood would tell of his feelings must start with *feng* . . . When feelings are informed with *feng* it is like the body containing breath . . . That which can draw deeply on *feng* will express the feelings clearly . . . When the thought is unfinished, and [the work] decrepit and flagging, this is a sign that it is lacking in *feng*. ('Feng ku' chapter.)

Feng, then, bearing in mind the basic meaning of 'wind', is the flowing force which animates writing, the intangible element which bridges the gap between writer and reader, the thing which enables the author's feelings as set down on paper to affect the reader.

Mechanically speaking, *feng* is contrasted with *ku*, literally 'bone'. *Ku* is concrete, structured, and resides in the semantic aspect of words. As Hsü Fu-kuan points out,[15] *feng* is more associated with lyricism – the subjective, warm and flowing; *ku* is associated with narrative and discursive writing – the objective, cool and calm. With regard to diction *feng* comes into being through the manipulation of 'functional words'

[14] 'Chung-kuo hsiu-tz'u hsüeh yen-chiu', *Chung-kuo yü-wen*, I, 6 (1952). Generally speaking the action of the wind would be more exactly described as 'influencing' or 'pervading'.

[15] *Chung-kuo wen-hsüeh lun chi*, pp. 319 and 321.

(*hsü tzu*), while *ku* is manifested in the sparing use of 'concrete words' (*shih tzu*). Hsü quotes Hsieh Shih-hou: 'You look for reasoning in the concrete words, you observe the spirit in the functional words.' With this last Aoki agrees: he is content to surmise that *feng* is the author's 'lively spirit'.[16]

The terms which we discussed in the previous chapter, belonging to literary theory, were almost manageable, but the exceeding difficulty of defining, let alone translating, all these terms which belong to literary appreciation shows how peculiarly Chinese they are. It is not that modern Western alternatives were not available, it is that Chou preferred not to accept the Western cast of mind as other critics did, but instead to be Chinese.

The value that we will next examine is as Chinese semantically as *ch'ü-wei*, and is even more typical of the Chinese mentality, measured by the degree of respect paid to it. It is the linked pair of concepts *p'ing-tan tzu-jan*.

[16] *Chung-kuo wen-hsüeh ssu-hsiang shih kang* (Outline History of Chinese Literary Thought), p. 54.

4

'BLANDNESS' AND 'NATURALNESS'

Like *ch'ü-wei, p'ing-tan tzu-jan* was a colour that Chou Tso-jen defiantly nailed to his mast, despite the criticism it attracted because of its untimeliness and 'negativism'.[1] *P'ing-tan* means something like bland, mild, muted; *tzu-jan* means natural.

Chou's best known confession of attachment to this principle is in his preface to *Yü t'ien ti shu*, 1925:

> Recently in my writing I have aspired to the state of *p'ing-tan tzu-jan*. But this kind of composition I have found only in classical or foreign literature, and I cannot imagine the day will ever come when I shall be able to achieve it, for it is bound up with character, situation and age, and cannot be forced. A person of my mean and hasty temper, born in China at this time in history, can hardly hope calmly and unconcernedly to produce gentle and mild essays. (p. 6.)

Thereafter he continued to express admiration for these two qualities of *p'ing-tan* and *tzu-jan*, though he still never claimed, out of becoming modesty, to have achieved the effect in his own writing. He was aware however that as early as 1922 Hu Shih had given him credit for it.

This is what Hu Shih wrote then:

> In the last few years the most notable development in prose writing has been in the *hsiao-p'in* form which Chou Tso-jen and others have advocated. This kind of *hsiao-p'in* adopts an undemonstrative [*p'ing tan*], conversational style which is profoundly evocative below the surface; sometimes it gives the impression of obtuseness, but it is in fact very witty. (*Wu-shih nien lai Chung-kuo chih wen-hsüeh*, quoted in Chou's 'Compendium' introduction, pp. 5–6.)

Chou reluctantly declines to accept such a compliment in 1936,[2] when he was at the height of his powers. He says there that he is

[1] See for example the essays of Hsü Chieh and Han Shih-hang in *Chou Tso-jen lun*. Hsü Chieh's essay is also to be found in Mao Tun, ed.: *Tso-chia lun*.
[2] 'Tzu-chi ti wen-chang' (One's own Essays), *Kua tou chi*.

pleased when people say his essays are *p'ing-tan*, for this is what he has aimed at – but he has only achieved irascibility. Similarly, in 1935,[3] he deplores the fact that at his age he is still writing 'with sword drawn and bow taut' when he should set his sights on *ch'ung tan* (temperate, unimpassioned) essays. What he means by his age or time of life is explained in Chou's quotation from Yeh Sung-shih in the same collection: 'In youth one loves the beautiful, in full manhood the heroic, in middle age the brief and condensed, in old age the mild and distant (*tan-yüan*)'[4]. This I suppose is the Chinese scholar's answer to the English country squire of Shakespeare's 'seven ages of man'.

References to *p'ing-tan* abound in Chou's essays, but nowhere does he attempt to define the term, since again he could assume a shared cultural background with the reader, and because too his aim was to communicate a pleasure, not to produce a literary theory. But one can show in what contexts he tended to use the word.

In 'Samples of Nan-t'ang's poetry' (1937)[5] he approves the judgement that Fang Chen-kuan's (i.e. Nan-t'ang, 1679–1747) poetry is 'indirect and poignant, the words short but the sense prolonged, the more calculated at length to create *p'ing-tan* and approximate to nature'. Clearly *p'ing-tan* here is not synonymous with *p'ing-yung* 'commonplace' and *tan erh wu wei* 'insipid'. On the contrary, the verse is stated to be both subtle and to have a fund of meaning, though expressed in a style – essential to the idea of *p'ing-tan* – that is undemonstrative ('indirect' is the pointer here, more often it is 'simple') and pregnant.

Many more such examples could be adduced, but their implications could only be brought out by a similar process of tenuous logical deduction, and this does not recommend itself. It would be more direct to go to some other formulations of Chou's which do not actually use the word *p'ing-tan* but do in fact describe it. One aspect of the idea is described in his comment on Yen Chih-t'ui's *Yen shih chia hsün* (Family Precepts):

> The 'Chung chih' [Mourning for Parents] chapter at the end of *Family Precepts* is a fine piece of writing, the like of which it would be hard to find in any age. It shows a thorough understanding of life and death, so the sentiments are down to earth, the diction likewise

[3] 'Wei t'ien min jen' (Fearing Heaven and pitying People), p. 137, *K'u chu tsa chi*.

[4] 'T'an wen' (On Literature), *K'u chu tsa chi*, p. 289. The quotation dates from 1880.

[5] 'Nan-t'ang shih ch'ao' (Samples of Nan-t'ang's Poetry), 1937, *Ping chu hou t'an*, p. 10.

concise and plain. Its lack of novelty is the most admirable thing about it. (*Yeh tu ch'ao*, 'Yen-shih chia hsün', p. 175.)

Somewhat more positive virtues emerge from Chou's comments on another writer, Ho Lan-kao (1757–1825), who, he says, writes as he himself would like to, but cannot:

> He uses simple words, is able to put across his meaning well. He expresses himself casually, as if entirely unconcerned, but brings out most sharply his feelings of affection or chagrin. (*Ku-chu tsa chi*, 'Mo-hu' [Muddle], p. 188.)

To put across deep feelings and serious thoughts in a flat and unemotional way, as these passages describe, is the secret of *p'ing-tan*. It was of course a quality sought after by English essayists. As early as 1668 Thomas Sprat praised Cowley's essays for their 'natural easiness and unaffected grace where nothing seems to be studied yet everything is extraordinary'.[6] No doubt Chou was thinking principally of the English essay when he mentioned having found *p'ing-tan* in foreign literature. However, we are concerned here with the other repository for *p'ing-tan*, namely classical Chinese literature, literary criticism, and the Chinese way of life.

Again we are lucky, since Chou Tso-jen omits to give one, to have a Chinese definition of *p'ing-tan* from Chou Chen-fu. He compares the effect of *p'ing-tan* to strong drink which is not stimulating to the taste-buds: it encourages one to drink more, and intoxication overcomes one unawares. He continues:

> In *p'ing-tan* works the words must needs be simple, without affectation, without embellishment. Rhetorical flourishes are not prized; instead, 'well-temperedness' is striven after. As Wang An-shih said: 'What appears to be pedestrian is the most imposing: the performance looks easy but is in fact arduous.' The content is pithy; it 'goes in deep and comes out shallow',[7] as if it were facile. In the writing it requires repeated turning over in the mind, and weighing of words – a very laborious process. When finished it is easy to read, easy to understand. (*Shih tz'u li hua*, p. 236.)

Chou Chen-fu adds that *p'ing-tan* is closely associated with *tzu-jan*, but not identical with it, particularly in that *p'ing-tan* is always plain, while 'natural' is not always so.

Historically both *p'ing-tan* and *tzu-jan* are central to the Taoist tradition. Clearly, the state of mind which can produce such effects in

[6] Quoted Atkins, *English Literary Criticism*, p. 47.
[7] *Shen ju ch'ien chu*: meaning that profound thoughts are so refined and condensed as to be capable of expression in simple language.

writing is the reverse of agitated or excited, and such disturbance Taoists strenuously – no, unstrenuously – avoided. As Chuang-tzu said, typically: 'In his social intercourse the superior man is bland, like water; the small man is sweet, like must.'[8] The age in which Taoist thought pervaded the arts most widely and deeply was probably the Wei-Chin period, incidentally a time much to the taste of Chou Tso-jen and Lu Hsün. On the philosophical side we might extract some typical observations relevant to the matter in hand:

from Ho Yen, commenting on the phrase *pu ch'ien nu* 'did not transfer his anger' (*Lun Yü*, 2,ii): 'If a man gives way to his feelings in showing joy or rage, he is in the wrong';[9]

from Wang Pi: 'In his feelings the sage responds to things but is not burdened by things';

from one of the greatest poets, Hsi K'ang: 'Knowing that fame and standing harm [Taoist] virtue, one neglects them, and does not seek to engineer them; it is not a case of wanting them but strenuously interdicting them. Knowing that strong flavours injure one's self, one sets them aside and disregards them; it is not a case of hankering after them but forcibly repressing [that desire]. External objects are not held on to because they burden the mind; spiritual endowments are brought to the fore on account of their purity';

and, from slightly later, this example of T'ao Ch'ien's philosophizing:

> 'Too much concern harms my existence; it is right to go along with fate. Cast yourself adrift among the myriad changes, without joy and without fear. When the end comes, then you must make an end; there is no need to worry particularly.' (From 'Shen shih', quoted with approval by Chou in '*Lao lao heng yen*', *Yao wei chi*, 1940.)

These thoughts in Taoist vein, urging as they do avoidance of strong sensations and vehemence of emotion and expression, are the counterpart in philosophy to *p'ing-tan* in aesthetics. Such an outlook was not of course the exclusive preserve of Taoism. The idea runs right through one of the Confucian Four Books, the *Doctrine of the Mean*. In the first chapter the idea of moderation is stressed:

> While there are no stirrings of pleasure, anger, sorrow, or joy, the mind may be said to be in the state of Equilibrium. When those feelings have been stirred, and they act *in their due degrees*, there

[8] *Chuang tzu chi chieh, Chu tzu chi ch'eng*, III, 125.
[9] Quoted Jung Chao-tsu, *Wei Chin ti tzu-jan chu-i* (Naturalism in the Wei-Chin Period), p. 14. Wang Pi is quoted on p. 14 also, and Hsi K'ang on p. 49.

ensues what may be called the state of Harmony.' (Trans. Legge, p. 384.)

There is a specific reference to *tan* in Chapter 33:

The superior man characteristically is mild [*tan*], yet people do not tire of him; he is simple yet his manner is cultured; he is genial yet methodical.

The combination of Taoist and Confucian influences was irresistible: the *p'ing-tan* syndrome came to be firmly embedded in the established Chinese culture. It may have been the *Doctrine of the Mean* that gave this ethos the looked-for authorization for the scholar-official; what is certain is that it has for a very long time been powerfully present in his self-image. Li Ch'en-tung points out[10] that two prominent officials, Chang Hua of Chin and Chiang Yen of Liang, felt bound to subscribe to the associated ideals of humility, modesty, purity, naturalness and non-interference, in spite of the fact that their life-long and successful pursuit of high office belied them. And Ch'ien Mu describes how the traditional scholar 'invariably quietly and unassumingly (*p'ing-p'ing tan-tan*) retired to his village, chose a plot with a view of clear mountains and living waters, good fields and fine trees, had his house built and lived out his remaining days there.'[11]

These two illustrations will serve to demonstrate the attraction of the *p'ing-tan* ideal in life. What of it in literary criticism? The element *ch'ung-tan* had a place, with *tzu-jan*, in Ssu-k'ung T'u's *Shih p'in* among the twenty-four categories of poetry, but his adumbration of it is obscure, to say the least. My impression is that *p'ing-tan* was held in the highest critical esteem in the Sung dynasty; this would fit in with the general trend towards favouring simplicity of style in that period.[12] Two famous Sung poets set great store by *p'ing-tan*. The slogan of Mei Yao-ch'en (1002–60) was: 'The question of ancient and modern in writing poetry is irrelevant; the difficulty is in creating *p'ing-tan*.'[13] Chang Chien comments that the word 'create' (*tsao*) here indicates the planning and polishing which goes into producing the effect of *p'ing-tan*. The other poet is Su Tung-p'o. He wrote: 'In youth writing should generally aim to make one's personal presence felt, to bring out colours vividly; but with increasing age and mellowness the aim becomes to create *p'ing-tan*. Actually this is not *p'ing-tan*, but vividness

[10] In his *Wen-hsüeh hsin lun* (New Discussion of Literature), pp. 52 ff.
[11] *Chung-kuo wen-hua shih tao-lun* (Introduction to Chinese Cultural History), p. 129.
[12] Described by Aoki, 'Outline History', pp. 80–2 and 101.
[13] 'Tu Shao Pu-i hsüeh shih shih', quoted Chang Chien, *Chung-kuo wen-hsüeh san lun* (Desultory Discussion of Chinese Literature), p. 56.

in its ultimate form.'[14] Su Tung-p'o also talked about *k'u-tan* 'dry and dull': 'What is praiseworthy about *k'u-tan* is when, dry outside, it is fat and fertile (*kao*) inside; when it seems dull but is really beautiful, as with T'ao Yüan-ming, Liu Tsung-yüan, and their like. If both outside and inside are "dry and dull", then it is not worth wasting words on it.'[15]

In his estimate of T'ao Yüan-ming, Chu Hsi seems at first to contradict Su Tung-p'o:

> Everybody says T'ao Yüan-ming's poetry is *p'ing-tan*, but as I see it he has heroic vigour, only the sense of it overtakes one unawares. (*Chu-tzu yü lei*, quoted Chu Tung-jun, op. cit., p. 178.)

If Chu Hsi had remembered the implication of strength beneath the surface in *p'ing-tan* – in Su's words, of it being 'vividness in its ultimate form' – he would not have found it necessary to frame his comment as a contradiction.

Yüan Chung-lang also took up Su Tung-p'o's evaluation of T'ao, and his view in turn appears to differ. He wrote:

> Sung Tung-p'o had a passion for T'ao Yüan-ming's poetry, valuing its mildness and relaxed manner. In nature fermenting makes sweet, baking makes sour; only *tan* cannot be fabricated [*tsao*]. The impossibility of being fabricated is the true soul of literature ('Hsü Wo Shih Chia sheng chi', *Yüan Chung-lang ch'üan chi*, p. 10.)

Now Su did apply the word *tsao* to *p'ing-tan*, but there is no real contradiction, for Yüan uses the word, as translated, to mean 'fabricate', to produce at a secondary stage by mechanical means, while what Su meant by it was to subject to control at the formative stage.

Chung-lang's younger brother, Chung-tao, expressed similarly high regard for *tan*. In the following extract he refers immediately to painting, but the relevance is wider:

> To take the mountain scene as an illustration, many are the changes the four seasons bring, but only in the wake of the rigours of winter is there a kind of superior charm, mild and serene, which excels over the splendid and gorgeous. ('Ch'en Wu-i Chi sheng p'ien hsü', *Wan Ming hsiao-p'in hsüan chu*, p. 51.)

In the world of men, he goes on to say, great work is not produced by the well-fed, but by those who have been reduced to the depths. This repeats the point, on a different plane, that *tan* only comes about through reduction, through a tempering process.

As a last word, to show how widely shared the value of *p'ing-tan*

[14] Quoted Aoki, 'Outline History', p. 82.
[15] *Tung-p'o shih hua*, quoted Aoki, ibid.

was, Yao Nai, the leader of the T'ung-ch'eng school, to whom the Yuan brothers were anathema, joined cause with them in this:

> Of all the states of sensibility in literature, none is finer than *p'ing-tan*. The use of words, the outflow of ideas, seem to be self-begotten. ('Yü Wang T'ie-fu shu', quoted Chiang Shu-ke, *T'ung-ch'eng wen p'ai p'ing shu*, p. 40.)

If *p'ing-tan* was popular in Chinese culture, then the related ideal of *tzu-jan* 'natural' was even more so. As it is easy to understand why naturalness recommended itself, we will not need to spend so much time explaining it. However, as every work of literature is an artifact, and so not 'natural', we might take a look at what the Chinese generally associated with the term. As Wu Hung-i pointed out in an article on Wang Kuo-wei's literary theory,[16] *tzu-jan* is broadly speaking understood in two ways: one is identical with *p'ing-tan*, namely the reduction of the complex and colourful to the plain and unextravagant – the painstaking work of the craftsman; the other, represented by Liu Hsieh and Chung Hung, sees it as spontaneity, the words flowing immediately and easily from the pen. It is the second line we want to pursue now, along the path he indicates.

Liu Hsieh's philosophy is summed up in a passage we have had occasion to quote before:

> Man is endowed with seven emotions, which are activated in sympathy with events; when moved by events one lifts one's voice to express one's feelings. The process is entirely spontaneous [*tzu-jan*]. (*Wen-hsin tiao lung*, 'Ming shih' chapter.)

This however only brings us to the starting point of artistic creation. It is true that in his 'Shen shih' chapter Liu elaborates the idea of fitting response to stimulus, of being 'vacant' and purifying the spirit to be responsive to influences, and that he gives the creative process over to Chuang-tzu's butcher and wheelwright, who worked purely intuitively, yet he does recognize that certain great poets only wrote slowly and laboriously, which could not be called 'natural' in the 'spontaneous' sense. It is still part of Liu's outlook that treatment should be natural in that the words should fit the subject and that *extraneous* embellishment should be ruled out.

Chung Jung, less of an aesthete, went further than this in rejecting any heightening or embellishment at all, preferring directness. This attitude inclines more to the 'plain words' (*p'ing shuo*) persuasion than to that of spontaneity. He wrote in his *Shih P'in* preface:

[16] 'Wang Ching-an ti ching-chieh shuo' (Wang kuo-wei's theory of 'worlds'), *Chung-yang jih-pao* fu-k'an (Central Daily News supplement), Taipei, 17 May 1967.

> As to expressing one's nature and one's feelings, what virtue is there in using allusions? 'I think of you like flowing water'[17] appeals directly to the eye; 'On the high terrace it is mostly the sad wind that blows' is also simply what is seen; 'On a clear morning ascending Mount Lung' has no antecedents; 'The bright moon shines on the piled up snow' does not derive from the classics or histories. The great lines of both past and present are rarely padded out or borrowed: they all come from direct apprehension. (In Hsü Wen-yü, *Wen lun chiang shu*, p. 172.)

He summed up: 'You rarely meet with anyone capable of the natural and noble [in poetry].'

So with Chung Jung, 'natural' embraces both relying on one's own resources, in that what is written about is apprehended, observed or experienced without intermediary, and simplicity, in the sense that expression should be direct and free from all elaborations or extraneous matter. The same applies to metre in poetry, to which the poet should not be enslaved. He wrote in the same preface:

> The *shih* and *sung* forms in ancient poetry were written to music, so, in order to harmonize, the [words] had to be distributed according to the five tones . . . Hence in the verses of the three emperors [of the Wei dynasty] the literary art may not have always been perfect, but the cadences were adapted to song. This is the reason for giving weight to tone and harmony; it is different from the talk of high and low tones nowadays [i.e. the tone theory of Fan Yeh and Shen Yüeh]. Since poetry is now no longer written to music, what is there to be gained from metric rules? (ibid., p. 176.)

He concludes:

> In my opinion it is basic to a composition that it can be read aloud without any impediment. As long as the 'clear' and 'cloudy'[18] flow together and the words trip off the tongue, this is sufficient. (ibid.)

This last description of natural harmony makes some contribution to the description of naturalness in action. It is much easier to say what naturalness in action is not than what it is. As Chiang K'ui (1155? –1235?) said in *Pai-shih tao-jen shih hua*, when accounting for the four kinds of 'masterly effect' (*kao-miao*) in poetry: 'The masterly effect of naturalness refers to: not being strange or outlandish; being stripped of rhetoric; knowing [the poetry] is marvellous, but not knowing how it comes to be marvellous.'[19]

[17] For the source of these lines see Hsü Wen-yü, *Wen lun chiang shu*, pp. 173–4.

[18] 'Clear' and 'cloudy' epitomize opposite qualities of the kind of minor/major in music and voiced/unvoiced in phonology.

[19] *Li tai shih hua*, II, p. 440.

Only half deterred by such a consideration, however, Su Shih described the natural flow of his own writing by means of a natural simile:

> My writing is like a copious fountain which issues forth regardless of the terrain. On level ground it sweeps along, covering with ease ten thousand leagues in a day. When it meets with hills and rocks, twists and turns, it describes configurations according to the object, all unpredictably. What can be predicted is that it always goes on when it should go on, and stops where it cannot but stop. As for the rest, even I cannot tell. (*T'ung-p'o t'i pa* 'tzu p'ing wen', quoted Chang Chien, op. cit., pp. 51–2.)

It would be impossible to withhold recognition of the spontaneity of the process Su Shih describes, but unfortunately the description is vapid. Lu Chi's rival description is even more so (quoted p. 58). Their use of analogies from nature, however, suggests others quite commonly used, which do not betoken headlong rush, and in fact form a third category of naturalness: those which compare the forming of a work of art to the gradual maturation of a plant. We have already had an intimation of this organic theory from Wang Ch'ung, Hsü Kan and Chu Hsi. As far as I know the analogy was not pursued at very great length, as it was by Coleridge.[20] The majority of scholars, indeed, seem to have mixed natural metaphors indiscriminately. Sung Lien, whose life spanned the transition from Yüan to Ming, is a good example:

> The Way of the sages filled them internally, manifested itself externally, took shape in their words. Literary form [*wen*] was begotten without it being striven for. This is the ultimate in letters. Now letters is like water and trees. The maker of waterways does not worry about the water not flowing on, he is afraid of the source not being deep. The planter of trees does not worry about the branches not being prolific, he is concerned about the root not being fed. If the root is fed and the source made deep what is there to impede the flow and prevent the prolificness? The sages never learned that art of letters, it came from them like a torrent, was written down all at once; yet none of those who study the art of letters have surpassed them, on account of their root being flourishing, their source being vast. If someone said 'I am learning the art of letters', I would know he was incompetent: how can the art of letters be the object of learning? Those who seek proficiency in mellifluousness of phrasing, preciosity in abstruseness of allusions, pursuing these ideals with all their resources and only desisting in death, it still remains but a matter of technique, however skilled they become – and what if they do not become skilled? ('Wen shuo tseng Wang Sheng-fu', reprinted in Wang Huan-piao, op. cit., pp. 134–5.)

[20] See Abrams, pp. 220–5.

Apart from the dismissal of and contempt for superficial technique, so common among Chinese writers, presumably because of the frequency of its occurrence, certain principles may only be *inferred* from this passage that are made explicit by Coleridge, such as that the work of literature, like a plant, grows independently of imposed controls yet in strict obedience to natural laws; but another derived principle of Coleridge's, put forward in 'On poesy or art'[21], that of 'co-instantaneity of the plan and execution' had, and still has, a prominent place in Chinese aesthetics.

If one regrets the failure of Chinese critics to develop the critical implications of their premises and move on from the language of rhetoric to the language of science (though they might after all have showed superior judgement in this), then the work of Wang Kuo-wei (1877–1927) will be greeted with pleasure and relief, for he was the first systematic modern literary historian, and probably remains the most respected one. Modern or not, like so many Chinese scholars before him, he gave naturalness the first place in the literary scale of values. The excerpt that follows is an appreciation of the literary principles inherent in the Yüan plays (*tsa-chü*); it identifies several characteristics that Chou Tso-jen values:

> Wherein lies the excellence of the Yüan plays? It can be summed up in one word: simply, 'naturalness'. Great literature of all ages owes its success to naturalness, and none is more prominent in that respect than the Yüan plays.
>
> None of the authors of the Yüan plays had rank or learning. In writing their plays they did not have in mind creating literary masterpieces or handing their work down to posterity. They wrote as they felt like writing, and pleased others by pleasing themselves. Awkwardness of plot they paid no attention to, banality of thought they did not shy away from, inconsistencies in character did not concern them. They simply wrote of the feelings within them and the state of the times. In the process their underlying sincerity and their nobility of character often revealed themselves. So it is quite permissible to refer to the Yüan plays as China's most natural literature. As to naturalness of diction, that necessarily follows, and is a secondary consideration. (*Sung Yüan hsi-chü shih*, chapter 12, reprinted in Hsü Wen-yü, op. cit., pp. 523–4.)

As an appreciation, the main formal virtue of this passage is just its plain words. Where Wang Kuo-wei does set up systematic criteria, they are not simply 'naturalness', or whatever, but still they rest on naturalness. So in *Jen chien tz'u hua* he identifies two modes in the *tz'u*:

[21] Abrams, p. 222.

> There is 'creating of scene' and 'describing of scene'; from this distinction derive the schools of 'idealism' and 'realism'. But the two are very difficult to differentiate, because the scene the great poet creates inevitably corresponds to nature, and the scene he describes must approximate to the ideal. (ibid., p. 435.)

And, on the same theme,

> However much a scene might be the product of imagination, its material must be sought in nature, and its structure must follow the laws of nature. Hence the idealist is also the realist. (p. 438.)

We can now extend Wu Hung-i's two kinds of 'naturalness' to four:

1. Avoidance of artifice and reduction to essentials (equivalent to *p'ing-tan*).
2. Easy, undirected, and self-generative writing (spontaneity).
3. Organic growth of a composition, in accordance with the laws of nature.
4. True projection of the author's thoughts and sensibilities, dependent on such things as 'sincerity', 'direct apprehension', and self-sufficiency.

The first three refer to style and structure, the last to matter. I do not recall any nod of Chou's in the direction of number three. For the first and fourth we have already adduced sufficient evidence to show they fit into Chou's scheme of things. That he consented to the second proposition can also be demonstrated by citing his approval of the opinion of Wang K'en-t'ang (late Ming) that unplanned, unpremeditated writing is far superior to that method of composition where all is seen in the mind before brush is put to paper.[22] Chou's own practice, too, followed this rule: his young friend Feng Fei-ming testifies that he never drafted his essays in advance, but just wrote the whole piece out at one go[23] (which is something the reader can detect for himself, also).

On this whole question of *p'ing-tan tzu-jan*, Chou's attitude once more corresponds, partly because he also was reacting against neo-classicism (of the Ch'ing dynasty in his case), to the position of the English

[22] 'T'an shih wen' (On Poetry and Prose), *Chou Tso-jen tai-piao tso*, p. 46.

[23] 'Chou Tso-jen', in *Erh-shih chin-jen chih* (Biographies of Twenty Contemporaries), Shanghai, 1935.

Romantic poets. But there is an important difference. Abrams sums up one of Wordsworth's propositions in this way:

> It is essential to poetry that its language be the spontaneous and genuine, not the contrived and simulated, expression of the emotional state of the poet.
>
> On this thesis, Wordsworth . . . based his attack on the 'mechanical adoption' of figures of speech to which he attributed the debased diction of eighteenth-century poetry. On it depends also the general romantic use of spontaneity, sincerity, and the integral unity of thought and feeling as the essential criteria of poetry, in place of their neo-classic counterparts: judgement, truth, and the appropriateness with which diction is matched to the speaker, the subject matter, and the literary kind. (op. cit., p. 102.)

On all Wordsworth's positive points, Chou appears to have been in complete agreement; and if the discussion is restricted to poetry, doubtless he would have agreed too that 'judgement' and 'truth' had little place in poetry. But he certainly did not devalue judgement and truth in literature as a whole. One reason why, on the contrary, he showed great respect for both (see Chapter 7, 'Perspectives') was that Chinese neo-classical literature was in his view sadly lacking in both.

So is an attitude to literature in general moulded by the history of a person's own national literature.

5

SECONDARY VALUES

'Extempore' and 'Impromptu'

It is of course a condition of naturalness that work should not be written under any constraint, but should arise spontaneously from the situation in which the writer finds himself, that it should be consistent with the writer's feelings at the time. This condition Chou describes as *chi-hsing*, often translated as 'spontaneous', but more nearly 'extemporaneous'. Chou uses it in *Yüan-liu* as an antonym of *fu-te* 'prescribed', which denotes something written to a given theme.

In Lecture Three, after criticizing *pa-ku wen* and its counterpart in poetry, *shih t'ie*, he says that though skilful examples of this kind of writing may give the impression of powerful feelings, they are in fact very far from being true literature, as they are brought into being by the prescribed theme. He then proposes that 'extemporaneous' could well serve as an alternative to *yen chih*, and 'prescribed' to *tsai tao*:

> The famous works of literature down the ages have all been extemporaneous literature. There were for instance no titles in the *Odes*, and originally there were no chapter headings in *Chuang-tzu*. In both cases there was first the idea, the writing followed immediately on the thought, and only when it was finished was the title abstracted from what had been written. 'Prescribed literature' starts with the topic, and the writing proceeds from it. (p. 70.)

Chou had said almost exactly the same thing two years before, in a somewhat lighter vein, for in writing his essay 'Chin yü' ('Goldfish') he himself had had recourse to a dictionary for a topic, and so had to chide himself:

> I feel all compositions can be divided into two kinds: one has a title, the other does not. Normally the act of writing is preceded by an idea, but there is no definite title . . . In this kind of composition it would seem easy to produce fine work because you can express yourself comparatively freely, though making up a title afterwards is a nuisance, and is sometimes actually more difficult than writing the

> piece itself. But there are times too when you cannot gather your stray thoughts together and do not know what to write for the best, in which case it is not without benefit to first decide on a title and then write the piece – only this is getting close to 'prescribed literature' and courts the peril of producing an 'examination-style poem'. ('Chin yü', 1930, *K'an yün chi*, p. 29.)

These sentiments are very close to those in a passage he quotes from a book he had read over a period of thirty years, namely *Chiang-chou pi-t'an* , by Wang K'an:

> The ancients only explained the whys and wherefores of a poem after the poem was written: they did not fix on a topic first and then take up the pen to write the poem. ('Chiang-chou pi-t'an', 1934, *Yeh tu ch'ao*, p. 216.)

And Ku Yen-wu had made the same point before him in his *Jih chih lu.*[1]

Though Chou may have used the term 'extemporaneous', and also 'impromptu' *ou-ch'eng*, which, also being an antonym of *fu-te*, was synonymous with it, in other places in a casual way, it was only in this kind of context that their use was considered and specific. That is to say, their relevance was to Chinese literary practices, or, more exactly, it was intended to contrast with literary malpractices. As on the question of *yen chih* and *tsai tao*, his unqualified approval of 'extemporaneous' literature and sweeping condemnation of 'prescribed' literature are largely dictated by emotion. Once more we shall call on Chu Kuang-ch'ien for a more balanced view:

> In general, literary creation has no more than two starting points. The first is where at the outset there is no intention to write anything; then it happens that the feelings are engaged, an emotional state or train of thought [emerges] which one feels is worth putting in writing, so one takes up the pen and writes it down. The other kind is where one predetermines the topic, and with the intention of writing a literary composition, directs one's thoughts to that topic; then, when the thoughts have matured, one writes them down. In previous times, when writing old-style poems, people used to add the phrases 'impromptu' [*ou-ch'eng*] or 'to a given theme' [*fu-te*] to the titles. The 'impromptu' ones arose from a spurring of interest, and were put into verse immediately. The 'to a given theme' ones have a set theme and rhyme pattern: the word selected is used as the rhyme for the poem . . . In principle only impromptu works accord with the ideal of pure literature, but in fact the majority of extant works belong to the prescribed category, as an examination of the works of any great writer would demonstrate. There are of course good

[1] Quoted Fu Keng-sheng, *T'ung lun*, p. 56.

> compositions in the prescribed group. Not only were good poems written on social occasions and in poetry gatherings, even such things as treatises, memorials, and epitaphs cannot be entirely discounted . . . 'Prescribed' is a kind of training, 'impromptu' a kind of harvest. If a writer has not gone through the 'prescribed' stage, there might never be 'impromptu', or if there is, it could not amount to much. (*T'an wen-hsüeh*, pp. 76–7.)

No more need be said.

Simplicity

An idea closely related to naturalness is simplicity, related mainly in their common rejection of contrivance. Simplicity both in life and letters has been so widely held to be a virtue in China and the rest of the world that there is little point in adducing evidence of the fact. We need therefore only fill in some circumstantial details.

It is not only in the West that there is the idea of 'classic simplicity'. Yang Hsiung stated the conventional view in answer to the question: 'Heaven and Earth are simple and easy to understand, and since the sages followed this principle, how is it that the Classics are disordered and disparate?' His reply was: 'They *are* simple and they *are* easy to understand. Where did you get the idea that they were disordered and disparate?'[2] Though one might well be inclined to take the part of Yang Hsiung's interlocutor, the point is that the Chinese Classics were generally *assumed* to enshrine the quality of simplicity in style along with teaching simplicity in life and thought. Perhaps the Chinese scholar was more conscious than say his Greek counterpart of the value of simplicity because of the firm Chinese theory that luxury and extravagant display invariably caused the ruin of the state, but he seemed to share with the Greeks the 'Attic taste' in aesthetics. This taste is probably best exemplified in the value of *ya* (elegant, cultured, refined), but it embraces too the criterion of *tz'u ta* (lucidity or communicability of language), laid down by Confucius: 'Words should simply convey.'[3] The implication is that words should not be wasted, but be straight and to the point. One might compare this requirement also with the predominant style that Robert Lowth discerned in Hebrew poetry – 'sententiousness', that is, 'marked by the utmost brevity and simplicity.'[4]

[2] *Fa yen*, chapter 8, 'Wu pai', quoted Lo, I, 88.
[3] In *Lun yü*, 'Wei ling kung' chapter; *tz'u ta erh i i.*
[4] Quoted Atkins, *English Literary Criticism*, p. 190.

As a teacher of Chinese literature and, according to report, a typical old-fashioned gentleman in behaviour, Chou Tso-jen almost inevitably prized the classical ideals of simplicity and directness for themselves, as self-evident virtues. Thus he thinks it sufficient to describe the strength of T'ao Ch'ien's poetry as in the 'sentiments being sincere and the language lucid (*tz'u ta*).'[5] And he went so far as to say, as we have seen in another context, that the author's duty was discharged if those same two conditions were met.[6] Even more extreme was his claim that all works of literature only needed to be 'genuine and concise' (*chien-ming*),[7] an opinion he repeated in 1935: 'There is no other secret to literary composition: one word sums it up, and that is simplicity (*chien-tan*).'[8] Consistent with this principle, from at least as early as *T'an lung chi* (published in 1927, but containing essays from several years before) through to his last wartime collection, he accords selected authors and art forms recognition for their 'plainness' (*p'u-chih* or *chih-su*).

Both as regards taste and practice, Chou allied himself with the school of prose writers described by Lafcadio Hearn, the American author who took Japanese nationality and a Japanese name, Koizumi Yakumo. This school avoids modifiers, does not directly describe but instead plays down emotion. Its strength lies in its simplicity. Its effect derives from worthy sentiments and accurate judgements which in turn depend on discipline in observation. It contrasts with the type of prose (practised for instance in modern China by Hsü Chih-mo), which has extravagant ornamentation, excessive complexity, harmonious sound and beautiful colours, relies on the author's 'beautiful inner feelings' and uses exquisite phrasing to express the emotional force of these sensibilities.[9] This description does not fit Chou's own prose exactly, but it is useful in polarizing the alternatives in style, and there is no doubt that Chou favoured the first. It need only be added that to him simplicity is associated with suggestiveness (*an-shih*), not explicitness (*ming shuo*).[10]

Admittedly the preference for simplicity is not only a question of literary values; it reflects a persuasion in favour of a whole way of life, which Chou found exemplified in Japan rather than China.[11] Never-

[5] 'T'ao chi hsiao chi', 1943, *K'u k'ou kan k'ou*, p. 133.
[6] 'Meng-hsiang chih i', pp. 6–7.
[7] 'Mei wen' (Belles Lettres), 1921, *T'an hu chi*, p. 42.
[8] 'Pen-se', *Feng yü t'an*, p. 35.
[9] In 'T'e-shu san-wen ti yen-chiu' (Studies in a Special Type of Prose), quoted by Li Su-po in *Hsiao p'in san-wen yen-chiu*, p. 90.
[10] 'Lun hsiao shih' (On the short Poem), *Tzu-chi ti yüan-ti*, p. 61.
[11] See, for instance, 'Jih-pen ti tsai jen-shih' (Reacquaintance with Japan), 1940, *Yao wei chi*.

theless to apply the standard of simplicity wholesale to literature, even allowing for critical licence and ambiguity in phrasing (the second example quoted above seems to refer to prose), suggests that Chou is measuring the whole against a yardstick suited only to a part. This question will be explored further in the chapter on perspectives.

For the present section, some words of Liu Ta-k'ui can form a fitting conclusion. They not only help to prove that Chou inherited his respect for simplicity from the tradition, they also show, from the grouping of simplicity together with other qualities that had Chou's approval, that he inherited these aesthetic notions as a whole complex:

> Letters [*wen*] prize simplicity. In all forms of letters, a mature hand makes for simplicity, as do in turn genuine sentiments, pertinent diction, proper sense, mild flavour, latent power, nobility, detached spirit yet infinite suggestiveness. Hence simplicity is the ultimate in letters. (*Lun wen ou chi*, reprinted Wang Huan-piao, pp. 167–8.)

To cap the conclusion, it was Lu Hsün's judgement that simplicity – or in his words, 'avoidance of abstruseness' – was not simply an element in the Chinese tradition, but 'the soul of China', and 'the national character'.[12]

'Bitterness' (k'u) *and 'Asperity'* (se)

Ou-yang Hsui once said of Mei Yao-ch'en:

> His recent poetry is more old and unyielding. When you chew it over it is bitter and hard to get the teeth into; or again, it is like eating olives: the true flavour grows to time. ('Liu-i shih hua', in *Li-tai shih hua*, I, p. 159. Cited Aoki, op. cit., p. 80.)

The taste of olives – invariably classed as *se* 'asperity' – and the taste of *k'u* 'bitterness' both appealed very much to Chou Tso-jen.

Chou's predilection for *k'u* is apparent from the frequency with which the word appears in the titles of his books and in the name of his studio, K'u yü chai. *K'u* is not a joyous thing. If that is not obvious, Chou spells it out in an essay called 'A line of Tu Mu's' in *K'u chu tsa-chi*. The line in question is: 'To tolerate wrongs can give cause for rejoicing [*jen kuo shih k'an hsi*].' Chou says he appreciates the 'mental world' (*ching chieh*) the line conjures up:

> This is like drinking bitter tea. Bitter tea is not nice at all. The child will not drink even ordinary tea until he is in his teens. To feel

[12] 'Tang T'ao Yüan-ch'ing chün ti hui-hua chan-lan shih' (At the Time of the Painting Exhibition of Mr. T'ao Yüan-ch'ing), *Lu Hsün ch'üan chi*, III, 411.

> invigorated after a swallow of strong tea is the sad lot of an adult, life's 'bitter-sweetness', as the Greek poetess called love. As the *Book of Odes* ['Ku feng'] says: 'Who said the sow-thistle is bitter? Its sweetness is like the shepherd's purse.' (p. 80.)

These comments reflect more on life than literature. They point to a man saddened by experience who has come to find a kind of solace in his sorrows, who is inclined to lick his wounds. But there is fortitude in Chou's attitude too; it comes out in the essay 'Reading by lamplight':

> Perhaps you can say I read to educate myself. There is neither any profit in it nor much pleasure. What is gained is only a little knowledge, and knowledge is bitter [*k'u*], or at least knowledge is tinged with bitterness.
> The Hebrew preacher said:
>
> > And I gave my heart to know wisdom, and to know madness and folly;
> > I perceived that this also is vexation of the spirit.
> > For much wisdom is much grief: and he that increaseth knowledge increaseth sorrow.
> > (Ecclesiastes, 1, verses 17–18)
>
> This is very true, but grief and sorrow are unquestionably an education; and even 'vexation of spirit' [the Chinese translation is actually 'grasping at shadows' (*pu feng)*] is not at all an uninteresting thing. I once said before, 'To know such madness and folly, and to ponder on the individual's ageing and death, sickness and travails [*k'u*] is a great task. Vain it may be, but, knowing it is vain, to still enquire and seek out is a very meaningful thing, and rates the name of great 'vexation of spirit'. (*K'u k'ou kan k'ou*, p. 34.)

Though one might harbour the suspicion that Chou was less determined to confront facts fearlessly than willing to confirm gloomy prejudices, there is still the flavour of Confucian steadfastness, summed up in the words 'to know a thing cannot be done and yet to do it' (*chih ch'i pu k'e wei erh wei chih*), in his attitude. This phrase was actually used by Chou, of Confucius' feeling that life was not too pleasurable, but not able to be ignored.[13]

Applied to literature this philosophy might simply signify that Chou liked reading distressing things for the good of his soul, but there is more to it than that. He had a theory that painful experiences admit more of sharing than pleasurable ones. This theory he put forward most clearly in 1944:

> In my humble opinion sharing in pleasure is a very shallow thing. Apart from the fact that honeyed words about the never-to-be future are totally unreliable, even a wholly factual picture of

[13] In 'Han wen-hsüeh ti ch'ien-t'u', *Yao-t'ang tsa wen*.

> everyone eating sweets together is not very interesting; at the most it could only arouse the envious delight of children.[14] More important and more interesting is in fact the sharing in distress. It was said of old: 'One can share in disasters but one cannot share in pleasures', which shows that sharing in distress is easier than sharing in joyfulness. Joyfulness is close to competition, while distress, on the contrary, draws together, like fish moistening each other with their slime [when stranded].[15] When we learn of the trials and tribulations of others, if the medium of words is effective, naturally our sympathy is aroused; there is a feeling of 'I and you are like him' or I *am* you. This is the most elevated kind of moral or religious feeling. ('Ts'ao t'un yü mao-wu' [Rustic Cradles and Thatched Huts], 1944, *K'u-k'ou kan'kou*, p. 108.)

If he had had a mind to, Chou could have found some classical quotations more favourable to the idea of sharing pleasures, but he has a valid point about distress being more likely to engender sympathy than joy. Whatever the merits of the proposition it does interestingly link up with one of the vital reasons Chou had for writing – that of establishing a bond with the reader (see p. 41).

The quality of *k'u* that Chou Tso-jen appreciates is not the same as the *k'u* which forms the basis of the theoretical work of Kuriyagawa Hakuson called 'Symbols of Discontent', made popular in China through Lu Hsün's translation '*K'u-men ti hsiang-cheng*'. In that work *k'u* stands for the exacerbation which stimulates artistic creation, and it arises from the inability of the artist to reconcile his ideals with reality, whereas Chou speaks of it as present in the finished product. Actually both aspects had received a good deal of attention from a long line of Chinese theorists stretching from Ssu-ma Ch'ien through Ou-yang Hsiu down to Wang Kuo-wei.[16] There seems to have been very wide agreement that the subjection of the artist to extreme hardship produces the best work, aesthetically speaking, and also that 'bitterness' of content makes the work richer, on the assumption that joy is fleeting, sadness is lasting, joy is simple, sadness is complex. It is the latter train of thought that Chou takes up and amplifies.

As to 'asperity' or 'astringency' (*se*), this belongs exclusively to aesthetics, and has no philosophical overtones. It typifies a preference

[14] Though this attitude is particularly evident in the war years, it was already formulated in 1928. He stated then that an objective appraisal of history is more interesting than dreaming of utopia or salvation, though it might entail descending into hell, with no prospect of re-emergence. (Preface to *K'ung ta ku*, wrongly entitled 'Preface to *Tien ti*', in *K'u yü chai hsü pa wen*, pp. 14–15.

[15] The reference is to *Chuang tzu*, chapter 6, 'Ta tsung shih'.

[16] See Fu Keng-sheng's summary in *T'ung lun*, pp. 63–6.

for the rough or rasping over the smooth, the opaque over the clear, the implicit over the explicit, the dense over the thin. In dividing modern Chinese prose into these two camps in his 'Compendium' introduction Chou made clear which he preferred. So when he described Yü P'ing-po and Feng Fei-ming's style as 'having the asperity of the olive'[17] he was paying them a high compliment. As both Yü and Feng were acknowledged disciples of Chou Tso-jen himself, he was perhaps conceding that his own work was along the right lines too.

Again Chou, to my knowledge, never went out of his way to explain what was involved in *se*, but there is a description of its effect from the pen of Fu Keng-sheng which is enlightening:

> Reading a work of genuine feeling is like eating an olive. At first one is put off by its asperity [*k'u-se*], but the aftertaste is like sweetmeats, and its fragrance lingers long in the mouth. The opposite kind is like chewing sugar-cane: at first it is like cliff-honey giving off its sweetness, then suddenly it is lees in the mouth; since it no longer has any taste, it is a relief to spit it out. (*Chung-kuo wen-hsüeh hsin-shang chü-yü* [Intimations of Chinese Literary Appreciation], p. 16.)

Bearing in mind Chou's knowledge and appreciation of Japanese culture, it is quite likely that in picking out *se* as a desirable quality he was influenced by the Japanese penchant for *shibumi*, the taste for the subdued and sober (in Chinese *se-wei*, 'astringent flavour'). Aoki Masaru attributes this Japanese aesthetic of the 'plain and unvarnished' to the importation of the values of the Sung dynasty, when, in reaction to the ideals of the T'ang, preference was shown for the solid over the beautiful, the simple over the ornate, the rude over the pretty, the unlovely over the resplendent.[18] Which country's tradition was to the forefront in Chou's mind it is hard to say, but Aoki's ascription of Japanese to Chinese makes the question ultimately futile.

[17] In 'Chih-mo chi-nien', *K'an yün chi*, p. 122.
[18] *Chung-kuo ku-tai wen-i ssu-ch'ao* (Trends in Literary Thought in Ancient China), p. 17.

6

THE ESSAY

As we have come to expect with Chou Tso-jen, nowhere does he attempt an exhaustive definition of the essay, whether it be classed as *mei-wen* 'belles lettres', *hsiao p'in wen* 'the short form', or *pi chi* 'jottings' – all these being terms he used to designate the said phenomenon. He did however make several excursions into the theory of the subject, the first being in *Mei wen*, (Belles Lettres), which is short enough to quote in full:

> In foreign literature there is a form called 'the essay' [*lun-wen*]. These essays can be divided into two general categories. The first is 'critical', of a scholarly nature, the second is 'descriptive', which is artistic in character, and has an alternative name of 'belles lettres'. The latter can be further divided into narrative and lyrical, but many combine the two. This type of belles lettres seems to be most developed among the English-speaking peoples: such figures well-known in China as Addison, Lamb, Owen and Hawthorne have very good belles lettres to their credit, and in more recent times Galsworthy, Gissing and Chesterton are also experts in belles lettres. Reading a good essay is like reading a prose poem, because it is in fact a bridge between poetry and prose. In Chinese classical prose, prefaces, descriptions, discourses, etc. may also be said to be a form of belles lettres. But in contemporary vernacular literature this kind of composition has not yet appeared. Why do not those who are active in the new literature try their hands at it? I believe there really is a connection between form and content in literature: there are a lot of thoughts which can neither be turned into stories nor are suitable for making poems of (here I am only talking about literary forms; as to character, belles lettres are indistinguishable from fiction, and fiction from poetry – Kuprin's 'Evening Visitor'[1] can stand as an example); in which case they can be expressed in the essay form. Its requirements, common to all works of literature, are just genuineness and conciseness. We may consult foreign models in writing essays, but we must use our own words and thoughts – we

[1] Translated by Chou in his *Tien ti* collection.

> may not imitate them. Some pieces which appeared before in the 'Twaddle' [*lang-man t'an*] column of the *Ch'en-pao* came near to matching the requirements, but later on (excuse my bluntness) they fell into the old rut, made use of lots of expressions drawn from nature, adopted a feeble, plaintive tone, and were pretty lifeless things. I hope everyone will clear the ground for a new start, and open up new territory for the new literature. There couldn't be anything wrong with that. (*T'an hu chi*, 1921, pp. 41–2.)

Up to the time of Chou's writing the literary columns had been filled with prose pieces, usually subsumed under the heading of *tsa kan* 'random thoughts'. These pieces would probably fall into Chou's 'critical' category, since the majority aired views on matters of public and personal interest, and certainly no bridge could span the gulf between them and poetry. Evidently it was the other type, then in a minority, that Chou wished to promote, and for this type he chose the name 'belles lettres', perhaps more wisely than he knew, for there came to be about them more than a suspicion of the arty-craftiness that accompanied the English belles lettres much in vogue at the time in England but now deservedly in disrepute. However, though Chou was pointing in the direction of the 'artistic' essay, he was clearly dissatisfied with current manifestations of it, which could have been summed up by the rather derogatory term *feng hua hsüeh yüeh* 'flowers in the wind and moon on the snow'; his prescription of genuineness and conciseness would have the effect of tightening up the slackness and giving body to the vapidness of this kind of essay. It also should be borne in mind that while Chou excludes the 'critical' essay from the discussion he does not disparage it. Part of his idea in recommending the purely literary essay surely was, in Hu Shih's phrase, to disprove the myth that 'the vernacular cannot be a medium for fine writing'.[2]

Despite the references to Chinese prose both ancient and modern, pride of place is here given to the English essay. It is a strange thing that Chou nowhere enlarges on the virtues of the English essay, though he does refer to it again for comparison. At least it seemed strange until Chou in his memoirs[3] confirmed one's suspicion that he never got far into English literature: he confesses there that he had only used English as a means of acquiring knowledge. As it was almost indecent to mention Chinese literature except as an afterthought during the May Fourth period, his pretension to familiarity with the English essay is understandable, but fortunately it was soon discarded and his attentions turned to Chinese prose, where his knowledge lay. The change in

[2] From *Wu-shih nien lai Chung-kuo chih wen-hsüeh* (Chinese Literature of the Last Fifty Years).
[3] *Chih-t'ang hui-hsiang lu*, p. 709.

his approach is evident in his preface to *Tao-an meng-i* by Chang Tai (1597–1684?), written five years later:

> I often reflect that modern prose is the form of the New Literature which has least been influenced from abroad: it is rather the product of literary revival than literary revolution, though in the course of the development of literature revival and revolution are alike progress. Before Neo-Confucianism and 'ancient prose' [*ku-wen*] reached the height of their influence, lyrical prose had already advanced considerably, but in the eyes of the literati naturally enjoyed little esteem. On reading some compositions of the 'dilettante' school [*ming shih p'ai*] of the Ming and Ch'ing we find they have almost the same emotional ambience as modern literature. Admittedly in thought there is inevitably a certain distance between them, but, as in the reaction of the Ming writers against the Confucian rules of propriety, they have quite a modern air. (*K'u yü chai hsü pa wen*, p. 147.)

In a letter to Yü P'ing-po, dated 2 February 1926, he extends the tradition back to Su Tung-p'o and Huang T'ing-chien. Also, instead of using the general term 'prose' (*san wen*), he adds the name *hsiao p'in*, literally 'small piece' or 'small form', denoting a work of art small in scale and scope, but self-contained and artistically whole. He wrote:

> I often say that present-day *hsiao p'in* are by no means an invention of the May Fourth movement, but 'have been known since ancient times': it is only that they have taken on a new lease of life. From Pan-ch'iao[4] and Tung-hsin[5] back to those Ming writers, and further back even to Tung-p'o and Shan-ku, it would seem possible to edit an anthology which would provide source material for prose *hsiao p'in*. I think this would be very worthwhile, and would incidentally be helpful to teachers. Certainly there is some difference linguistically between modern prose and the works of Sung and Ming writers, but in manner [*feng-chih*] they are truly the same – except perhaps that the modern writing has been somewhat influenced also by the West, which has given it a kind of fresh breath. (*Chou Tso-jen shu hsin*, pp. 161–2.)

Two years later, in 1928, he returns to the same theme, this time including the T'ang dynasty in his perspective:

> T'ang and Sung writers also wrote prose pieces which revealed their inmost selves, but most of them regarded them as literary recreation; when they came to write 'proper' compositions, they wrote their 'ancient prose' in compliance with the rules. It was the same in Ming and Ch'ing, but in Ming literature the arts had more life in them, and

[4] i.e. Cheng Hsieh (1693–1765).
[5] i.e. Chin Nung (1687–1764).

literature had quite a reformist look about it. The Kung-an school could disregard the 'ancient prose' orthodoxy and write everything in lyrical vein. Although critics of later generations dismissed them as facile and empty, they expressed themselves truly and individualistically, and they were better than the Chin-ling school. Previously the attitudes of writers to their work could be said to be dualistic; theirs was monistic, and in this they were identical with modern writers ... Previously people thought literature was for 'conveying the Way', but there was a particular kind of composition that could be written for diversion. Now they have been brought together, writing or reading can be said to be basically for diversion, but at the same time it is for spreading the gospel, or hearing the word ... Such being the case, it is no cause for surprise that modern literature – now we are only referring to prose – is similar to that of the Ming dynasty, though there is no question of imitation – probably very few people read Ming works. Also, due to the times, there are many instances of Europeanization in vocabulary, and there have also been marked changes in thought compared with four hundred years ago. Modern prose is like a river buried in the sand which has been dug up many years later downstream. It is an old river, but it is also new. ('Tsa pan erh pa' [Postscript to Tsa pan erh], K'u *yü chai hsü pa wen*, pp. 150–2.)

From these comments we gather that Chou, subsequent to the '*Mei wen*' essay, found enough, or became willing to find enough, in Chinese prose for modern writers to associate with, which fulfilled the conditions that he recognized, basically that of 'giving vent to the feelings' or 'revelation of the inmost self', but including the spirit of revolt against conventions, and not assuming a special portentous style for 'serious' writing. All this Chou may have most powerfully and potently believed, and it may well be true, but then it was not untrue of the English essay either. Where then do the early Chinese 'essayists' gain over the English? Apparently in their closer emotional affinity with their modern successors: they have the same *feng-chih*, that is, manner, or way of conveying a state of sensibility. As a case in point, Yü P'ing-po has the kind of 'manner' which is 'characteristic of Chinese literature; it is so old, but again so new' (ibid., p. 150). Since Chou later says that Yü resembles the Ming people in the 'civilized' (*ya*) quality of his style (*ya* is then defined as 'natural' and 'generous-minded', *not* as observing linguistic taboos or putting on gentlemanly airs – p. 159), we must assume that *ya* also describes the typically Chinese manner. As the word is really untranslatable doubtless he is right on that point.

There is another factor, an external one this time, which presumably contributed to forming this manner, the manner at least of the Ming essayists, which Chou states in his postscript to another work of Yü P'ing-po:

> The source of the new Chinese prose is, as I see it, in the confluence of the essays [*hsiao p'in wen*] of the Kung-an school and the English. But the situation in China now seems to correspond exactly to that at the end of the Ming dynasty: it is not really surprising that literary men who can't hold a bamboo pole should have to take refuge in the world of art. (*'Yen chih ts'ao pa', 1928,* K'ü *yü chai hsü pa wen*, p. 160.)

In other words both they and the moderns belonged to a world gone haywire in which the man of refined sensibility had to express his defiance, his resentment, and his aspirations in a literary form. This gave their work a feeling that the English essay did not have.

In these generalizations Chou was not really being very general. Yü P'ing-po can hardly represent the new prose as a whole. But he can fairly represent that type of essay cultivated as an art form for which Chou has in these remarks introduced the term *hsiao p'in wen*. What Chou meant by *hsiao p'in wen* can be seen in the last-mentioned preface:

> That type of prose which is not simply ratiocinative and narrative but is principally lyrical – as someone called it, 'chatter'.[6] To be readable it has to have asperity and simplicity, so the diction has to be modified. The hard core of the ordinary spoken language has to admit and assimilate elements of Europeanization, classical language, and dialect, and the whole has to be organized suitably and sparingly, and submit to the control of good sense and taste. (ibid., p. 159.)

If these are the elements of style that Chou liked to see, the content is a combination of 'scientific common sense as the basis', together with 'unsullied feelings' and 'penetrating intelligence'.[7] Beyond style and content, there is something more that has to come through, and that is *ch'i wei*, which in this sort of context would normally mean something like 'temperament', but which Chou initially seems to take more in the sense of 'smell':

> *Ch'i wei* might seem to be a rather abstruse and mysterious term, but actually it is not. *Ch'i wei* is a very palpable thing: a man may have about him the rank odour of sheep, the smell of garlic, or a kind of unctuousness. These are all things that everybody can distinguish. (ibid., p. 154.)

He continues that it is a pleasure to listen to men of all times and parts speaking their mind, but the pleasure of conversation with friends of

[6] That someone was Hu Meng-hua; see p. 118.

[7] 'Tsa pan erh chih erh hsü' (Second preface to *Tsa pan erh*), 1932, K'u *yü chai hsü pa wen*, p. 155.

like temper (*ch'i wei hsiang t'ou*) on any and every subject is greater. Here Chou is cheating, because the *ch'i wei* of *ch'i wei hsiang t'ou* is not the easily perceptible kind he gives examples of; but it is clear that apart from style and matter the thing that counts is the sense of the kind of man the author is, which somehow communicates itself in the writing. (This is exactly what Chou asked for in the preface to his book *I-shu yü sheng-huo* in 1926.) If Ch'ien Mu is correct, Chou was only looking for what there was plenty of, for Ch'ien thinks it characteristic of Chinese literature that the author is visible in his work. Taking the mirror as an analogy, Western literature uses it to give back the exterior, while Chinese literature stresses the aspect of throwing light on the interior; put another way, Western literature belongs to the fire element, lighting up what is round about, while Chinese literature belongs to the water element, allowing one to see the inside.[8]

So far Chou's discussion of various aspects of the essay, being very general, has not been very controversial. There is a further desideratum he put forward which is more limiting, for it is an aesthetic principle that takes the question of how something should be said very close to what should be said. It is that there should be a balance between the serious and the frivolous, that there should be a lightness of touch even with the most solemn subjects. It is in the collection *Yao wei chi* (1940) that Chou actually formulates this requirement, though it is implicit in much of his earlier criticism (he complained for instance in 1925 that the Chinese either regard a thing completely seriously or not seriously at all.)[9] In his comment on the style of Yü Yüeh in that collection, Chou wrote: 'To be playful and yet restrained, grave yet totally at ease, this is the characteristic of good writing; just like the two sides of a shield, one can't have one without the other.'[10] Taken in conjunction with his judgement that Yü Cheng-hsieh's prose shows fairness in argument and funniness in style,[11] which seems to exemplify the same two sides, it would appear that Chou wanted an essay to have humour or wit, but not the self-amused type of humour that Ling Yutang was associated with.

The subject is put in its proper perspective in Chou's discussion of *p'ai-wen* in two essays in *Yao wei chi*. In both essays, 'T'an p'ai wen' ('On *p'ai-wen*') and 'Tsai t'an p'ai wen' ('On *p'ai wen* again'), Chou discusses the mode in Chinese and Japanese literature. For our purposes it is

[8] *Chung-kuo wen-hsüeh chiang-yen chi*, p. 38.
[9] 'Hua-chi ssu pu to' (Humour apparently in Short Supply), *Yü Ssu*, no. 8.
[10] 'Ch'un tsai t'ang tsa wen', 1939, *Yao wei chi*, p. 112.
[11] 'Yü Li-ch'u ti hui-hsieh' (The Wit of Yü Li-ch'u), 1937, *Ping chu hou t'an*, p. 47.

more convenient to see them separately. In Japanese *p'ai wen* (*haibun*) means a prose piece written in a poetic style reminiscent of the *haiku*. It was Matsuo Bashō (1644–94) who pioneered the *haibun* and made it into an art form which embodied thoughts on 'nature and human life' (p. 195). *Haibun* fall roughly into three categories: the first is lofty, detached, elegant; the second ribald and satirical; the third is an intermediate kind, rich in inferences and implications and humorous as well. All three put a premium on conciseness, show a preference for 'overtones', and avoid digressions. The language is a blend of recondite and everyday words, with the addition of some Chinese terms. It would appear from this account that in proposing a formula for Chinese *hsiao-p'in wen* Chou has been more or less describing, both qualitatively and linguistically, the Japanese *haibun*. Though he does not say so, we can reasonably assume from what we know of his tastes that it was the third group, which includes a humorous element, that Chou preferred.

It is in the second essay, 'On *p'ai wen* again', which deals mainly with the native Chinese counterpart to *haibun*, that Chou highlights the aspect of humour. Indeed, the nature of the Chinese terms allows of nothing else, for *p'ai wen* is not an authentic Chinese word: Chinese only has *p'ai hsieh wen* or *p'ai (hsieh) t'i*, which mean in themselves 'comic writing' and 'humorous style', hence the earliest manifestations of it that Chou mentions, from the Wei-Chin period, are straightforward comic cuts. However unpretentious these jokes may have been, the trend they initiated was a good one, because 'laughter and gaiety are after all part of the make-up of man' (p. 212), and because this kind of writing was able freely to extend its own range, not being 'a menial for others' (p. 209) – which presumably means being free from any pressure to conform. But Chou's real interest is engaged by what he calls the 'new *p'ai wen*', which is 'a new kind of composition which was a blend of the Kung-an and Ching-ling schools' (p. 222).

The man chosen to represent the new *p'ai wen* is Chang Tai (Tsung-tzu). Chou says of him that it was his aim to write right and proper compositions, but humour always crept in. For instance, his two collections, *Meng hsün* and *Meng i*, 'are both works on Tsung-tzu's pain at the ravage of his country and the loss of his home, yet the writing is notable for its wry humour' (p. 226). On the other hand, 'if you regard him as a humorous writer, the content is still serious, and there is sadness in it too' (p. 222). Chang showed absolute disregard for conventions of diction and linguistic taboos, the ideal being 'the mouth does not select the words, the words do not discriminate between subjects' (*k'ou pu tse yen, yen pu tse shih*) (p. 222). He did not pause either to consider questions of ancient or modern, decorous or uncouth. In this he was like the moderns.

Having thus described Chang Tai's writing, Chou is forced to admit that perhaps *p'ai wen* is a bad name for it, for the original type of *p'ai wen* was written only as a sideline or by entertainers, while the 'new' type recognizes no distinction between the playful and the serious. The genre he is thinking of would in fact include in its scope the work of Matsuo Bashō, Yokoi Yayū, Montaigne, Lamb and Milne, its essence being 'to want to speak for oneself, not to do the running about for politics or religion' (p. 228). In England it might be called '*essai*' (sic!), in Japan *zuihitsu*, in China *hsiao p'in wen*.

These two essays, since we finally discover they are about *hsiao p'in wen*, add to Chou's definition of that genre the element of humour or pleasantry, and confirm the points of conciseness, hidden depth, varied vocabulary, and a style natural to the man (*k'ou pu tse yen*). The last two points, bearing on the use of words, can now be enlarged upon.

In the section on the limitations of writing we saw that Chou believed the spoken word was superior to the written word as a form of expression, in that it was closer to the heart, so to speak. The line of reasoning is that followed by Yüan Tsung-tao:

> The mouth represents the heart, writing in turn represents the mouth. In the transitions there is alienation, so though one might write perspicuously, it must fall short of the mouth, and even shorter of the heart. ('Lun wen', reprinted Yang Chia-lo, op. cit., vol. III.)

The correct conclusion from this premise, and Yüan draws it, is that the test of literature is its ability to communicate, not that all literature should resemble conversation. It does however follow that there is a special virtue in writing being like talk, and the essay form is the best adapted to accommodate this virtue. So Chou accepts the way of looking at prose as talk written down on paper, as opposed to applying standards of weightiness (in a doctrinal sense) or musicality.[12] His reason is the same as that of Yüan Tsung-tao, that writing should have good sense and communicability. Similarly when he compared the pleasure in reading books to that of listening to the conversation of like-minded friends[13] he was referring to matter-of-factness and easiness of style. The point is that good essays give the *impression* of good conversation. In Chu Hsi's terms they are 'uttered' (*shuo-ch'u ti*), not 'fashioned' (*tso-ch'u ti*); according to him, the compositions of the ancients were mostly uncontrived talk (*p'ing shuo*), with the sense developing in its own way, while latter-day writers were keen to make their work pregnant with meaning and took great pains with their craft, with the opposite result to what they had hoped for.[14] Chou likewise

[12] 'Ch'un tsai t'ang tsa wen', *Yao wei chi*, p. 105.
[13] As note 7.
[14] See Chu Tung-jun, *Ta kang*, p. 179.

had a horror of contrivance (*tso-tso*). But he did not claim that the essay, or any form of prose, should actually be spoken conversation transferred bodily onto paper. Linguistically it could not be, since he thought undiluted colloquial language (*pai-hua*) inadequate. Furthermore he did on one occasion say that there was a qualitative difference between them. Unfortunately this was in a lecture that he did not include in any collection; it is not even known whether he approved its publication in *Ch'en pao fu-k'an* on 5–6 January 1928.[15] In it he states that literature is close to letter-writing or conversation in that it gives voice to discontents or visions of the future without any expectation of remedying the first or realizing the second. But letters and conversation are marked by casualness of delivery, commonplaceness of thought, and have no distinct character. Literature, besides relying on fullness of feeling and lively and acute thought, needs adequate artistic means of expression. In conversation meaning can be got across with the help of facial expressions and tone of voice, but literature has to use extra verbal means to supply this lack.[16]

This attitude conforms reasonably with other stated views of Chou's, such as his preference for opacity and suggestiveness, and ordered economy, which are not characteristic of conversation. And it is only sensible to recognize that a written composition obeys different rules from conversation. However, the point the article is making is that literature demands a product of high calibre, beyond the capacity of the ordinary person, who can only express himself in ordinary conversational style – hence the title, 'The aristocratic nature of literature' ('Wen-hsüeh ti kui-tsu hsing'). So with regard to the essay the only positive point it makes is that the writer must be an accomplished artist with words; it is not in conflict with his normal standpoint that it is the sense of hearing the voice of the writer that gives the feeling of intimacy which is so important a literary value.

Having put forward what Chou Tso-jen considered the main

[15] The text of it may be found in Juan Wu-ming, *Chung-kuo hsin wen-t'an mi lu* (Secret Records of the New Chinese Literary World), Shanghai, 1933.

[16] pp. 178–80. Though no comparison with Chou Tso-jen personally is intended, Aristotle made the same sort of qualification. G. M. A. Grube summarizes Aristotle's arguments like this: '. . . Lucidity is the only specific *areté* or excellence which fulfills the proper function of speech. Now current words make for clarity but the result is somewhat common, so we must use unusual expressions, though not as freely as poets do, to ornament our speech and make it pleasing, but the audience must not be aware of artifice, we must appear to speak naturally, not in a studied manner. Artifice is successful when the artist composes in the terms of common speech.' (*The Greek and Roman Critics*, p. 95.)

qualifications for a good essay, we should note the disqualifications. It goes without saying that any essay was declared out of court if it conveyed any 'way' other than the author's own. But Chou also deprecated the polemical essay as such, which one would have thought need not suffer from this defect. It was part of Chou's credo in his middle period, as we have seen in the section on the uselessness of literature, that the intention to effect social change or indeed achieve any object not only leads to waste of words, but in itself precludes good writing; it is, he said,[17] quoting Confucius, 'a slight on the words'. This position he did not attempt to justify in any concrete detail, but we can assume the mark of any polemical essay is more likely to be 'irascibility' than *p'ing-tan*. One of the factors involved was probably his own reluctance to enter into personal disputes, as his brother and perhaps the majority of contemporary essayists were wont to do: 'A fight might be entertaining for spectators, but the fighters might not think the spectacle elevating if they could see it.'[18] In fact he does state in the same essay that those like him had not 'the zeal and resolution to be thus severe and critical to the point of engaging in abuse'.[19] But apart from this personal factor, in terms of aesthetics the straight polemical essay left no room for all the little incidental things that Chou valued, which could perhaps be summed up in the word *jen-ch'ing*, 'humanity', or when differentiated are the personal qualities of the writer that breathe through the work, the so-called *ch'ü-wei*. It is the relaxed and leisurely essays that can bring out such qualities regardless of the subject matter – the more homely the better – that Chou particularly called *hsiao p'in wen*; the other more factious or irritable kind he called *tsa-wen*.[20] In suggesting such a clarification of nomenclature he was at one with Lu Hsün and other left-wing writers, though of course their preferences were opposite.[21]

The objection to polemical essays does not, let it be said, entail any suggestion of suppression of controversial views. On the contrary, the quality of *ta pu ching* 'flagrant irreverence' stood very high in Chou's estimation, and he bemoaned the scarcity of it in Chinese literature. It was however typical of the fourteenth-century Japanese *kyogen* plays, several of which Chou translated; and the Japanese stories about the thunder god have the same spirit: 'This kind of uninhibitedness pleases

[17] 'Kuan-yü hsieh wen-chang erh' (On the Art of Composition, 2), *K'u ch'a sui-pi*, 1935, p. 298.
[18] ibid., p. 299.
[19] ibid., p. 300.
[20] 'Liang ke kui ti wen-chang' (Essays of Two Demons), *Kuo-chü ti kung-tso*, p. 77.
[21] See Jen Hsin, *T'an hsiao p'in san wen* (On *hsiao p'in* Prose), section 13.

me very much because there is vigour and vitality in it.'[22] He is at pains to point out that 'uninhibitedness' is in no sense a vice: it does not denote violence and rudeness, but a lack of 'religious and moral hypocrisy'.[23] Having noted this general commendation of nonconformity or irreverence, it should not be confused with vehemence in attack on specific existing, and strongly defended, citadels, not at least if such attacks were part of a concerted campaign. It is still principally a literary 'flavour'.

In this taboo on social and political questions, Chou Tso-jen is recognized as heading a school of modern writers. The *Weltanshauung* from which their writing stemmed is summed up in the phrase 'to save one's skin in a chaotic age' (*kou ch'üan hsing-ming yü luan shih*), adopted by Chou in his essay 'Reading behind closed doors' (1928).[24] Since their world was beyond saving (an assumption that led to different attitudes on the part of different individuals, as for instance with the more active Chu Tzu-ch'ing to the 'philosophy of the moment', *ch'a-na chu-i*) the individual had best save himself from despair by putting a little distance between himself and the political situation, not necessarily by covering his eyes but by avoiding crippling involvement. Conversely they turned their gaze on eternity, taking pleasure in things of permanent interest, in nature, in man, and in art. Chou had already heralded such a trend in 1923 when he defended the love of the 'dilettante' for 'such things as works of art, historical relics, folkcrafts and toys': 'in this vast desert of China, at least, it is necessary, because a life prickly outside and succulent inside, like a cactus, is our only way, even if it is close to the hermitry now despised by the world.'[25]

In their own art the ideal relationship of members of this school to their subject matter was expressed by Yü P'ing-po, a disciple of Chou Tso-jen, in this way: 'To succeed in the business of writing there is a general rule, especially marked in the creation of *hsiao p'in wen* . . . in all our encounters with the external world we must not become absorbed, if we do, there is blockage; neither must we cut ourselves off, if we do, there is estrangement.'[26] Chou Tso-jen himself, though he did

[22] 'Kuan-yü Lei kung' (About the Thunder God), 1936, *Kua tou chi*, p. 16.
[23] 'Huai Tung-ching' (Fond Memories of Tokyo), 1936, *Kua tou chi*, p. 95.
[24] 'Pi hu tu shu lun', *Yung jih chi*.
[25] 'Wan-chü (Toys), *Tzu-chi ti yüan-ti*, p. 138.
[26] In 'Ch'ung k'an Fu sheng liu chi hsü' (Preface to the reprint of *Fu sheng liu chi*), quoted Sun Hsi-chen, *Hsien-tai Chung-kuo san-wen hsüan*, appendix, p. 13.

to some extent carry out his resolution to talk about harmless things, represented in the phrase *ts'ao mu ch'ung yü* (plants, insects, fishes), maintained in his essays this connection with the world at large; as Sun Hsi-chen wisely remarked:

> He was never willing to limit himself to the isolated topic under discussion; instead his aim was to identify the main source of value in the object and to enter into a critique of the whole culture.[27]

And, as A Ying[28] and other critics have pointed out, Chou's 'escapism', unlike Yü P'ing-po's, was involuntary. All through his work in fact one can detect an emotional resistance to the 'powers of darkness'. Perhaps this accounts for the tension underlying the appearance of scholarly remoteness that makes Chou's work superior to that of others of the same school. He was never able to swallow whole as Lin Yutang did, the philosophy of 'expressionism',[29] which meant self-projection, to the detriment of concerns which drew men together.

Having now sampled some of Chou's opinions on what the essay should be (though he was not clear what it should be called) we can see how they match other well-known definitions of the essay form current in China between the wars. The two most widely quoted come from Japanese sources. The kind of essay that Lafcadio Hearn tried to introduce to the East was the 'sketch'.[30] Hearn starts with the premise that the novel is dead, and the future lies with other prose forms. The sketch is peculiarly suited to busy modern life because of its shortness. By sketch he means 'any simple piece of prose whose matter is either a picture of real life as actually witnessed, or an impression of life felt in the heart'.[31] The sketch can have a multitude of forms, and gives scope to the highest powers of reflection, description, and expression of feelings. It is a Western form acceptable in Japan because Japan also had the form of old – difference between linguistic forms is not very important: what matters is the quality of the thought and the genuineness of the feelings. Hearn then goes on to quote some

[27] ibid., p. 9.
[28] In 'Yü P'ing-po hsiao p'in hsü', *Hsien-tai shih-liu chia hsiao p'in* (*Hsiao p'in* of Sixteen Writers of Today).
[29] Lin Yü-t'ang drew principally on Spingarn for the theory of 'expressionism'; he expounded it in an article in *Yü Ssu*, V,30 (1929). See also the critique by Hu Feng called 'Lin Yü-t'ang lun' in Mao Tun, ed. *Tso-chia lun*, esp. pp. 140–4.
[30] His treatise on the subject, translated into Chinese, has been reprinted in Ts'ao Chü-jen, *Hsien-tai wen-i shou-ts'e* (Handbook to Modern Literature), Hong Kong, 1952.
[31] ibid., p. 45.

examples, and comments in passing on such elements as humour – deep-seated, not just comicality – scientific thought, and the idea of macrocosm in microcosm. In conclusion he says the trend of the best thought and feeling in Western literature is towards compassion, which is equivalent to humanism, and the form of literature best suited to be the vehicle for humanism is '*hsiao p'in wen*'. Throughout the treatise the word used to translate 'sketch' is *pi chi wen*. Whether in this last instance *hsiao p'in wen* is the inspiration of the translator I do not know, but the change is to be welcomed, for *hsiao p'in*, like sketch, applies to painting as well as to writing.[32] It will be noticed that in its general principles Hearn's analysis largely coincides with Chou Tso-jen's, with regard to the scope of the essay, its basic elements – sound thought and genuine feelings – and in some incidentals.

The second description of the essay is from the hand of Kuriyagawa Hakuson; it was written in 1920 and translated by Lu Hsün in 1925. The most quoted passage[33] is this:

> If it were winter, seated in an armchair by the fire, if summer, sipping tea draped in a bathrobe; altogether casual, chatting freely with good friends: if these words were transferred just as they were onto paper, this would be an 'essay'. If the mood takes one, there can also be some serious discussion, short of the kind that gives one a headache. [The essay] has sarcasm and arresting phrases; there is both 'humour' and 'pathos'. As to the topics of conversation, apart from the great issues of the day, they may include the trivial matter of the market-place, criticism of books, news of mutual acquaintances, and reminiscences from the past: whatever occurs to you can be talked about regardless. When entrusted to a ready pen, this is what this kind of composition consists of. (*Lu Hsün i-wen chi*, 1958, vol. III, p. 113.)

This setting of slippered ease where talk can be unconstrained was cherished by Chou Tso-jen. He described it as 'worth ten years of worldly dreams'.[34] But there are more points of correspondence between their views, for Kuriyagawa goes on to say that it is essential to the essay that the author should 'richly express the colouring of his own individual personality; its interest lies in its personal note.' For both men, if this condition were met, it qualified the essay for the title of prose poem.

[32] For a eulogy of *hsiao p'in* paintings see T'ang Hsien-yüeh, 'Wen yü hsü', in *Wan Ming hsiao p'in hsüan chu* (Annotated Selection of Late Ming *hsiao p'in*), p. 70.

[33] Quoted for instance by Ts'ao Chü-jen in 'Handbook', and Jen Hsin in *T'an hsiao p'in san wen*.

[34] 'Ch'ih ch'a' (Drinking Tea), *Yü t'ien ti shu*, p. 73.

A third normative description of the essay, which has the term 'chatter' (*hsü yü*) Chou referred to, was by Hu Meng-hua.[35] Hu followed Kuriyagawa very closely, specifying only the additional characteristics of 'irregularity' and 'informality', and that surface ordinariness should belie striking thoughts (Chou's *p'ing-tan*).

It is apparent from these three descriptions that the key values in Chou's system find parallels in the Western – and particularly the English – essay as conceived of in China and Japan. There is in fact nothing which blatantly conflicts. On the other hand the works traditionally classified as *hsiao p'in* in China include straightforward and almost impersonal discussions and descriptions, and stern censure, as well as fiercely embattled diatribes which would quickly dispel any air of ease and serenity (as in the selection called *Huang Ming shih liu chia hsiao p'in*). So in terms of aesthetic theory it would have been more consistent for him to continue to advocate the English essay as a genre, since, even if he had not read many examples, he had got its characteristics right, instead of transferring his loyalty to the Chinese *hsiao p'in wen*.

Theories aside, looking at the nature of the beast, it was idle of him to pretend, except where the topics were timeless ones, that the modern Chinese essay had more in common with *hsiao p'in wen* than with modern Western literature. Chu Tzu-ch'ing denies this contention in his preface to his own *Pei ying* collection (1928), and asks where anything like Chou's own essays is to be found among the work of Ming writers. He would only agree that there is some similarity in 'emotional tone'. Overall Chu must be right. It must be the writer's outlook on life which determines the content and in turn the style of the work, and the outlook of the modern writer was radically different from that of any of his precursors in an imperial age. In essays, which do not refract but directly express the author's mind, the differences in his view of the world and his own place in the world should be especially marked. If a modern work was indistinguishable from an ancient one it would be because the author was following a convention and was not seeing things afresh, for himself. In Yü Ta-fu's view modern prose is clearly marked off from all that went before it by the acceptance of the philosophy of individualism: 'People of times gone by existed for their lord, for "the way", for their parents; only modern man knew he existed for his own self.'[36] But possibly because in an age of 'disintegration of

[35] 'Piao-hsien ti chien-shang' (Appreciation of [the art of] Expression), quoted by Chung Ching-wen, 'Shih t'an hsiao p'in wen', *Wen-hsüeh chou pao*, 1928.
[36] 'Compendium', VII, 5.

the power of the central state' the individual has some responsibility for the way society is to develop, there is also in modern times the consciousness of being a social unit, so Yü continues: ' "To see the world in a grain of sand", for a windblown flower to give rise to thoughts on human nature, this is a characteristic of modern prose'[37] – a characteristic, he says, determined by the tide of the times and the influence of society.

Though Yü Ta-fu might be regarded as indulging in a piece of special pleading (to justify his own habit of self-absorption), there is no reason to suppose that Chou would have disagreed with this analysis. He freely admitted that Chinese thought had changed over the centuries, in modern times under the impact of foreign materialistic, scientific thought.[38] He also consistently deplored the blind spots, deficiencies and fallacies in Chinese thought, so there is no question of ideological loyalty colouring his judgement. I do think, however, that when free from the obligation to say the right forward-looking kind of things, he was ready to affirm his cultural identity as a Chinese, and to write himself and his own time into Chinese history. On the particular issue of the use of classical Chinese, for instance, he insisted that modern writers could not cut themselves off from their linguistic heritage: by the very fact of using the Chinese language they could not avoid rhetorical devices common to the tradition.[39] But above all Chou's bias indicates the unusual store he put by emotional affinities. It is not an unreasonable assumption that there would be more community of feeling between two Chinese separated in time than between a Chinese and a Westerner separated geographically, with all the attendant historical, cultural, and linguistic divergences. If, as Chou claimed in a moment of enthusiasm in 'Belles lettres', the essay is a kind of poem in prose, the linguistic aspect would be of prime importance, and the skilful use of words is more open to appreciation in one's own language. It is noteworthy how frequently in recording a favourable response to a piece of writing Chou had recourse to the expression *miao*, which above all marks a happy turn of phrase.

It is a strange thing that even in his middle period, when Chou so insistently stressed the aesthetic requirements of the essay and seemed to embrace the *ars longa, vita brevis* attitude, he was rarely able in practice to set these aesthetic priorities above what might be broadly called ideological aims (I refer only to his genuine essays, not his scholarly jottings). So when he divided his own essays into two classes,

[37] ibid., VII, 9.
[38] ibid., VI, 11–12.
[39] 'Yang pien chi hsü', *T'an lung chi*, p. 67.

those in which style is important and those in which the object is important, in 1935,[40] he had to admit that the majority of them fell into the second class – which aim to arouse feelings and influence issues. This was because he 'could not completely forget about society and the state'. I would not wish to imply that he did not cherish the values he recommended as sincerely as he professed to (though he was undoubtedly forced to some extent into his extreme socially negative position by the underlying rivalry with Lu Hsün), but it is clear from this admission alone that what we have concentrated on so far tells only part of Chou Tso-jen's story. The other part we will consider in the next chapter.

[40] 'Kuan-yü hsieh wen-chang erh', *K'u ch'a sui-pi.*

7

PERSPECTIVES

We have seen how in his middle period Chou Tso-jen spoke out continually against literature being used as propaganda, how he regarded it as 'useless', and how he insisted that any function it did have was limited to giving vent to grievances. But this negative attitude pertains to the attitude the author should have to his work, and stems, as we have suggested, from his experience of finding stuff written *as* propaganda, in order to be useful, and to provide guidance to the public, wholly unreadable. He was not indifferent to the kind of 'humours' actually present in a work, in fact he consistently demanded that literature should be 'healthy' in itself.

After he 'shut up shop' with *'One's Own Garden'*, his own work was fairly consistent with his professions, writing not to propose or instruct, or please in any deliberate way, but as it pleased him, without any particular reader in mind. As he said: 'If my ideas are genuine, my language clear enough to convey them, then my side of the affair is done. Whether the readers are men or women, greybeards or youngsters, or whether they enjoy reading it or not, these things I can forget about.'[1] At the same time his laments that his writings are too 'positive' in spite of himself have some truth in them. Though his crusading days had a term, the point of view behind them was that of a mature man, and it was not very likely that the outlook manifested in his essays would change radically, though the tone and approach in fact did. The vast majority of them, even those which consisted largely of quotations from writers of the past, which earned him the title of 'Mister Quotation', continued to expose human folly, invariably with some reference to the present time. In his preface to *K'u k'ou kan k'ou* (1944) he confessed that none of his essays were without their moral and political import; 'if you extract this thought from them, what is left is only empty words and phrases, entirely valueless.' (p. 2.) Like Ku Yen-wu what he had always wanted to get some perception of was 'in

[1] 'Meng-hsiang chih i', *K'u k'ou kan k'ou*, pp. 6–7.

the sphere of "the source of order and disorder in the state" and "the strategy for providing a good living for the people" ', though for his material, unlike Ku, he did not reject scholarly marginalia and the pleasurable contemplation of nature.

Chou later ascribed this bipolarity of his interests to a split in his personality between the gangster and the man of the gentry, or in other terms, between the rebel and the recluse. The piece in question, 'Essays of Two Demons',[2] written at the end of his essay-writing career, interestingly surveys the whole of his active literary life. He says there that his opinions did not change after 1919, when he wrote 'Ancestor Worship' and 'Revolution in Thought';[3] what he advocated then, the eradication of the Confucian doctrine of fealty, and the old rules of propriety, the old idea of integrity, of setting an example to the people, and so on, he still advocated. But he did not like the slanging matches that this kind of diatribe inevitably tangled him up in, so his interests changed direction and he wrote 'idle and agreeable' *hsiao p'in wen* to pass the time after his 'Reading behind closed doors' essay in 1928. It was then that the 'gentry demon' fully emerged. Nevertheless, his basic attitudes of atheism and belief in the primacy of the people were not sympathetic to 'poetic' themes. So of his 'idle' and 'serious' essays, it was the latter which, he felt, embodied to the greater extent his thought and opinions, and to him were more significant. He concludes that those who prefer him to write 'idle' essays have mistaken the nature of his business (pp. 76–77).

It is particularly in these prefaces and special backward-looking essays, as opposed to the occasional extempore type in which he was more liable to express himself extravagantly, that we find Chou Tso-jen admitting the possibility that he has something to contribute to the world. Another example of the kind of essay devoted to a survey of his past work is 'What one can do oneself' (1937).

In it he says

> I don't like historical anecdotes, so I don't discuss politics; I don't believe in the supernatural, so I don't record strange happenings; I don't write historical treatises, so I don't evaluate the achievements of past ages. What is left is browsing among the writings of our forebears, discriminating between them, sifting the gold from the dross, polishing away at the wood to fashion something usable. Though these labours bring no credit, they should nevertheless be of benefit to man and *mores*, and are also work worth doing. ('Tzu-chi so neng tso ti', *Ping chu hou t'an*, p. 2.)

[2] 'Liang-ke kui ti wen-chang', *Kuo-ch'ü ti kung-tso*, 1945.

[3] 'Tsu-hsien ch'ung-pai' and 'Ssu-hsiang ke-ming', both collected in *T'an hu chi*.

Then, after describing how sensible traditional ways of thought in China had degenerated into an unholy mess, he comments:

> A small part of these inchoate things is written down in books, but the greater part is preserved in the skulls of men and women and in the whole range of social phenomena. We have no effective way of dealing with it, but at least we should still think of ways to probe into it, and criticize it in its different forms. The ancient Greek philosophers had a saying, 'know thyself'; although we ordinary mortals are incapable of soldiering for the cause of philosophy, since we have been fortunate enough to be born into this world as human beings, we have no choice but to exert ourselves to this end. (p. 3.)

What are the areas in which he feels confident to speak? He continues:

> Thirty years ago I was given to talking about literature, as if I had a thorough grasp of the subject, and was willing to offer wild opinions on many things besides. When I think back on it now I break out in a sweat. Later on the light dawned, and after giving the matter careful thought I no longer ventured to discuss things I could not be confident about. I put into practice the teaching of Confucius of not thinking one knows what one does not know. So then the literature shop closed its doors, but what about the other shops? Confucius also said: 'Recognize you know what you do know.' What after all was there that I knew? If it was nothing, well there certainly was nothing wrong with that, but after one subject after another had been pared away, the prospect of continuing until nothing was left was not something that an ordinary mortal like myself could easily face, so in the end it was like the case of the last cake on the plate that you want to leave just a little bit longer. We can't simply write 'zero' and go away contented. So inevitably I wanted to set up a stall in the road beside the closed shop as a sign that I still had some stock and was still in business. Literature is a specialized field, one I really did not know about; what I did feel I had a smattering of knowledge of was common or garden things, that is, middle school standard Chinese literature, history, physiology and natural sciences, apart from a little education derived from several decades of reading and experience. It was all in a very chaotic state, neither new nor old, yet both new and old. To use local slang, this knowledge was of the 'three-legged cat' variety. A three-legged cat is actually out of place in its environment, but that is just what I needed. Cats all have four legs; to have three legs is indeed peculiar: like the three-legged toad of Liu Hai[4] it qualifies to get into a painting. Those who are quite old only know the past, people who have yet to grow up will of course be quite new, and will pay no heed to the old things that are done with. Perhaps they will be very pleased to hear something about them. The half old, half new three-legged cat does indeed have

[4] Presumably the T'ang dynasty immortal.

> his advantages, rather like the old Reform Party member in a revolutionary age. Sometimes he is more extreme than the post-revolutionary youth, giving no quarter to the old forces and old thought, because he knows better the miseries they bring. For this reason I feel I have no right to belittle myself, believing I am not a babe in arms in these matters, and I want to do my bit and make some contribution to society. I don't understand literature, but I know whether style is good or bad; I don't understand metaphysics, but I know whether thought is sound or not. When I talk about literature I base myself on experience gained from writing myself and from reading Chinese literature, and I value equal amplitude in style and content. In talking about thought, basing myself on biology, cultural anthropology, the history of morals, the psychology of sex, etc, I have investigated the ideas of the Confucian, Buddhist and Legalist schools of thought, and after due deliberation have concluded that the palm goes to a happy combination of feeling and reason. My ideal is just the Middle Way. This might seem a very ordinary thing, but it is not necessarily very easy to find. So I always feel there are too few things to praise: on the one hand I seem to be clinging to things whose day is done, on the other to have a weakness for abusing things people feel are sacred. But it is truly something I cannot help. I am no doubt a sceptic, and in this believing age I am rather out of touch with the times, which is not very fitting, but for that reason it is just what is needed. The saying goes: 'Nasty medicine is the best cure'; that is what I mean.

It is noticeable that this theme of being of service grows stronger as the nation is threatened. It runs very strongly and undisguisedly through the collection *Yao-t'ang tsa wen*, written when China was locked in war with Japan (these essays incidentally make it plain, with their emphasis on the basic soundness of the Chinese tradition and the implication that all Chinese should recognize their common heritage and work towards their common well-being, where Chou's loyalties lay, despite his collaboration with the Japanese). So the humorous qualifications in the last essay give way to earnest lectures, and he resurrects some of the slogans of the optimistic May Fourth days, such as Andreyev's 'the great work of literature is to erase the various divisions and distances between people' (p. 30).[5] This sobering process he himself acknowledged:

> In times of peace and prosperity everyone feels exhilarated, consequently a lot of high-flown theories are aired. As long as they are acceptable in theory it does not matter if they are impracticable. But when, sadly, calamity descends, then sentiments and debates

[5] First quoted by Chou in 'Sheng-shu yü Chung-kuo wen-hsüeh', 1920, in *I-shu yü sheng-huo*.

> come closer to reality, and for the most part centre on the safety of the people and the state, so they come to resemble the platitudes of old wiseacres, which is only natural. ('Han wen-hsüeh ti ch'ien-t'u' (The future of Chinese literature). *Yao-t'ang tsa wen*, p. 32.)

Several times in this collection Chou quotes the passage from Mencius[6] on Yü and Chi, who three times passed their homes without entering them (so devoted were they to succouring the people), and elsewhere he attests that Yü is the only sage of old whom he admires.[7] It is a fair indication of the way his thoughts had turned back to active concern for the welfare of the people.

It was during the war period that Chou singled out Tu Fu's poems for a description I have not seen him apply elsewhere, 'the highest achievement of literature.'[8] The justification for this praise is significant. After citing several of Tu Fu's early poems Chou says: 'Although these poems could not make the gods weep, they do have the power to stir you to the depths. This comes entirely from the feeling of compassion in which no distinction is made between oneself and others. It can be regarded as the highest achievement of literature.' He adds that Tu Fu's best poems mostly 'grieve over the human condition and commiserate with those caught up in disorders', and says the thought behind them is directed to 'the benefit of the people and the country'.

The chief thing that Chou felt could make a contribution to relieving misery in this vale of tears, one that he had all along been looking for in his reading and drawing attention to in his writing, was a sane and sensible approach to the physical environment and a sympathetic understanding of normal human nature – summed up in the phrase *jen-ch'ing wu-li* 'human feelings and the natural order of things'. In the Chinese context his meaning could be expanded as a sensible and undogmatic recognition of the nature and needs of common human drives and emotions, as opposed to their sublimation and direction into narrow channels, and a clear-sighted understanding of the principles actually operative in nature, as opposed to uninformed speculation and superstitious credulity. In drawing attention to these things even in his most 'negative' period Chou was making a contribution in however small a way towards making this world a better place to live in.

As his writing became more positive in the late '30s and early '40s, the theme of *jen-ch'ing wu-li* was heard more often. This was coincident with Chou's reconciliation with the Chinese tradition, and the

6 'Li lou hsia' chapter, section 29.

7 'Yü chi ssu' (The Temple where Yü trod), 1939, *Yao wei chi*.

8 *Wen-i ti chih-chi*, in 'Chung-kuo wen-hsüeh shang ti liang chung ssu-hsiang' (Two Modes of Thought in Chinese Literature), *Yao-t'ang tsa-wen*, p. 22.

acknowledgement that he was basically Confucian.[9] Now 'human feelings', according to Confucian doctrine, are seven: pleasure, anger, sorrow, fear, love, hate, and desire.[10] Not all these feelings are given equal latitude of course, but Chou gives credit to the founding fathers of their culture for taking a wholly realistic attitude towards basic human needs. He quotes Chiao Hsün (1763–1820) as saying:

> Our enlightened predecessors have said that human life consists only of eating and drinking and sex. Without eating and drinking there is no means to live, without sex there is no means to give life. Granted I want to live, but other people want to live also; I want to give life, but others want to give life too. Mencius's pronouncements on 'loving material goods' and 'fondness for women' say all that need be said.[11] There is no need to put aside my livelihood or what I give life to, but one cannot forget other people's livelihood or what they give life to. ('Han wen-hsüeh ti ch'uan-t'ung', *Yao-t'ang tsa wen*, p. 3.)

Chou comments that this is a pure Confucian attitude: 'The idea is very banal, but because of that is also extremely profound and far-reaching; it is what I call common sense and hence is synonymous with truth.'

He next quotes from Liu Hsien-t'ing, 1648–95:

> I have observed that the meanest citizen likes to sing and go to the opera: this is the equivalent in nature to the *Odes* and *Music*; he likes to read novels and listen to storytellers: this is the equivalent in nature to the *Book of History* and *Spring and Autumn*; he believes in fortune-telling and sacrificing to the gods; this is the equivalent in nature to the *Changes* and *Ritual*. The teaching of the Six Classics of the sages was based on human feelings, but latter-day Confucians . . . prohibited and repressed with all their art, and were bent on obfuscating men's minds with the sacrificial straw dogs of Lo-yang. This is no different from blocking a stream so that it cannot flow; no wonder that it should lay waste the land when it breaks out. (p. 3.)

On this Chou's comment is: 'From this we can see that the rules of behaviour were codified and the laws drawn up by the wise men of yore entirely for the benefit of man. Not only did they extend their own feelings to others, they were also sympathetic to other people's points of view, hence were able to gain an understanding of human feelings and the nature of things.' (p. 4.)

One could cite numerous other instances of Chou's commendation

[9] Such an admission is made in 'Tzu-chi ti wen-chang', 1936, *Kua tou chi*, among other places.

[10] According to the *Li chi*, 'Li yün' chapter.

[11] Book 1, chapter 5, sections 4–5. The drift is that these 'weaknesses', if allowed to all the population, bring about contentment.

of similar strands of Confucian thought, for instance the saying of Mencius that 'man differs from the animals only in trivial things',[12] but this is fully intelligible only in the context of Chou's biological philosophy, which we will come to later. A more transparent example, and one from an earlier stage in Chou's life, occurs in *K'u chu tsa chi*, of 1935,

> I feel there is one excellent thing about China, and that is recognizing the facts of life. Her worst aspect is in not recognizing the facts of life. Every situation involves human feelings and provides examples of the natural order of things; it only needs someone to investigate them carefully. Then those who can comprehend can progress to the goal of sagehood, those who do not comprehend will be proven fools or rascals. The *Li Chi* says: 'Drinking, eating and sex; herein reside the main desires of man. Death and poverty; these are the things humankind most abhors.' The *Kuan-tzu* says: 'When the granaries are full then men know of the rules of conduct. When well-clothed and well-fed they know of honour and shame.' These famous sayings have been immutable throughout the ages, because they correspond to the facts of life. ('Ch'ing li' [Feelings and Order], *K'u chu tsa chi*, p. 281.)

Similarly he says one year later: 'Simplicity and accordance with the facts of life can be said to be a valuable outlook of the Confucianists.'[13]

One might ask why Chou makes so much fuss about a virtue both self-evident and made so evident. The answer is, as has been implied, that it had *not* been evident to the Chinese down the ages, because they had seen things through the prism of their preconceptions. As he puts it, the original down-to-earth Confucian thought has been smothered by a thousand years of speeches from the pulpit of the dogmatists, with disastrous results in the spheres of morality, politics, scholarship and the humanities.[14] An essay on an early twentieth-century collection of scholar's notes[15] provides some typical examples of his compatriots'

[12] 'Meng-hsiang chih i', 1944, *K'u k'ou kan k'ou*, p. 9.

[13] 'T'an yang niao' (On keeping Birds), 1936, *Kua tou chi*.

[14] 'Ku wen yü li hsüeh' (Ancient Prose and Neo-Confucianism), *Chih-t'ang i-yu wen pien*, p. 45. The same idea is expressed by Liu E in *Lao Ts'an yu-chi*, chapter 9. The winsome young lady immortal (?) there remarks: '. . . This love of women is fundamental to man's nature. The Sung scholars try to say we should love virtue and not love women. Surely this is self-deception? To deceive yourself and deceive others is the extreme insincerity! But they perversely want to call it "maintaining sincerity" – isn't that hateful? ' etc. (Trans. H. Shadick, *The Travels of Lao Ts'an*, p. 101.)

[15] 'Ch'ang t'an ts'ung lu ch'i erh', 1936, *Kua tou chi*.

'lack of soundness of mind'. Foot-binding is the abuse he chiefly deals with here, and he notes that even Ku T'ing-lin and Li Li-weng (Li Yü) did not oppose the custom, while Chou's culture hero, Yü Li-ch'u (Yü Yüeh), had some fantastic theory to account for it; but he also mentions the 'eight-legged essay', which was restored, after it had been abolished in 1664, in response to the demands of Chinese officials – and Yü-yang shan-jen (Wang Shih-chen 1634–1711) was one who lent his voice to the campaign (Chou's comment being: 'Chinese literary men and scholars were all equally unenlightened'); and he criticizes the men of letters for always talking about elegant verse and regarding everyday things as beneath notice. Arising from this last point Chou notes the lack of attention paid to natural history in traditional China, and elsewhere he has some fun at the expense of common Chinese anthropomorphic explanations of animal behaviour.

From these comments it is clear that though an understanding of 'human feelings and the natural order of things' was basic to the original Chinese tradition and persevered among certain individuals in later ages, it had long before Chou's time dwindled to an underfed stream. Even the few enlightened men were capable of startling misconceptions, because their knowledge was faulty. Evidently the much-needed remedy was a thorough grounding in the science of man and his environment. As Chou points out in 'My Experience of Study':

> How it came about I do not know, but I feel that the thought of Western savants like Havelock Ellis really comes from the same stable as that of Li Cho-wu, Yü Li-ch'u and the others. The only difference is that the latter relied on intuition to understand human feelings and the natural order of things, while the former came to it through science. Though the result was similar, it was more definite. Doubtless wisdom derived from knowledge is more soundly based. ('Tu-shu ti ching-yen', *Yao-t'ang tsa wen*, p. 36.)

The Western savant whose name appears most frequently in Chou's work is the same Havelock Ellis. Though Chou read all Ellis's essays with pleasure and respect, it was Ellis's *Psychology of Sex* which earned him his special place in Chou's affections, for that work, bought in Japan in his student days, opened his eyes on life and society.[16] The news of the suicide of a Japanese prostitute in 1936 elicited from Chou the admission that books on sexology had influenced him more than any others, apparently because – relevant to this case – they showed a sympathetic understanding of the necessary but disavowed class of prostitutes, and more generally because they laid bare the unpleasant

[16] As he says in 'Tung-ching ti shu-tien' (Tokyo Bookshops), *Kua tou chi*, p. 104.

truths that society wishes to keep covered. He says that the works of Ellis, Forel, Iwan Bloch and Hirschfeld gave him more than the sacred books of China, widened his vision, and made him understand 'human feelings and the natural order of things'.[17]

Chou's commitment then to the rational, scientific approach to the human environment and condition goes back a long way, certainly to his Japanese period (1906–11), when his brother was writing essays on science and civilization, all based on Western sources.[18] In the essay, 'Tokyo bookshops', the books he mentions as having bought in Japan include some by Andrew Lang (not specified here, but the titles *Custom and Myth* and *Myth, Religion and Ritual* are given in *Yeh tu ch'ao*[19]), Westermarck's *Development of Moral Ideas*, Samuel Butcher's lectures on Greece, and all available books by Ellis, from *New Spirit* to *Contemporary Problems*. During the May Fourth period Chou drew almost exclusively on Western authorities in his contributions to the general effort to inculcate a modern way of thinking in China. His range was wide, but his dominant theme was the biological creed expressed in 'Jen ti wen-hsüeh'.[20] This creed remained with him for the rest of his life. As he wrote in the postscript to the *Yeh tu ch'ao* collection in 1934:

> On the surface these essays seem to differ somewhat from those of ten years ago, but in fact my attitude is the same as at the time of writing *Tzu-chi ti yüan-ti*. I still do not believe that writing has any connection with the human heart or the way of the world. 'I do not believe there is any classic in the world that can be used over hundreds and thousands of years as a textbook for mankind; only "Biologie" [*sic*] which records the phenomena of life of living things can provide us with terms of reference and establish the standards for human behaviour.' This is what I said in 1919 in *Mei chou p'ing lun*,[21] and I still think the same to this day. (p. 310.)

His 'attitude' at the date of writing is expressed in an essay on a book of poems on small creatures from the same collection:

> Usually people revile others by calling them animals, but actually you cannot apply the terms of right or wrong, good or bad to the behaviour of animals, which is instinctive biological life. Because man has reason, although he is basically unable to act counter to biological principles, he is inclined to regulate them to some extent,

[17] 'Kui-nu-ch'uan shih-chien' (Incident at Kinu-gawa), *Kua tou chi*.
[18] See Angela Castro, M. Phil. thesis on 'Three early essays of Lu Hsün', Univ. of London, 1968.
[19] 'Hsi-su yü shen-hua' (*Custom and Myth*).
[20] 'Literature of Man': see my essay, 'Chou Tso-jen and cultivating one's Garden'.
[21] In the essay 'Tsu-hsien ch'ung-pai'.

thus giving rise to so-called civilization. But on the other hand he is at liberty to allow himself more licence, and uses reason to cover up for himself unreasonably, which is a business animals do not go in for. I am thinking of such things as burning heretics for the good of their souls, and occupying Manchuria under the aegis of the right royal way. If we observe the life of animals, and make a comparison with human life, it emerges that man has some points in common with animals, and these are necessary and sound; in some areas man can excel, but there are others too where he falls short of animals. Constantly to think along these lines is a more realistic way of self-improvement than absorbing oneself in moral philosophy, and has implications for a new morality. ('Pai nien ch'ung yin', *Yeh tu ch'ao*, pp. 228–9.)

'Juan fan', also in the *Yeh tu ch'ao* collection, has the same message:

Just as the Western savant[22] says: 'If you want to become a healthy person, you must first become a healthy animal.' Unfortunately men have forgotten their origins, and since the time they stood on their hindlegs the gain in dexterity has been at the expense of healthiness. When the deer and the antelope meet the tiger, if they run fast they keep their life, if they can't get away they are simply eaten. For his part the tiger has no compunction about eating his fill and going away contented. There is no nonsense about 'just retribution' and 'vanquishing evil and vindicating righteousness'.[23] In the mating season it is true there is a bit of a circus, but when they share a female they don't make the excuse of 'lack of issue being the great crime'; still less would they go with a piece of [their own] flesh in their mouth to curry favour with their dam. As to legends about 'deer-life grass'[24] and 'randy-ram epimedium'[25] there is naturally nothing in them. We block up natural outlets, become slaves to perverted passions, and then rely on the power of reason to fabricate a lot of mystical explanations. If you compare the behaviour of this kind of civilized man with that of animals, how mortifying it is! Once men became beasts retrogression was of course unavoidable, but a mankind given over to megalomania regards it on the contrary as the normal mode of life for living beings. It really makes you sick. To wake them from their delusions it would be best to direct them to learn from the ants – no, they could find wisdom in any insect, bird or beast. Far better to read an *Insect World*[26] than a pile of venerable scriptures. That is why I recommend it as the most beneficial prescribed reading for young people. (pp. 61–2.)

[22] Nietzsche.
[23] For just such nonsense see e.g. 'Kuan-yü Lei kung', *Kua tou chi*.
[24] The myth was that a deer could revive after this grass had been substituted for its innards: see Morohashi, XII, 905.
[25] Supposed to give a ram strength to serve 100 ewes in one day.
[26] This is the title of a serial work on insects by Henri Fabre. See 'Fa-pu-erh K'un ch'ung chi' (Fabre's *Insect World*), *Tzu-chi ti yüan-ti*.

Having now got an idea of what Chou meant by 'human feelings and the natural order of things', we can go on to see how he insisted on an understanding of the same evincing itself in literature, which would be in line with his early proposal of not 'art for art's sake', nor 'art for life's sake', but an 'art of life'.[27] Through most of the '20s Chou expressed this requisite in terms of 'scientific understanding',[28] or universal human nature – free, that is, from the distortions or any particular culture.[29] In those days he used the language of the Western books he was reading; in the '30s and '40s he was using the nearest native Chinese term. The substance was the same as before – he still did not deny the need for an education in the works of Western specialists in biology, anthropology, paedology, feminology, etc., along with a study of the healthy strains of the native Chinese tradition[30] – and the demand was as insistent as ever. For example, in the title essay of *K'u k'ou kan k'ou*, 1943, he asserts: 'Literature consists of nothing else than human feelings and the nature of things. If there is no understanding in this respect, the rest is all words.' (p. 4.) He puts the problem in terms of his own reactions in this way (the particular reference is to *pi-chi*):

> In reading a book, when I come across an enjoyable part I am already satisfied enough. I may find the reading unappetizing, but this is no cause for revulsion – what is the point of making great demands on the ancients? I am just mindful of the moments of browsing it provides me with. As the ancients said: 'Just aim to distract the eye': that is all I want to do. But sometimes I come on some passages whose style is quite good and whose content appears very estimable, but which reveal utter ignorance of human feelings and the nature of things, and then I feel irritated all over. This dissatisfaction goes beyond revulsion, it is quite close to terror. ('Yü Li-ch'u lun yu shu' [Yü Yüeh's letters on various evils], *Yao-t'ang tsa-wen*, p. 127.)

From the opposite point of view, the kind of writing he does like to read, and to quote, has a 'content which combines sound understanding of the nature of things and profound human feelings, and a style which mixes the plainness of free prose and the beauty of "balanced prose".'[31]

Granted that spreading the modern and ancient gospel of *jen ch'ing*

[27] In 'Hsin wen-hsüeh ti yao-ch'iu' (Requisites of the New Literature), 1920, *I-shu yü sheng-huo*.
[28] As in 'Shang-hai ch'i' (The Shanghai Style), *T'an lung chi*, p. 158.
[29] Hence he applauded Kuo-Mo-jo's assertion that a poet must be steeped in anthropology: see 'Ta Yün-shen hsien-sheng' (In Reply to Mr. Yün-shen), 1927, *T'an lung chi*, p. 162.
[30] See 'Han wen-hsüeh ti ch'ien-t'u', 1943, in *Yao-t'ang tsa wen*.
[31] 'Hou chi' (Postscript) to *K'u chu tsa chi*, p. 312.

wu li was desirable in China, because of the general lack of soundness in Chinese thought, but should these values, which pertain to the business of living and the quality of life, be transferred unaltered to the realm of literature? There was a time, when his literature shop was still open, when he recognized that different standards applied to literature and life, as in his justification of the 'wild romanticizing' in the novel *Ching hua yüan*[32], and when he conceived the artist's function – of planting flowers – as different from the practical tasks of feeding and doctoring society.[33] But after he ceased to regard himself as a literary expert, he took rather the ordinary man's view of literature, certainly not undervaluing the qualities of style that go to make up good writing, but essentially interested in telling and being told. When he was told arrant nonsense, naturally he complained. And as he read more Chinese literature, as for one thing his teaching duties required, the more he complained about the lack of good sense in it. Taken in the mass, there appeared in Chinese literature to be very little middle ground between the scholars' essays and 'jottings' (*pi-chi*) and the belles lettres of the dilettanti (*ming shih liu*) which bore the mark either of afflatus or flatulence, according to the point of view. The scholars' contributions were marred by an invalid world view, the outpourings of the artists by self-indulgent conceit. The strange thing is that it was the former more often than the latter which provoked the cry for *literature* to be based on *jen ch'ing wu li*. Now *pi-chi* in their most common manifestation are scarcely 'literature' at all; for them to qualify we would have to understand *wen-hsüeh* in the sense of the old term *wen*, which meant the record of all organized thought.

This faces us with the basic problem of the frame of reference for most of Chou's pronouncements on literature. Naturally it varied with the subject under discussion. If he was writing about a poet, clearly it would include poetry. But where there was no such obvious pointer his remarks tend to be dominated by what the essay form is capable of, or its ideal characteristics, and the potentialities and attributes of imaginative literature are left out of account. He is predisposed towards writing which has a practical bearing on life, not in the sense of laying down rules of behaviour, but of helping one to understand the world, a function Confucius pointed to positively in commending the *Odes* for teaching the names of birds, animals, and plants,[34] and negatively in stating that 'not to study the first two books of the *Odes* is like standing with one's face right to the wall'.[35]

[32] In the essay of that name in *Tzu-chi ti yüan-ti*.

[33] See the title essay in *Tzu-chi ti yüan-ti*.

[34] *Lun yü*, 'Yang huo' chapter, section 9.

[35] Ibid., section 10.

The following quotation, while not necessarily delimiting, does indicate the general trend of Chou's interest in the written word:

> Why are we so interested in seasonal changes and local customs? The answer is very simple: it is because of the tiny changes in these ordinary lives of ours. The history of peoples is actually the continuum of routine human affairs. Astronomy,[36] geography, the rhythms of nature, all exert an influence on human affairs, and so produce all sorts of patterns, mainly for utilitarian ends, but the fact of responding to the seasons is the same. In Chinese poetry and painting this kind of situation would also seem to be very marked. Generally speaking the common refrain in literature is 'flowers in the wind and moon on the snow' *feng hua hsüeh yüeh*,[37] but though the common refrain is objectionable (as all common refrains are), there is otherwise no fault to be found in *feng hua hsüeh yüeh*. Why object to it? Spring grasses growing by ponds, the garden willows becoming alive with singing birds, the emotions roused by these are as much responses to the transitions in nature as thinking of sowing when the ground is ready for it. It would not be right to call the one cultured and the other uncouth, but the concrete one is restricted to practical considerations, it affects in a limited way, while the aesthetic or abstract one can arouse a general enthusiasm, so would seem to be more poetic. If we add to this local considerations, [the response] is even more complex and multifarious: the customs of any place, whether they are the same as or different from one's own locality, are all of interest to us; if different they supply a comparison, if the same, then there is a sense of intimacy. ('Ch'ing chia lu', *Yeh tu ch'ao*, pp. 132–3.)

Because Chou takes an interest in any writing which deals with the 'tiny changes in these ordinary lives of ours', it does not follow necessarily that he is not also interested in imaginative literature. But it does show that relevance to daily life was an important criterion for reading matter, and that this criterion could enable him to see something valuable in a kind of literature – *feng hua hsüeh yüeh* literature – which was in his time usually dismissed as effete poetizing. The fact that he was willing to go out on a limb to defend this kind of literature, was prepared to see in it this supposed value, indicates that it was a consideration that habitually weighed with him. The normal response to this kind of writing would be to the literary skills involved, whereas Chou finds the matter interesting. The attitude is exactly the

[36] *T'ien wen*; Chou might be thinking of the *I ching*, chapter 22: 'Observe the patterns in the sky [*t'ien wen*] to discover the seasons' changes.'

[37] This phrase generally stands for rhapsodizing over nature in her diverse moods and raiments.

same as that of the comments on the *Odes* from the Yang-huo chapter of the *Analects* just quoted, which is in turn more exactly matched by another criterion for *pi-chi* put forward by Chou that they should 'explain the names and varieties of things, and elucidate their basic qualities'.[38] In more general terms his definition of the history of peoples as 'the continuum of routine human affairs' clearly eschews any reference to great exemplars in art and culture and points to a factual, down-to-earth turn of mind. With it can be bracketed Chou's admission that he had previously always looked on literature and the fine arts as a window onto the culture of a people – not primarily for their aesthetic qualities.[39]

Chou Tso-jen's 'impure' approach to literature comes out clearly in his essay on Andrew Lang in 1933. He quotes adverse comments on Lang's style, then presents his own views:

> Regarded as a purely literary man, he does admittedly have the fault of mixing styles, but in my personal opinion this in a sense can be counted an advantage, because the kind of writing which displays many-sided learning has a particular charm that the purely literary man cannot achieve. Moreover, the essays which 'delve into the by-ways of learning', which are of course even farther removed from pure literature, also please me very much. Among Lang's works one called *Historical Mysteries*, in sixteen chapters, has long had a place in my affections; this may be a personal fad, as I have not seen anyone else express the same preference. I have the same attitude to the works of the Japanese Mori Ōgai: I often dip into his '*Notes from a Mountain Home*' and a lot of his lives of medical men, probably more than I do into his novels. ('Hsi-su yü shen-hua' [*Custom and Myth*], 1933, *Yeh tu ch'ao*, pp. 30–1.)

What Chou is really admitting here is that works which deal with the real world, and from which he can learn something, are more to his taste than the artifacts of the imagination – hence his preference for essays and studies as reading matter.

In Chou's opinion Chinese writers were rarely equally competent in the two fields of sensible and realistic comment and belles lettres, as the following extract from 'The wit of Yü Li-ch'u' shows. After quoting a passage from Yü's *Kui ssu ts'un kao* he comments:

> Mr Yü was not a literary man, but I found the above excellent both in sense and style. It is really a first-class piece of writing ... Recently I have had nothing to do, so I have re-read my collection of Ch'ing *pi-chi*. This month I have looked into roughly twenty-odd collections, over 400 volumes. In the end I only picked out 230

[38] 'Ch'ang t'an ts'ung lu', *Kua tou chi*, p. 148.
[39] 'Yüan jih' (Day of Worship), *Yao wei chi*, p. 158.

examples – on a rough average a ratio of one example to two volumes. But what surprised me more was that good *pi-chi* material, that is to say, what I thought worth selecting according to my two standards of common sense and interest, came mostly not from the works of famous literary men and scholars but from the books of plain pedants, like Yü Li-ch'u's *Kui ssu ts'un kao* and Ho Lan-kao's *Shai-shu-t'ang pi lu*. As regards scholarship and belles lettres, Ku T'ing-lin and Wang Yü-yang of early Ch'ing are people to be reckoned with in anybody's book, but one does not find in their *pi-chi* as much of this as one would have expected. Why? On the whole Chinese literary men and scholars all have their separate tradition, whether it be the stern moralist school or the romantic genius school; though they have their own system they lack the qualities of 'gentleness and staunchness'[40] and 'calm and tranquility'. These are essential to *pi-chi* literature, hence whatever their other achievements, in this regard they could hardly be otherwise than defective. This minor matter is actually of great significance: it not only demonstrates the way of reading *pi-chi*, it also taught me how to write essays. ('Yü Li-ch'u ti hui-hsieh', *Ping chu hou t'an*, pp. 46–7.)

Though Chou is arguing here that Ch'ing writers famed for their literary ability suffer from comparison with 'plain pedants' only in the field of *pi-chi*, not a pure art, his general remark about Chinese literati lacking 'gentleness and staunchness' and 'calm and tranquility' is seriously disparaging (the former is, according to the *Li-chi*, the 'teaching for poetry'): these virtues, essential as he says to *pi-chi*, are not to be confined to the same. Moreover, the traditions of the literati that he specifies, the 'stern moralist' and the 'romantic genius', are not calculated to engage sympathy. These points, taken in conjunction with Chou's final acknowledgement that good *pi-chi* taught him the way to write, add up unavoidably to a bias in favour of 'impure' literature. Significantly, what inspired these remarks, and earned Chou's rare commendation as a 'first-class piece of writing' is a well-chosen selection of comments on the denigration of women in China, linked together by pointed, laconic and ironic commentary – and nothing more.

We all know that Chou Tso-jen's chosen form was the essay, but essayists do not invariably like to read essays more than any other kind of literature. In that Chou did have this preference, as one could justly conclude from the above evidence, he placed himself in the main tradition of Chinese civilization, one which valued 'matter' over

[40] *Wen jou tun hou*; the phrase comes from the *Li chi*, 'Ching chieh' chapter. Chu Tzu-ch'ing has an essay on the subject in *Shih yen chih pien*.

'manner'.[41] Where manner was valued, it was for the human qualities that lay behind it. Such, it seems to me, was the basis for Chou's appreciative literary criticism. It falls into the third of Abram's three categories of critical activity:

> The first type is primarily an investigation of literary causes; . . . the attempt is to isolate and explain the special quality of a work by reference to the special quality of character, life, lineage and milieu of its author. The second type is biographical in aim; it sets out to reconstruct the author as he lived, and uses the literary product merely as a convenient record from which to infer something about his life and character. The third, however, claims to be specifically aesthetic and appreciative in purpose: it regards aesthetic qualities as projections of personal qualities . . . in F. L. Lucas's . . . rendition of this ideal:
>
>> I have found by spontaneous experience more and more that even the aesthetic pleasure of a poem depends for me on the fineness of the personality glimpsed between the lines; on the spirit of which the body of a book is inevitably the echo and its mould.
>
> In the critical discourse of such readers therefore the primary qualities of a good poem are, literally, attributes of the mind and temper of its composer: sincerity, integrity, high seriousness, shrewdness, benignity – and so on, through the whole of the characterological resources of the language. (*The Mirror and the Lamp*, pp. 227–8.)

Compare with this Chou's admission (already quoted): 'I just try to make out the author's character and qualities as revealed in the poetry', and his choice of such terms as 'generous', 'sincere', 'far-seeing', 'having integrity' to characterize books (or authors?) he had read.

I have suggested that Chou's formulations of the aesthetic requirements of literature tend to be limited by the characteristics of the essay. Let us reconsider his ruling in 'Belles lettres' that '[the essay's] requirements, in common with *all works of literature,* are just sincerity and conciseness.' How many literary masterpieces would have to be thrown on the scrapheap if these conditions were accepted? Though this was written in Chou's outward-looking period he could not have been thinking of world literature, since anyone brought up on the great comedies, satires, tragedies and novels would never have thought the qualities of sincerity and conciseness, admirable though they be, sufficient to use as a guideline for 'all works of literature'.[42] They do

[41] The attitude was expressed acidly by Chang Hsüeh-ch'eng: 'Poetry is at best bad prose, its art adding nothing to its value.' (Quoted Nivison, p. 137.)

[42] I am not altogether convinced by my own argument. 'Conciseness' could be understood as leaving out what should be left out, invariably a

embrace a much larger proportion of Chinese literature, lacking as it is in sustained imaginative constructions, but even there they are surprisingly restrictive. Their real province is the short poem and the mature prose piece. Chou did not only disregard long works, he positively distrusted them: as he said in 1937, the danger in grand and lengthy works is that it is hard to avoid the manner overcoming the matter.[43] Even where Chou does allow a role for grand works it is only to pass on to things nearer his heart. In the passage from 'On the short poem' we have cited, he says:

> The more intense and profound emotions, like the bitterness or sweetness of love, the joys of parting and reuniting, birth and death, naturally can give rise to all sorts of great works grandly conceived, but our daily life is full of feelings which are not so vital but just as real. They are born in an instant and die as quickly; they cannot be sustained for long, so cannot cohere to form a gem of literature. But they are enough to represent the moment to moment transitions in our inner life. In a sense this is actually our real life. ('Lun hsiao shih', *Tzu-chi ti yüan-ti*, p. 53.)

It might be objected that Chou passes over 'great works grandly conceived' because his express intention is to recommend the short poem; certainly that is the case, but when did he ever recommend the former? Far from apologizing for the triviality of the short poem he claims that it deals with matters more relevant to us than the peaks of experience, matters which represent 'our real life'.

Such an attitude is consistent with Chou's support for humanistic literature in his seminal essays of the May Fourth period, 'Literature of man' and 'Requisites for the New Literature'. The aspect of humanism that Chou dwells on is its concern with the quality of everyday life, not the achievements of the human spirit that give man a touch of divinity. He allows no doubt, in 'Requisites', that 'all things beyond human

---

good thing, and 'sincerity' would always be relevant if one took the view that all good creative literature is an emanation of the author's personality, however dressed up it might be. Chou himself adopted that view, stating that even the fiction of Zola viewed the hard facts of life through the prism of the author's personality (note to 'Wan-chien ti lai-k'e' [Evening Visitor] in *Tien ti*); and Wang Kuo-wei insisted that the Yüan plays were a form of self-expression. However, as in later life Chou ceased to read novels, apart from *Shui-hu chuan* and *Don Quixote* (see 'Tokyo Bookshops' in *Kua tou chi*), my conclusion seems reasonable.

[43] 'Ho I-sun lun shih' (Ho I-sun's Poetic Criticism), 1937, *Ping chu hou t'an*, p. 32.

feelings and human powers, the prerequisites of the gods, are excluded from our requirements.'[44]

If I might speculate in conclusion on the fundamental reason why Chou Tso-jen was attracted to the essay above all other forms of literature, the key I think is in its special relationship to humanism. In the early part of this century humanitarian values determined to a much greater extent than they do today aesthetic theory in general. So Wilson Follett, whose work Chou was acquainted with,[45] wrote on the notion that 'the purpose of art is to give pleasure' the following:

> The highest pleasures are the social emotions which come from a rational and truthful view of our status as fellow mortals – pity, compassion, fellow feeling, fraternity, solidarity; the pleasure of 'truth of intercourse'. (*The Modern Novel*, 1923, pp. 275–6).

As we have seen, Lafcadio Hearn, an interpreter not an originator, saw the essay as the best vehicle for this compassionate humanism. There is indeed logic in his affirmation that the essay was the medium *par excellence* through which man talks to man about man. It is something that has been recognized for a long time: T. H. Green (1832–82), for example, described *The Spectator* as 'the first and best representative of that special style of literature – the only really popular literature of our time – which consists in talking to the public about itself. Humanity is taken as reflected in the ordinary life of man and . . . copied with the most minute fidelity.'[46]

If we accept that the essay is uniquely adapted to this end, then it is natural that the cultured man, who belonged to a literate class which has always believed in literally leaving its mark, and yet did not consider himself a poetic genius, who did value 'the truth of intercourse' perhaps above everything else, and who was interested in the commonplace things of everyday life, should turn to the essay both as a source of pleasure and as a vehicle for self-expression. Chou Tso-jen was such a man.

[44] 'Hsin wen-hsüeh ti yao-ch'iu', *I-shu yü sheng-huo*, p. 34.

[45] See the quotation from Follett in 'Sheng-shu yü Chung-kuo wen-hsüeh', *I-shu yü sheng-huo*, p. 68–9.

[46] Quoted Ian Watt, *The Rise of the Novel*, Peregrine Books, 1956, p. 53.

APPENDIXES

A

THE T'UNG-CH'ENG SCHOOL

An examination of the theory and practice of the *T'ung-ch'eng p'ai* (hereafter abbreviated to TCP) is called for, not only because Chou Tso-jen held pronounced views about it, but because of its relevance to the conception of the New Literature movement: as Chou says in *Yüan-liu*, Lecture 3: 'The end-of-Ming literature is the origin of the present literary movement, but Ch'ing literature is the *cause* of the present literary movement.' (p. 55.) The malpractices in Ch'ing literature able to set in motion such a sea-change would have had to be many and various, but as the leading school of thought the TCP can be taken as representing its characteristics and limitations.

In presenting a general picture of Ch'ing literature, Chou first explains that *pa-ku wen*, the examination essay that all scholars had to practise if they wanted an official appointment, was an exegesis of the Classics given its procrustean form in the Ming dynasty. It had eight sections, made up of matching pairs, and followed a prescribed logical pattern. He then continues:

> In *pa-ku wen* the main consideration was form; in content it expressed the Way of the Confucian sages. The ancient-style prose of the TCP gave equal weight to form and thought. The starting point of balanced prose (*p'ien-wen*) was feelings, and it also had a slight bias towards form. What gave equal weight to feelings and form was the new literature of the succeeding period. Of these, *pa-ku wen* and the ancient-style prose of the TCP were very close: it has already been said that the TCP wrote *pa-ku wen* in free prose. Balanced prose and the New Literature both take feelings as the starting point, so these two are also very close; the difference was that balanced prose was too much inclined towards form. Afterwards, opposition to the TCP and *pa-ku wen* could have been channelled . . . either towards balanced prose or the New Literature. But the strength of balanced prose in the Ch'ing dynasty was minimal, so only the way to the New Literature was open. (pp. 59–60.)

Inveighing against *pa-ku wen* and similar literary aberrations was a pre-occupation of Chou Tso-jen's, because the word play they involved led only to sterility in letters. On a vulgar level the effect could be laughable, as in the instance Chou quotes of a pedant passing a stable; he is pleased by the first half of the couplet on the gate post: 'With the left hand we lead out a "thousand-mile" horse', but to achieve the proper balance amends the second half, 'With the right hand we lead forth a thousand-league colt' to: 'With the right foot we lead out a ten-thousand-league colt' (p. 61). But in all seriousness, Chou thought the concentration on purely formal characteristics at the expense of meaning that this type of exercise encouraged quite disastrous.

In practice the TCP was not unaffected by the *pa-ku wen* style, as Chou rightly says, but what its members stood for was a quite complex body of literary ideas. Let us look first at what Chou says about them in Lecture 4:

> They carried on the tradition of the Eight Masters of T'ang and Sung, following Tso (Tso-ch'iu Ming) and Ssu-ma Ch'ien, but giving pride of place to Han Yü of T'ang. They added Kui Yu-kuang of Ming to the pantheon, then after him Fang Pao. However, there were some differences between them and the Eight Masters of T'ang and Sung. Though the latter advocated 'literature as a vehicle for the Way', what they emphasized was the ancient-style prose, and only wanted to put the thing called Way into their compositions as content: so they were still only literary men. The members of the TCP were not merely literary men, they were at the same time 'moralists'. They thought Han Yü's style was all right, but in respect of moral philosophy his achievement was not high; the neo-Confucianism of the two Ch'engs and Chu Hsi was all right, but their compositions were definitely poor. So with the idea of combining the strengths of both camps they resolved to 'be the heirs of Ch'eng and Chu in learning and behaviour, in style to stand with Han and (Ou-yang Hsiu)'.[1] They believed 'letters *are* the Way', the two being indivisible. Such proposals are very close to *pa-ku wen* [in intent]. Moreover Fang Pao was a very good hand at *pa-ku wen*. . . .
>
> They did not regard themselves as writers, but as effecting a grand union of moral philosophy, textual scholarship, and literary style. Actually, ever since the Eight Masters of T'ang and Sung advocated 'literature as a vehicle for the Way' ancient-style prose and moral philosophy had been indivorceable, while Han learning (i.e. textual scholarship) was supreme in the Ch'ing, so they naturally paraded themselves as experts in Han learning too. In fact, what Fang Pao and Yao Nai knew of textual scholarship was very limited. . . .
>
> With regard to diction, they proposed the so-called 'T'ung-ch'eng right method [*i-fa*]'. This 'right method', though they set much store by it, in our view is no profoundly mysterious thing; it is just a

[1] From 'Wang-hsi wen chi hsü' (Preface to the works of Fang Pao) by Wang Chao-fu.

variety of stylistics. Their statements can be summed up in the following two points:

One, letters must 'be connected with the Saintly Way'. Fang Pao said: 'If something does not expound the Way or support the doctrine, does not bear on proper human relationships or educating the people, it should not be carelessly undertaken.' Yao Nai used a similar form of words, considering that 'if one cannot shed light on the moral import of the Classics then one may not lightly put pen to paper.' So letters must 'illuminate the thinking of the Classics and uphold the morality of the people'. Actually this is the same as the programme of 'literature as the vehicle for the Way' of Han Yü and company. There is no higher principle involved.

Apart from this the odd points they put forward, such as following the *Tso chuan* and *Shih-chi* in style and modelling themselves on Han and Ou-yang, are trivial and unsystematic. Reasonably representative is this passage, from Shen T'ing-fang's postscript to the biography of Fang Wang-hsi [Fang Pao]:

> From Southern Sung, Yüan and Ming times, it has been an age since there has been any concern for the right method in ancient-style prose. The [Ming] loyalists of the southern coastal provinces [Wu and Yüeh] were particularly feckless, either allowing novelettish adulterations or imitating the old style of the Han-lin academy, not one of them having an elegant and clear-cut style. The following are beyond the pale of ancient-style prose: expressions from colloquies [*yü lu*], the florid parallelisms of the Wei-Chin-Six Dynasties people, the sonorities of the Han *fu*, the euphuisms found in poetry, and the witty levities of the histories of the Northern and Southern dynasties.

If you draw together the ideas here they just about add up to the part of their 'right method' which constitutes the second point, namely that writing should be elegant and correct [*ya cheng*].

There is another bewildering thing, which present-day writers of the T'ung-ch'eng persuasion cannot explain either, and that is the eight things which they say a composition should have – *shen, li, ch'i, wei, ke, lü, sheng* and *se*. Yao Nai says in *Ku wen tz'u lei ts'uan hsü*:

> There are thirteen different forms of writing, and there are eight things which go to make up writing, namely *shen, li, ch'i, wei, ke, lü, sheng* and *se*. The first four are the subtle elements, the last four are the coarse elements.

Li is moral philosophy, what we call the Way; *sheng* is rhythm, the musical element in a composition; *se* is colour, the [visual] beauty of a composition. These few we can understand. But *shen, ch'i, wei, lü*, etc. are wholly vague in meaning, and very difficult to make sense of . . .

No matter what their arguments were, what they produced was still the ancient-style prose of the Eight Masters of T'ang and Sung. Furthermore, the more their work conformed to their arguments the worse it was. The pieces included in 'Fang and Yao's Selected Prose' they themselves regarded as the finest examples, and they may be seen as representative, but we cannot see where their fineness resides. However, compared with the fake antiques of the Former and Latter Seven Masters of the Ming, I think the TCP had some positive qualities. At least, compared with those fake antiques, their style was more fluent, and some pieces have a little literary flavour. And in their blandness, simplicity, pregnancy, and in leaving an after-taste, the works of the TCP are sometimes better than those of the Eight Masters. Nevertheless we can never agree with their thought and 'right method', and in their programme for compositions they are ultimately closest to *pa-ku wen*. (pp. 77–85.)

Having let Chou have his say, let us see to what extent modern scholars agreed with him. First, there is unanimity on the relative lack of effort that went into moral philosophy and textual criticism among the TCP. Chiang Shu-ke in his *T'ung-ch'eng wen p'ai p'ing shu*, p. 37, sums up the achievement of Yao Nai, chief advocate of the triple pillars of moral philosophy, textual criticism and literary style, as:

> What he himself achieved in moral philosophy and textual criticism was negligible. What he should be remembered for is only literary style. The first two are what Fang Pao called 'substance in writing'; the last one is 'order in writing'. Tseng Kuo-fan's criticism is indisputable: 'There is order in plenty, but substance is in short supply.'

Kuo Shao-yü is of the same opinion, though he is more charitable:

> In moral philosophy and textual criticism their discussions did not amount to scholarship; they just stood for the attitude they took towards certain branches of learning. In respect of moral philosophy and textual criticism the questions they concentrated on were how to achieve their integration, their intermingling, even their application. They did not want to confine themselves to any particular branch of learning so they should not be condemned for their scholarship not amounting to scholarship.[2] (Kuo, p. 572.)

Chou is also quite right that the celebrated 'right method' of the TCP was not different from the philosophy of 'literature as a vehicle for the Way' of the T'ang *ku-wen* movement. According to Chiang the term 'right method' derives from the *Shih-chi* 'Shih erh chu hou nien piao hsü': 'When Confucius edited the *Spring and Autumn Annals* he abbreviated the text, eliminating its laboriousness, in order to establish

[2] The same point of view is put very sensibly by Tseng Kuo-fan in 'Liu Meng-jung shu', quoted by Wu Wen-ch'i, *Chin pai nien lai ti Chung-kuo wen-i ssu-ch'ao* (Trends in Chinese Literary Thought over the past Hundred Years), p. 7.

the right method' (op. cit., p. 22), but despite its impeccable origin the term itself was not taken up by the *ku-wen* protagonists, though Li Ao revived the idea in his dictum: 'When literary style [*wen*], moral science [*li*] and rectitude [*i*] are combined together, [one's work] can stand out in one's own age and survive through later ages' (quoted Chiang, op. cit., p. 35); however there appears to have been no significance in their neglect. The passages quoted by Chou from the TCP on the necessary orthodox moral content of all writing are indeed typical of the 'literature as a vehicle for the Way' philosophy, and they fairly represent the formal pronouncements of the TCP on the subject.

Given that the TCP was what it was, namely the main body of literary opinion under a rigidly and dangerously conservative dynasty, things could hardly have been otherwise. However, if the 'right method' of the TCP was not different from the 'literature as a vehicle for the Way' philosophy, it was also more than that. As a 'variety of stylistics' it added up, with the contributions of Fang Pao, Yao Nai and Liu Ta-k'ui, to quite a comprehensive and not unsubtle aesthetic. Fundamental objections could be made against it because of the assumptions underlying it, such as the insistence on the *tao* being immanent in the Confucian Classics and the works of the Neo-Confucian philosophers rather than in the facts of ordinary life, but once this hurdle has been taken (Chou Tso-jen of course balked at it), much of their argument can be seen to be reasonable and perceptive.

There were two difficulties that Chou had to contend with; one was to know what TCP doctrine was, and the other was to separate common practice, especially later common practice, from original doctrine. Though Chou was extremely well read in Ch'ing literature, he had not made a special study of TCP theory, nor as far as I can tell, had anyone else at the date of his writing, with the exception of Chiang Shu-ke, whose short guide on the subject, published in 1928, has already been cited. Chiang did make a start on building up an over-all picture of their theory from scattered sources in the collected works of the chief exponents – nowhere unfortunately are the various strands brought together conveniently. Since the war, however, Kuo Shao-yü has dealt with the school at greater length in his 'History of Chinese Literary Criticism', the relevant volume of which was not published till 1947, and since revised, and in 1963 a wide-ranging collection of essays called *T'ung cheng p'ai yen-chiu lun-wen chi cheng p'ai yen-chiu lun-wen chi* (Researches into the T'ung-ch'eng school – *TCPYCLWC*) was published by the Anhui People's Press. From these it is possible to build up a clearer picture of TCP doctrine, despite the smoke-screen put up by individual contributors to the latter work. On the second point, it was quite legitimate for Chou to pronounce against the TCP on the grounds that on the whole its adherents produced poor writing, but it is our responsibility to see that its ideas are fairly represented, and not to accept uncritically that because the writing of members of the TCP was inferior (which is only a personal judgement) they were therefore bereft of fruitful ideas. Moreover, in this case particularly, we cannot pass Chou's motion on the nod. Like the other pioneers of the New Literature movement he was deeply committed against the TCP, who were after all the representatives of the old order that they were seeking to overthrow. Abuse of the TCP was commonplace during the May Fourth period. To quote just two examples, Ch'ien Hsüan-t'ung wrote: 'As I see it, what these people wrote was simply high class *pa-ku wen* (which is still a polite expression, to tell the truth one should say frankly 'deviant *pa-ku wen*'); literature, never! ' ('Compendium', Vol. I, p. 80). and Ch'en Tu-hsiu himself described Fang, Liu and Yao as 'demons', found their more ambitious works incomprehensible, thought them empty inside and their only skill in the confidence trick of imitating the ancients. He summed up the TCP as a 'mixture of Eight Masters and eight-legged essays' (ibid., pp. 73–4). Among the previous generation great scholars and educators like Liu Shih-p'ei, Chang T'ai-yen and Liang Ch'i-ch'ao had also dismissed the TCP as either dull or out of date.[3]

All very well, but we still have not found out very much about the famous 'right method' of the TCP. Since there is no dispute about Neo-Confucianism being the ideological framework they fitted into, that is the main point at issue. The school actually came into existence through the promotion of Yao Nai, and included Liu Ta-k'ui, his teacher, and Fang Pao from the previous generation, all natives of T'ung-ch'eng in Anhui province. It is therefore fitting that we examine the contribution of each of them to the body of TCP theory.

I-fa was the standard that Fang Pao ran up for himself. The term may be taken in two ways, either as a conjunction of *i* and *fa*, rectitude and method, or as a binom *i-fa*, right method or scheme, when it applies only to style. Fang himself separated the two:

> Rectitude is what the *Changes* calls 'words having substance'; method is what the *Changes* call 'words having order'. When method is made the woof to the warp of rectitude then the composition can stand up. ('Yu shu *Huo chih chuan* hou', quoted Kuo, p. 551.)

Such a division is implicit in Fang Pao's allegiance to the Sung philosophers on the one hand and the *ku-wen* stylists on the other. In conjoining the art of letters and Confucian ideology (for 'substance' in the above context means weighty Confucian thought) Fang was only serving up the old fare, so this line leads nowhere very interesting.

With *i-fa* used in its second sense, the two elements are not

[3] See quotation in *TCPYCLWC*, p. 192.

considered separately; the question becomes one of marrying form to content, of cutting the coat according to the cloth, and so enters the province of aesthetics. In this context *i* may be taken as meaning 'purpose', or 'what one wants to say' (that the thought should be correct is axiomatic but beside the point). To bear out this contention, and also to give an indication of TCP hagiography, I quote from the preface to Fang Pao's *Ku wen yüeh hsüan* (*TCPYCLWC*, p. 173). I should remark in passing that Fang's discussion of *i-fa* was always confined to ancient-style prose (*ku-wen*).

> The origins of *ku-wen* are far off in antiquity. The Six Classics, the *Analects* and *Mencius* are its source. Of the works fed by their waters and embodying 'right method' in crystalline form, none compares with the *Tso chuan* and *Shih-chi*, but each is a complete work with a beginning and ending and cannot be cut up [for this anthology]. After them, the *Kung-yang chuan, Ku-liang chuan, Kuo Yü* and *Kuo ts'e* do provide models in individual passages, but they all give a comprehensive account of words and deeds in several hundred years of history, and scholars must survey them in their entirety to get their essence. However, the letters and expositions of Han times and the writings of the Eight Masters of T'ang and Sung each encompass one matter only. The best of them may be included, but the choice must be severely restricted to bring out the essence of the right method. Hence twelve have been selected from Han Yü, eleven from Ou-yang Hsiu, and from the other six Masters one out of twenty or thirty. Of Han letters and expositions only two or three per cent have qualified.

It would seem from this that since the 'right method' can best be exemplified in whole short works as opposed to longer ones whose thought or purpose cannot be fully divined when fragmented, it is concerned with the *relationship* between idea and execution, that is, with the form most fitted to embody a given purpose.

In a letter to Sun I-ning, quoted by Kuo, pp. 552–3, Fang commended Ssu-ma Ch'ien's selection of material for his biographies under the rubric 'what is recorded must fit the stature of the person concerned', and in another letter in reply to Ch'iao Chieh-fu (Kuo, p. 553) he held that the *Kuo Yü* and *Ch'un-ch'iu chuan* were justified in giving quite different emphasis to the same subject on the grounds that 'all forms of writing have their own right method.' Perhaps the clearest statement of this principle is this:

> Among narrative literature only *Tso chuan* and *Shih-chi* have the right method. In each chapter the veins flow into one another and cannot be increased or reduced, but the inter-connectedness of the narrative as it develops may be concealed or apparent, may be partial or complete, the variations depending on what is appropriate, no one

course being held to . . . The variation in *fa* is necessitated by *i*. ('Shu *Wu tai shih* An Chung-hui chuan hou', quoted Kuo, pp. 553–4.)

If this is a correct picture of 'right method', then as a general proposition it is unexceptionable. If not very exciting it would on the surface appear to encourage flexibility of approach and to discourage the production of stereotypes. But there were two major limiting factors in Fang's attitude to letters that militated against flexibility; they had to do with diction and veneration for the tradition.

We have already quoted from *Yüan-liu* Shen T'ing-fang's description of the linguistic standards of Fang Pao. The reasons for prohibiting adulterations from the vernacular or poetic coinages are clear enough. If you believe that the great men of the past were morally and intellectually superior and therefore seek to emulate them, the task is made more difficult if you discard the language they expressed their thoughts in: all translation is distancing. This idea is put into words by Han Yü in a passage we have translated before:

> In applying myself to *ku-wen* I am not of course merely attracted by its diction being different from that of today. One cannot make the men of old appear by thinking of them. In attempting to follow the ancient way one needs to be conversant also with their language. In being conversant with their language, one's mind is basically on the ancient way. ('T'i Ou-yang sheng ai tz'u hou', *TCPYCLWC*, p. 7.)

In other words, if you seek the ancient way you can only find it cached in the language of the ancients, which is *ku-wen*.

In attempting to find a descriptive term for this ancient style, Fang hit on the word *ya-chieh* (rather than *ya-cheng* as Chou says). Fang says in 'Ku wen yüeh hsüan hsü -li': 'In *ku-wen* style what is valued is pellucid clarity without any dregs' (*TCPYCLWC*, p. 29); and in 'Ta Ch'eng Jo-han shu': 'No writing can be overgrown and at the same time proficient. It is the same as in heating gold and tin: when the crude ores are removed, the dark and turbid influences are dissipated and the sheen emerges.' (ibid., p. 220.) Fang's adverse criticism is often directed at 'language verging on commonness and suffering from verbosity' (Kuo, p. 555). In contrast *ya chieh* denotes classical elegance and purity, clean lines, an Attic quality. *Chieh* 'clean(ness)' is summed up separately as 'elucidating the essential matter, with the language free from admixture' ('Shu Hsiao hsiang kuo shih chia hou', Kuo, p. 556).

Yao Nai was wholly in agreement with his predecessor on the subject of an acceptable style. Like Fang he favoured brevity, or concentration:

> The *Changes* says: 'Auspicious men are sparing with their words.' When utterance is made only from inner fullness, words are correct in reasoning and feeling. In such circumstances, as one would not

feel satiated were the words to run into thousands and ten thousands, it is tantamount to their words being few. 'Ta Lu Pin-chih shu', *TCPYCLWC*, p. 6.)

He also agreed that the vulgate should be taboo. He wrote:

I have heard that 'without elegant composition words will not go far'.[4] Tseng-tzu refused to accept a mode of expression which could not rise above vulgarisms. How much more firmly to be rejected are vulgarisms in those expositions of the holy writ for educational purposes which are handed down to later generations! In T'ang times the priests had no literary background and so wrote down their teachers' words in the colloquial language and called it 'colloquies' (*yü lu*). The disciples of the Sung Confucians seem to have taken a leaf out of their book; however, in the case of students being afraid of unfaithfully recording their teachers' words, there is something to be said for it. But there is nothing to be said for those who lived in Ming times who wrote on their own account and yet still imitated their style. I would hope that you, sir, would change all those expressions which verge on the colloquial, such as are found in 'colloquies', so that the finished work is respectable. ('Fu Ts'ao Yün-lu shu', *TCPYCLWC*, p. 7.)

Furthermore, Yao went further than Fang in that he rejected letter style. Mei Po-yen, Yao's student, said: 'My teacher instructed scholars: "Good writing does not admit the modes of commentary, colloquies or private letters." Seemingly letter style is distinct from good writing.' ('Yao Chi-ch'uan hsien-sheng ch'ih tu hsü', quoted Chiang, p. 40.)

Despite the admonitions against the use of any but the strictly classical language, the TCP did not advocate mechanical imitation of the ancients or verbal plagiarism. Though the spoken language of their own time was not admitted, the literary man was supposed to be so versed in the language of the Classics (through the process of *lan shu* – being able to recite backwards) that to them it could be a natural mode of expression, allowing room for individual styles, rather like Latin was for medieval European scholars. The man who spoke out most strongly against plagiarism was Lui Ta-k'ui. Liu stated his position unequivocally:

In literature stale phrases must be got rid of. Han Yü in his discourses on literature gave priority to their removal. Later generations put this down simply to his liking for novelty, not knowing that all writers of *ku-wen* avoid stale phrases. They should look to see if Ou-yang Hsiu and the Sus ever directly used a word of their predecessors.

The 'Epitaph to Fan Tsung-shih'[5] says: 'In ancient times it was

[4] Attributed to Confucius, in *Tso chuan*, Hsiang Kung, year 25.

[5] 'Fan Tsung-shih chih ming'. Fan (fl. early ninth century) was highly praised by Han Yü.

the attitude to words that they should come from oneself. When the power was lost in degenerate days plagiarism became the thing. Those who came after designated their predecessors and borrowed openly from them. This same practice has prevailed from the Han to the present day.' Nowadays authors actually pride themselves on being derivative in using ready-made phrases from the masters of the past, preening themselves on their classical elegance, unaware that it is plagiarism and pillage.

To put it briefly, language is a thing that is daily renewed. If one writer follows another in lifeless fashion, how could their brew be thought anything but rancid? Even when one's ideas are the same as those of the ancients, when it comes to putting them down one must cast the metal anew. Even to say the same thing one must not take over the words of the ancients without modification. (*Lun wen ou chi*, quoted Kuo, p. 562.)

In taking the great prose works of the past as their models, what the TCP sought to capture from them was the elusive 'tone' of greatness. We will let Yao Nai's disciple Fang Tung-shu introduce the subject:

If scholars want to study the letters of the ancients, expert recitation must come first. After long and profound mulling over and savouring of the text, and becoming cognisant of their *ch'i* (animus) at the points where it manipulates ideas, fixes on words, accepts or rejects and makes its dispositions, then one comes into one's own and the piece is written . . . Otherwise, if the ancient ways are strange to one's mind and heart, invariably the pitch and measure of one's writing are uneven and inharmonious. Although this is applying oneself to minutiae, and is not the basic thing in writing, it is in fact the key to the ancients' achieving fame in their own age and being held up as models in later ages, and the secret of that which despite the profound and subtle competence of a lifetime they were unable to communicate to others. Today there are *littérateurs* in plenty, but few experts in recitation; they throw off their works lightly, and limit their expectations to making a bright show and thus gaining favour. No wonder they fall far short of the ancients. ('Shu Hsi-pao hsien-sheng mu chih hou', *TCPYCLWC*, p. 13.)

Liu Ta-k'ui anticipated the point about the relative unimportance, but absolute necessity, of studying the phraseology of the old masters:

Spiritual animus [*shen ch'i*] is the quintessence of literature; cadence is the relatively crude aspect, and words and phrases the most crude aspect . . . Cadence is the traces left by spiritual animus; words and phrases are the yardstick for cadence. Spiritual animus cannot be seen: it manifests itself in cadence. Cadence cannot be gauged: the gauging is done through the words and phrases. ('Lun wen ou chi', Wang Huan-piao, p. 166.)

This confirms that in their concentration on the diction of their great predecessors, the real objective was the latter's spirit or genius. If by way of comparison an English writer set out to capture the spirit of Shakespeare we might be doubtful of his chances of success, but would probably be content to wish him luck.

However, the TCP undeniably believed in imitating in the broad sense, and this was in principle unacceptable to the moderns. Yao Nai's statement in a letter to Kuan I-chih (quoted Kuo, p. 569) is representative of the school as a whole:

> The ears of men have been filled in recent times with the special pleading of Ch'ien Shou-chih[6] and they are contemptuous of the imitation practised by Ming writers, but if writing does not go through the stage of imitation how can it be resurgent? If we look at the way the classical authors learned from the pre-classical ones, those who imitated by synthesis and with subtlety are obviously worthy of emulation; those who imitated dully and constipatedly can obviously be dismissed. ('Yü Kuan I-chih', quoted Kuo, p. 569.)

Similarly and equally undogmatically Yao wrote on the subject of strict orthodoxy:

> With regard to composition, the ambition should be to create new worlds. The imaginative range of those who stick to strict orthodoxy is soon exhausted, and their best efforts are easily overshadowed by the ancients. Modern men are ignorant of the fact that poetry has an orthodox form and read only latter-day verse, with the result that their style is debased, and their determined quest for novelty ends up in triviality and vulgarity. This is repellent indeed, but sticking to orthodoxy to the exclusion of change in turn entails narrowness. (From a letter to Shih Fu, quoted Kuo, p. 570.)

Mei Tseng-liang (1786–1856, a follower of Fang and Yao) wrote in like vein that a writer's work must be in tune with the times, of the man and of his place; the world had moved on since ancient times, and the writer had an inexhaustible store of new material (see *TCPYCLWC*, p. 36).

Not only are the attitudes of the TCP towards their exemplars less dogmatic than Chou Tso-jen and his contemporaries would have us believe, in other respects too they show a sympathetic understanding and appreciation of literature that one would not expect from self-righteous defenders of the faith. One of the things they enjoyed for its own sake was the writer breaking through the conventions under his own colours, a feat Fang Pao distinguished in Liu Tsung-yüan: 'In [two named works] he has let himself go and has found his own way: there is no trace of borrowing or indebtedness.' ('Shu Liu wen hou', *TCPYCLWC*, p. 23.) Yao Nai likewise showed himself appreciative of

[6] i.e. Ch'ien Ch'ien-i (1582–1664).

individuation when he concluded his exposition of the opposite and complementary elements, *yin* and *yang*, 'hard' and 'soft', that make up a composition with the remark on the end product: 'When you look at the writing, when you intone the sounds, then the nature and appearance of the writers are all thereby differentiated.' ('Fu Lu Hsieh-fei shu', *TCPYCLWC*, p. 12.)

It is particularly in the free form of *chi* 'description' – a term which covers a lot of ground – that the TCP both allowed and encouraged a great deal of manoeuvre on the part of the author. Fang Pao wrote:

> Among prose forms only *chi* are difficult to compose. Disquisitions, refutations, epistles and expositions have their matter for discussion; annals, biographies, memorials, and obituaries bring out noble deeds. Only *chi* have no solid backbone: simply to detail the time-scale of the beginning to the completion of an edifice, the position of palaces, temples and pagodas, all set out mechanically, so that it palls on the reader, is hardly worth the trouble. Therefore when Han Yü wrote *chi* their 'waves and ripples' derived from the copiousness of his emotions; Ou-yang Hsiu and Wang An-shih sought in their own way for a moral philosophy in which to fit their private thoughts. Liu Tsung-yüan simply in his description of scenery etched out the myriad forms of life and was able to affect people's feelings. ('Ta Ch'eng K'ui-chou shu', *TCPYCLWC*, p. 22.)

Even more interesting to modern theorists is a passage on the accidental nature of great writing; from Yao Nai:

> Kui Yu-kuang was able to talk inconsequentially on inconsequential subjects, but he had a grace and harmony and an air of detachment which made him one in manner with Ssu-ma Ch'ien. This ambience is not one you will easily attain to. Writers have 'deliberate' gems which can be realized through effort, and 'unwitting' gems where effort is of no avail. After you have applied yourself long and studiously they may be left to appear of themselves. ('Yü Ch'en Shuo shih, *TCPYCLWC*, p. 23.)

Passing over the bit about inconsequentiality, which would have gladdened Chou Tso-jen's heart, this recognition of the phenomenon of things falling into place of their own accord lets in the idea of inspiration. It is not at all an isolated recognition, but it occurs in passing remarks, and was not a central part of TCP doctrine. Nevertheless it is worth taking a little further.

Though he did not give a name to the agency, Fang Pao also spoke of the spontaneous birth of a work of literature, as in his letter to Wu Tung-yen: 'Whenever I write I have to wait until the feelings and the vision came to life, and only then can I apply my intellect.' (*TCPYCLWC*, p. 221.) Now in Chinese literary theory the scholars most fond of talking about the ineffable thing we now call inspiration (the modern Chinese term *ling-kan* is of course of recent coinage) were those touched by Ch'an Buddhism, so if the TCP were at all interested in the subject one might expect some acknowledgement of their ways of thought. Indeed, Yao Nai provides this in another letter:

> The 'Model Styles for Composition' you sent me is the work of a miserable pedant . . . It is necessary to rise above this level of understanding to become a real writer. You should know that it is like a Ch'an riddle – it cannot be explained! How can you hope to enter into the subject by means of 'model styles'? ('Chi Ch'en Shuo shih', quoted Kuo, p. 568.)

Yao Nai really threw caution to the winds in a letter in reply to Lu Hsieh-fei, where he exclaimed: 'The supreme in literature comes from communion with the gods; it is not in the gift of human power.' (*TCPYCLWC*, p. 14.)

The sources of inspiration, the 'gods' of the TCP, may have been different from those conceived of by their modern critics, but they were unlikely to have been conjured up at all by the despots masquerading as men of letters of Ch'en Tu-hsiu's imagination.

Now Chou Tso-jen had his fun, and was entitled to it, at Yao Nai's expense over his famous eight elements, *shen, li, ch'i, wei, ke, lü, sheng*, and *se*. But it is neither unusual to find such tabulation nor maddeningly puzzling what roughly the eight elements might be. Let us recall what Chou said about them:

> *Li* is moral philosophy, what we call the Way. *sheng* is rhythm, the musical element in a composition, *se* is colour, the [visual] beauty of a composition . . . But *shen, ch'i, wei, lü* are wholly vague in meaning, and very difficult to make sense of.

One cannot help feeling that Chou is rather overplaying the plain man act. The elements he pretends to understand certainly have wider currency in everyday language, but they are not more definable than the others, which would be quite familiar to anyone acquainted with literary criticism. *Shen* is the presiding spirit; *ch'i* is 'animus', or the vital force; *wei*, 'taste', is a term that Chou himself frequently used, as we have seen; *ke* is structure; *lü* is measure (Chou unconsciously (?) omitted *ke* because the two tend to merge together). The only question is what particular kind of *shen, ch'i, wei* etc. Yao Nai had in mind. It is impossible to enumerate them all, but Hsü Wen-yü quotes two passages in his notes on Yao's '*Ku wen tz'u lei tsuan* hsü' that throw some light on the main ones. The first is a gloss by Hsieh Ying-chih:

> Literature is founded on reason, *shen* moves it, *ch'i* fills it. It gets its flavour from its density, its harmony from its lilt. With sound the ability to sink and soar is prized; colours should be muted but not dark, beautiful but not dazzling. (From *K'uai-chi shan chai wen chi*, in *Wen lun chiang shu*, p. 381.)

With this Hsü associates another passage of Yao Nai:

> When *ch'i* is full but still, the sound is strong but not agitated; when the feelings are expressed clearly but under restraint, the colours are shining but not superficial. (From 'Ta Lu Pin-chih shu'.)

It is ironical that Chou should have dissociated himself from these requirements, as the kind of literature they would give rise to, reasoned, having conviction and feeling, but restrained and muted in tone and colour, is the same as Chou himself tried to write.

As all literary coteries tend to be, the TCP were unpleasantly self-righteous and intolerant, but so far it seems reasonable to conclude that they were neither as narrow nor as obscurantist in their views as Chou pretends. The main remaining charge against them is that what they wrote was *pa-ku wen*. This is a very complex problem which admits of no clear answer. The issue is beclouded by two facts, that all scholar-officials had to be proficient in *pa-ku wen*, and that ideologically there is nothing to distinguish the *de rigeur* Confucianism of *pa-ku wen* from the relatively freely espoused Confucianism of the TCP. Theoretically judgement of a sort could be reached by comparing a representative sample of TCP writing with a book of *pa-ku wen* essays, but that I am unable to do. Most of my evidence will be what the TCP leaders said about *pa-ku wen*. But first the caveat should be entered that clearly only to a certain type of prose could the conventions of *pa-ku wen* apply: *chi* (descriptions) for example could with regard to formal characteristics have little in common with *pa-ku wen*. So even if they were convicted out of their own mouths for favouring applying *pa-ku wen* principles to other forms of writing, not everything they wrote could bear this hypothetical family resemblance.

What did the founding father of the TCP have to say about *pa-ku wen*? First of all, Fang Pao is compromised by his personal record. He spent most of his youth teaching this essay form to make a living. At the other end of his life, at the age of 69, he was invited by the Ch'ien-lung emperor to select several hundred model examination essays from Ming and Ch'ing (see *TCPYCLWC*, p. 59). He accepted. However, his comment on the labours of his youth was: 'I used the examination essay as a sign to attract students, so could not be rid of it; thereby my days were reduced and my vitality diminished' (*TCPYCLWC*, p. 187), which would seem to qualify his approval. Wang Ch'i-chung has collected some passages which demonstrate beyond doubt Fang's positive disgust with the common practices of the examination essay. All are from prefaces. In the first[7] he deplored the blinkered concentration on examination topics to the neglect of the wide world, of true scholarship and of self cultivation, because therein

[7] 'Sung Kuan Shu-ch'ang chin sheng hsü', *TCPYCLWC*, p. 17.

lay recompense. In the second[8] he dated back to Southern Sung the refusal of scholars to step out of the ruts made by their predecessors (for fear of being unorthodox), whereas, as Fang says, 'the examination essay relative to prose writing as a whole, is like an inferior grade of skill. Those who were famed in their time for it, like Kui Yu-kuang, T'ang Shun-chih, and Chin Sheng (1598–1645), as you will discover if you look into their hearts, did not want to be known for their examination essays.' In the third[9] he bewailed the practice of scholars of devoting themselves to one classic and wearing out their youth on the examination essay, thus leaving insufficient energy for exploring the ancient world. He seems to condemn the whole business in the fourth preface[10]: 'I have remarked before that there is nothing more demoralizing or destructive of talent than the examination system, and the examination essay is the worst part of it. From its inception those who have had commerce with it have been eager either for profit or renown.'

Indeed Fang did condemn the examination essay business, but it would be wrong to suppose that he was opposed to that kind of essay in itself: the criticism just noted applies more to abuses and deluded attitudes than to inherent evils. Approached as a discipline among other disciplines, rather than as a means to an end, pursued exclusively of other ends, Fang approved of the examination essay. This is implied in a comment in 'Yü Han Mu-lu shu': 'In the field of the examination essay, if one aspires to make it capable of being disseminated among one's contemporaries and handed down to posterity, the difficulty and elevatedness of it is not different from that of *ku-wen*.' (ibid., p. 187.) The inference is that the examination essay is a not inestimable art that requires painstaking application.

Fang's placing of the examination essay on a level with *ku-wen* gives the key to his strategy. It was, as his friend Wang Shu-chih said, 'to use *ku-wen* to write examination essays' (ibid., p. 188), in other words, to raise the status of the examination essay, which was repeatedly stigmatized by less orthodox writers, by effecting a marriage with *ku-wen*. This he plainly advocated in '*Ku wen yüeh hsüan* hsü': 'Through discovering the "right method" in the *Tso chuan, Shih chi, Kung-yang* and *Ku-liang chuan, Kuo-yü* and *Chan-kuo ts'e*, one's apprehension transcends genres, and one has abundant resources for applying it to writing examination essays and setting out disquisitions and treatises.' (ibid., p. 151.) What he thought could be done by this method he indicated in '*Ch'in ting ssu shu wen* fan li': 'The writers of the Cheng-te and Chia-ch'ing periods (1506–66) were the first to be

[8] 'Yang Ch'ien-mu wen kao hsü', ibid.
[9] 'Tseng Ch'un An-fang wen chou hsü', ibid.
[10] 'Ho Ching-huan i wen hsü', *TCPYCLWC*, pp. 16–17.

able to use *ku-wen* to write examination essays; distilling the Classics and histories, they were able to deal exhaustively with the obvious and hidden meanings inherent in the subject, thus producing the acme of Ming prose.' (ibid., p. 137.) This was Fang Pao's method of reconciling his loyalty to the dynasty and his instinctive orthodoxy with his painful consciousness of the sterility of the examination essay as practised.

There is no logical inconsistency in Fang Pao's approach, for the examination essay was in fact only a highly circumscribed form of *ku-wen*. All three of the TCP leaders recognized the relationship. Witness Liu Ta-k'ui: 'Those who talk about *ku-wen* are often contemptuous of the examination essay: what they do not realise is that the examination essay can be taken as one form of *ku-wen*.' ('Hai-feng shih wen lun', ibid., p. 153.) And Yao Nai also stated that, like Fang, after reading the examination essays of the Cheng-te and Chia-ch'ing periods, 'I perceived the basic form of the original "exegesis of the classics" [i.e. the examination essay] and the purpose behind the composition of T'ang Shun-chih and Kui Yu-kuang, and the light dawned: this too was *ku-wen*; how could their paths be different? ' (Hsi-pao hsüan kao hsü', ibid., p. 153.) Indeed, the aesthetic principles of the examination essays, such as they were, were practically identical with those laid down for *ku-wen* and hence subscribed to by the TCP. Liu Chi-kao (*TCPYCLWC*, p. 55) has drawn up a comparison. The stylistic guideline for the examination essay was 'purity and classical elegance' (*ch'ing chen ku ya*), which corresponds to the *ya chieh* of the TCP; it was limited to a few hundred characters, which of course conforms with the principle of 'valuing brevity' of the TCP; and its slogans 'moral pregnancy' and 'words must have substance' coincide with the 'purport' (*i*) of the TCP. This comparison has the weakness that the programme for the examination essay is taken from 'Chin ssu shu wen hsüan piao', whose author was none other than Fang Pao, but it probably gave rise to little dissent.

Yao Nai did not share the ambivalent attitude of Fang Pao to *ku-wen*. Perhaps by his time, when the counterblasts of the end-of-Ming stalwarts had faded into the distance, he could feel more secure in its conventions. At any rate he showed few scruples about embracing its cause – indeed on some occasions he advocated 'using the examination essay to write *ku-wen*', thus setting Fang's formula on its head. Yao confessed: 'Never in my life have I dared to look down on the exegesis of the Classics; indeed I have had the ambition of leading the country in practising it. When those who practise it are multitude, a genius who can use the exegesis to write *ku-wen* will come forth from their ranks, and be fêted by the world.' ('T'ao shan ssu shu wen hsü' ibid., p. 189.) An even more fulsome tribute to the potentialities of the examination essay form is to be found in 'T'ing yün t'ang i wen hsü'. First Yao deplores the antagonism of the aesthetes and methodical scholars towards the essay, then claims:

> If intelligent and talented men, abiding by Sung Confucianism, and beyond it penetrating to the essence of the sages, reach the supreme literary spheres of the ancient works while using the contemporary idiom, it need hardly be said that the 'exegesis' form would be infinitely superior to those of the *littérateurs* and Han scholars. It could be the crown of belles lettres, besides which it enjoys the support of the nation's laws, so how sad that it should be held in such low opinion! (*TCPYCLWC*, p. 189.)

The extravagance of Yao's language might in part be due to eagerness to show himself in milk-white hind in an age of literary inquisitions, but evidence from his personal life, like paying for printing of *pa-ku wen* collections, show it to be consistent with his normal conduct (see ibid., p. 189).

There seems no need for further evidence to prove the partiality of the TCP for *pa-ku wen*. Their own words, as well as the weight of opinion among Ch'ing and Republican critics, show that they favoured applying the convention of the examination essay outside that particular context. In terms of technique probably the most substantial element in the TCP approach coincident with *pa-ku wen* practice was the emphasis on measure and tone, which derived from the same injunction, namely 'compose in the tone of the ancients' (from 'Ming shih hsüan chü chih', quoted *TCPYCLWC*, p. 120). In the case of *pa-ku wen* this ideal was reduced to mere mechanics.

I do not doubt that this and other theories of the TCP likewise dictated by convention had a deleterious effect on their writing, but it must be remembered that the theories were mostly formulated with what one might call 'serious' prose in mind. They shared the traditional dichotomy of outlook between the highly formal kind of writing which contributed to a person's reputation or status and what was written just for amusement. Now Chou Tso-jen's conception of literature left out altogether the first category, and the TCP said little about the requirements for the second category, so there was little common ground between them.

When it comes to literary *values*, the TCP cleaved firmly to the Chinese tradition. Where those values were embodied in the more occasional forms of literature, which could best accomodate them, they emerged as qualities that by and large Chou could and did endorse. The four that he picked out were blandness, simplicity, pregnancy and having after-taste, and we have shown how attached he too was to these. More that he did not mention were quite in conformity with his outlook.

In view of the bias in the present summary towards presenting the case *for* the TCP, highlighting their more enlightened views, we ought to remind ourselves before concluding of the gravamen of Chou's case against them, and for this we had best go farther afield than *Yüan-liu*. His case could be summed up in the phrase *lin ching tu*, 'classical poison', or bigotry, which he adopts in *K'u-chu tsa-chi*, 'About Wang T'ao'. Some of the chief characteristics of this bigotry are set out in the diatribe of Chiang Tzu-man that Chou quotes, and underwrites, in *Chih-t'ang yi-yu wen pien*, 'Ku-wen and Neo-Confucianism':

> Now the three (Fang, Liu and Yao) in their writings mistakenly regard the teachings in the colloquies of the Neo-Confucians as the Way. They have nothing worth recommending in the province of human feelings or the natural order of things. What they talk about is the Way that belongs to grandiloquent theorizing; the Way they refer to is wrong. The prose of the Eight Masters is the work of T'ang and Sung men; at that time there was no such thing as the examination essay style we have nowadays, so they each developed a technique of their own. Ever since the adoption in the Ming dynasty of *pa-ku wen* as the statutary means of selecting officials, those familiar with the *ku-wen* of the Eight Masters adapted the technique of the Eight Masters to the format of the examination essay. Thereafter the obligatory twists and turns of the examination essay were invested with the vestigial notions of the Eight Masters. Once the practice had become inveterate it was as if a thousand faces wore a single expression, and a contemporary style persisted while the ancient style was lost . . . Taking, (as the three do), unparallel examination essay prose for *ku-wen*, their so-called 'method' is wrong. ('Ku-wen yü li-hsüeh', p. 42.)

To this Chou adds the criticism that those like Fang and Yao who edited *ku-wen* anthologies, by selecting those pieces closest to the examination essay, falsely restricted the scope of *ku-wen*, and only by this means were able to extract their celebrated 'right method'.

Other criticisms Chou levelled at the TCP included their absorption with sound effects, thus compounding an inherent weakness in Chinese literature[11], and of course their insistence on ideological correctness, which sometimes masqueraded behind the seemingly innocent demand that 'words should have substance' (*yen chung yu wu*).[12]

All these objections are real ones and are enough to explain and justify the marked hostility Chou showed towards the TCP. It is surprising that anathema for their thought should have gone hand in hand with concurrence in many of their literary judgements. Perhaps the values they shared belonged to the central literary tradition of China.

[11] In 'Han wen-hsüeh ti ch'uan-t'ung', *Yao-t'ang tsa-wen*.
[12] In 'Ch'un tsai t'ang tsa wen', *Yao wei chi*.

B

THE KUNG-AN SCHOOL

Chou Tso-jen's writings are interspersed with references to the *Kung-an p'ai* (abbreviated to KAP). His interest in them antedated that of Lin Yutang, the first collection of short prose pieces from the end of Ming and beginning of Ch'ing, in which they figure prominently, being published by a disciple of his, Shen Ch'i-wu.[1] His attitude towards the school is expressed most judiciously in *Yüan-liu* (pp. 42–52), and we will now translate the bulk of what he has to say there. He has previously been discussing the Seven Former and Latter Masters (*ch'ien hou ch'i tzu*) of the Ming dynasty, who laid down strict rules on what period of literature should be copied.

> Those who unfurled the banner of revolt against this revivalist trend were the Kung-an and Ching-ling schools. The three leading lights of the KAP were the three Yüans, namely Yüan Tsung-tao, Yüan Hung-tao and Yüan Chung-tao. They belonged to the Wan-li period, in Western dating the period spanning the end of the sixteenth and the beginning of the seventeenth centuries. They acquired the name of KAP from the fact that they came from Kung-an in Hupei province. Their doctrine was very simple; it could be said to be roughly the same as Mr. Hu Shih's. The difference is that their time was the sixteenth century, before [Matteo] Ricci came to China,[2] so it lacked Western thought. If you subtract from the present-day Mr. Hu Shih's doctrine the Western influence, in the several respects of science, philosophy, literature, and thought, you are left with the KAP's thought and doctrine. And their view of the evolution of Chinese literature is perhaps clearer than that of modern commentators. Their theories and compositions were both right and good, but alas their luck was bad: in Ch'ing their works were proscribed, and

[1] I refer to *Ping hsüeh hsiao p'in*, which was prepared for publication in 1930, but only appeared two years later as *Chin-tai san-wen hsüan*. Chou referred to the end-of-Ming movement as early as 1923, in 'Ti-fang yü wen-hsüeh' ('Place and Literature'), *T'an lung chi*, p. 13.

[2] In fact Ricci was established in Peking by 1601.

their movement was overthrown by an eighteenth-century scholar.[3]

'Just give rein to the spirit, do not be bound by form,' this was the KAP's doctrine. In his 'Hsü Hsiao-hsiu shih', Yüan Chung-lang (Hung-tao) said:

It [his poetry] has its good and bad points. The good points we need not discuss, the bad points mainly consist of terms peculiarly fashioned by his own persona. As for me, I delight in the bad points, and the so-called good points I cannot help detesting as prettifying and conventional – he has not been able to free himself entirely from recent popular literary practices. Poetry and prose have in recent times deteriorated to a wretched condition. Prose has to take its standard from Ch'in and Han, poetry from the Golden Age of T'ang. [It is all] plagiarism and imitation, following like shadow and echo. Whenever anyone is discovered using an unsanctioned phrase they all condemn him as a pariah. What they do not realize about prose taking its standard from Ch'in and Han is that the men of Ch'in and Han never modelled themselves word for word on the Six Classics; similarly with regard to poetry taking its standard from the Golden Age of T'ang, the men of that time never followed word for word the poetry of Han and Wei. If in Ch'in and Han they had imitated the Six Classics, how could there ever have been a Ch'in-Han prose style? If in the Golden Ageof T'ang they had imitated Han and Wei how could there ever have been a Golden Age of T'ang poetic style? Know then that dynasties rise and fall and techniques do not succeed unchanged. Each maximizes its mutation and follows its bent to the end, and should be prized for this; talk of superiority or inferiority is out of place. Now of all things in this world, those which are unique cannot be dispensed with; if they cannot be dispensed with, even if there was a will to do away with them it would be in vain. If something is a mere replica of something else, then it may be dispensed with; if it may be dispensed with, even if one wanted to retain it one could not . . .'

These words are very much to the point, and are very like those spoken in modern times.

In his preface to Chiang Chin-chih's *Hsüeh t'ao ke chi*, Chung-lang explains his view of the way literature has evolved:

Ancient times belong to antiquity, present times to the present. To appropriate the vestiges of the language of the ancients and lay claim to antiqueness is to persist in wearing summer clothes in the depths of winter. The reason why the *sao* form broke away from the *ya* was that the *ya* gave poor scope for complaint, and only the *sao* form could accommodate it. In later times people attempted to write in imitation of *sao*, but never achieved a true resemblance. Why? Because they sought directly for *sao* in

[3] The person meant is Chang Hsüeh-ch'eng.

sao. But when it came to the leave-taking of Su Wu and Li Ling, the Nineteen Songs, etc., the rhythms and form of *sao* had changed, but we still have to recognize them as true *sao*. . .

Then he gets on to the subject of *fa*, what we now call 'philosophy' or 'style':

Style originates in degeneracy and culminates in excess. To correct the 'cake-stand' style [i.e. using ready-made slabs of rhetoric to construct a passage] of Six Dynasty prose, mellifluousness was found to be the best method. The cake-stand style was truly the origin of mellifluousness, but the excess of the latter lay in daintiness, and the writers of the T'ang Golden Age corrected this with expansiveness. But once expansive, the expansiveness gave rise to wildness, so those who followed the T'ang Golden Age corrected it with realism. Once realism was established it gave rise to vulgarity. Hence after mid-T'ang this was corrected with esotericism and abstruseness. But esotericism narrows the scope, and abstruseness necessarily leads to competition in non-essentials. So the course of poetry became increasingly confined in late T'ang. In Sung, Ou-yang Hsiu and Su Shih came to the fore in succession and radically changed these latter-day practices. They encompassed every subject and every style, every emotion and every scene, flowing and spreading like the Yangtze and Yellow rivers. People of the present day only see that the Sung did not style itself on the T'ang; they do not realize that the Sung only had its style because of T'ang.

This view of the history of literature is much more enlightening than saying: 'The path that China's past literature took was entirely the wrong one, and only the path taken now is correct.'

In criticizing Chiang Chin-chih's poetry he used the words: 'Trust to the wrist, trust to the mouth, and all the words will find their fit measure.' These words may be said to be the permanent philosophy of the *shih yen chih* school, and to this day there has been no more incisive expression of it; even Mr. Hu Shih's 'Eight don'ts'[4] do not get closer to the heart of the matter.

Because they opposed the revivalist movement of the Former and Latter Seven Masters, they opposed imitation with all their strength. In Chung-lang's preface to *Hsüeh t'ao ke chi* just quoted, there is the following statement:

When plagiarism is used to revive the ancient, matching phrases and copying words, with the insistence on forcing things together, ignoring the present scene, and picking up worn-out and hackneyed terms, the man of talent, being unversed in the technique, does not dare to demonstrate his genius, while the man of no talent pastes together a few vacuous phrases and produces a poem. The intelligent man is hampered by the practice, while the

[4] Originally put forward in 'Wen-hsüeh kai-liang ch'u-i' (Tentative Proposal for Literary Reform) in *Hsin ch'ing nien*, 1917, and repeated in more quotable form the following year.

> fool rejoices in its simplicity. One man proposes and a million consent; actors jump on the bandwagon and join the debate on 'the civilized way'. Alas, how shameful that poetry should be in such a state!

We cannot from our modern standpoint criticize his 'actors jump on the bandwagon and join in the debate on "the civilized way" ' as having feudal overtones; that is due to the times he lived in. His opposition to imitating the ancients is really quite correct. Imitation does not require thought, so the malpractices he refers to are to be expected. In school examinations nowadays they are always asking questions on such things as 'the thought of Tung Chung-shu' or 'the thought of Yang Hsiung'[5] for the Chinese test, and this can easily lead to such faults as Yüan Chung-lang mentioned, so that those who can write essays write away without coming to grips with the subject and those who cannot feel altogether at sea. The questions in the entrance examinations for foreign universities are mostly of the 'pleasure of travel' variety, not the 'on Shakespeare's plays' variety. China ought to change in her turn; in my opinion it would be rather more suitable if subjects like 'the sun' or 'willows' could be used as themes for composition, because those who are relatively more accomplished in literature could produce good essays on them.

Po Hsiu's (Tsung-tao's) understanding of the problems is somewhat inferior to Chung-lang's. In his 'Essay on literature' he also expressed his opposition to following the ancients:

> Today's round collars and loose robes are the way of imitating the patchwork of leaves and skin garments of yore. Today's whole variety of fried and stewed foods are the way of imitating eating hirsute meat and drinking blood of yore. How is this? The men of yore aimed to fill their mouths and bellies and cover their frames; the men of today aim to fill their mouths and bellies and cover their frames: there is no difference. Taking the words and phrases of ancient writers into one's own work is the same as sticking leaves and skins between the sleeves (of modern dress) or mixing bristle and blood among our culinary delicacies. In general the first aim of the ancients' writing was to convey their meaning, and the first aim of the moderns' writing is not to convey their meaning. To emulate conveying through non-conveying, can this be called emulating the ancients?
>
> A school of learning comes to evolve a philosophy; from the philosophy is created a type of language. If the language does not have a philosophy behind it, it is vacuous; if it is vacuous then one voice will be a hollow echo of another. Those who greatly rejoice will of course be convulsed with laughter, those who are greatly grieved will wail in anguish, those in great ire will roar fit to make the earth tremble, and their hair will stand on end. But those on the stage, who have nothing to rejoice about but have to force a laugh, or have nothing to grieve over but have to force a

[5] Two eminent Confucian dogmatists of the Han dynasty.

> tear, are in a situation where they can only borrow and imitate. Present day literati, vapid as they are, have never made a study of anything. If you knock on their breasts you find them dim and lacking the least thread of thought. They have merely apprehended that the ancients had the saying about leaving a literary legacy for the ages, and that their seniors are famed for their prowess in poetry and prose, so they too want to grasp their brush, spread their paper, and get into the business, and with a stream of papers and a sheaf of scripts they solicit men's praise. To conceive such foolishly grandiose schemes with such clouded minds, they have to lean on Tso Ch'iu-ming and Ssu-ma Ch'ien, and collect droppings and dig among the dung heaps, or else they cannot fill their pages. If you were to take one of these gentlemen's works and strike out all the archaisms and hackneyed phrases, ten to one you would end up with nothing . . .
> However, the root of the trouble does not lie in copying but in ignorance. If one's breast were filled to bursting point with one's own genuine perceptions, then one would not have time for grinding ink or wielding one's brush; even if one were to dash it off, one would still be afraid of failing to get down all one's ideas. How can one have time to use phrases of the ancients? But if scholars can gain genuine understanding from their studies, and their writing can issue from this understanding, though you drove them to imitate you would not succeed in it.
>
> Though this is written half for amusement, half to make mockery, the views in it are well worthy of notice.
>
> From these passages the general approach of the KAP to literature can be made out. Regarding their own prose compositions we might sum them up as 'fresh and flowing'. Their verse was also ingenious and easy to understand. They did not put on airs in their compositions, did not talk in high-flown style about ways of bringing peace and order to the world. You need only have read the spurious antiquarian pieces of the Former and Latter Seven Masters to appreciate where their strength lay.
>
> However, their subsequent decline had its seeds in this same thing. Their compositions were too empty and facile, clear without being deep. As with a pool of water, it obviously does not do for it to be too muddied, but if it is so clear that the eye can see straight to the bottom, and all the plants and fishes in it can be sharply discerned, there is no interest in it.

Though the tone of Chou's appraisal here of the KAP is cooler than at other times, this passage fairly represents his considered opinion of them. His approval of their oeuvre is qualified. His criticism of their verse above is not very enthusiastic, and in his preface to Chung-lang's collected works he only says Chung-lang's poetry has negative value – that is, in being unlike that of the Seven Masters. In that essay he picks out very much the same qualities in their prose as he does here, freshness, natural charm, and the ability to coin striking phrases. He does not claim pre-eminence for Chung-lang in any field of literature, understandably in view of the criticism made above: his writing was too transparent and had no great depth.[6] By contrast the style of Chang Tsung-tzu (Chang Tai) did draw the highest praise from Chou, and this he described as a combination of KAP and Ching-ling p'ai styles: that is, the shortcomings of the KAP style had been corrected with a measure of the indirectness and density of the Ching-ling school.[7] Again while he did claim that the short lyrical and descriptive pieces of Chung-lang and Liu T'ung-jen[8] were unique, he had reservations about the style of the theoretical works of both schools.[9]

The reason for Chou's special attachment to the KAP, who do not figure very prominently in normal histories of Chinese literature, and his frequent recommendation of them to his readers, lies clearly in their approach to writing. The main points in their diatribes that Chou quotes are rejection of imitation and classicism, support for spontaneity, idiosyncracy, contemporariness, truthfulness to one's own experience and understanding (*ch'eng*), and belief in continuity in literature (even if it manifests itself in reaction against, not conformity with). Naturally all these are points with which Chou agreed, and as he said with reference to Hu Shih, they were guiding principles for the New Literature movement – all except the last. Chou Tso-jen was exceptional in seeing the New Literature as part of the whole of Chinese literature; the view he cites of the New Literature as a complete break with the past was practically an article of faith with the majority of the participants. Despite this broad measure of agreement with their ideas, however, Chou expressly declined to identify himself with the KAP, on the grounds of his eclecticism and the inevitable fact that ways of thought had changed over the years.[10]

Though, as I have said, references to the KAP abound in Chou's later essays, they do not generally introduce any further aspects of their thought, though the perspective varies, as for instance when he picks up the normally derogatory term 'heterodox' (*p'ang men*) as applied to the end-of-Ming authors, and comments: 'But my prejudice is that heterodoxy in literature and thought is invariably more interesting than orthodoxy because it is more courageous and more vital;'[11] or when he

[6] 'Chung k'an Yüan Chung-lang chi hsü', 1935, *K'u ch'a sui-pi*.
[7] 'Tsao yü Ch'iao ti hsü', 1931, *K'an yün chi*.
[8] A member of the Ching-ling school.
[9] 'Mei hua ts'ao t'ang pi t'an teng', 1936, *Feng yü t'an*, p. 185.
[10] In 'Ch'ung k'an Yüan Chung-lang chi hsü'.
[11] Mei hua ts'ao t'ang pi t'an teng', *Feng yü t'an*, p. 183.

credits the KAP with influencing later writers to identify morality with what comes from the heart;[12] or when he sees in them 'genuine individuality'.[13] One new claim he does make is that the KAP and Ching-ling p'ai were superior to the moderns in making a break with the past and seeing the *Shih ching* anew as poetry; no such revaluation had been made by contemporary critics.[14]

Chou says he is prejudiced in favour of the KAP; prejudice is in fact the vital thing in determining attitudes towards them, as there is very little dissent about their influence or artistic achievement. The bibliography to the *Ssu k'u ch'üan shu*, a work that one would expect to be at the opposite critical pole to Chou Tso-jen, says this of them:

> Their poetry and prose changed the solemn and ponderous into the light and agile, changed ornamentation into following the natural bent. When they had given the world a new view of things they were in turn followed heedlessly. But the Seven Masters still based themselves on learning, while the Three Yüans only relied on intelligence. The imitators of the Seven Masters only faked an air of antiquity, while the followers of the Three Yüans, proud of their cleverness, broke all the rules. They claimed to be remedying the abuses of the Seven Masters, but their own abuses were still more serious. (*Ssu k'u ch'üan shu shu mu,* VI, p. 3714.)[15]

This recognizes that the KAP had a historical role to play and pronounces the same critical verdict as Chou, though its premises are different from his.

The things that the KAP stood for, at least the things Chou thought worthy of mention, were by no means their monopoly. Kuo Shao-yü has a very useful chapter on 'The precursors and cohorts of the KAP' which shows how indebted the KAP were for their ideas to their predecessors, and that certain of their contemporaries held similar views. Li Chuo-wu (1527–1602) is their most obvious source of inspiration. Yüan Chung-lang was something of a disciple of his. Chung-lang's brother, Chung-tao, wrote: 'Only when [Chung-lang] met Lung-hu [Li Chuo-wu] did he realize that up till then he had been culling worn out phrases and had thoughtlessly stuck to conventional opinions, and was dying under the subjection to the language of the ancients; a vital spark, he had been covered from view. But then the

[12] In 'Yüan yüan ch'ang ho chi', *Yao wei chi.*

[13] 'Tsa pan erh pa', *Yung jih chi,* p. 172.

[14] 'Ho I-sun lun shih', *Ping chu hou t'an*, p. 28.

[15] The school of Ronsard in France suffered a similar critical fate to the KAP at the hands of a generation concerned about its unsettling ideological influence. See J. W. H. Atkins, *English Literary Criticism*, p. 4.

floodgates opened, and like a down feather carried along by a favourable wind, like a giant fish sporting in a huge waterway, he was able to be master of his thoughts, not mastered by them, was able to manipulate the ancients, not be manipulated by them; when he gave utterance, each word flowed out from his innermost being.'[16] Li Cho-wu was in turn inspired by Wang Yang-ming, apparently accepting the latter's doctrine of 'subjectivism', that is, confidence in innate knowledge, and primacy of the individual conscience. The Yüan brothers' eagerness to challenge accepted standards, as the above quotation shows, was very much in the Li Cho-wu mould. Li's ideal of preserving the 'child-like mind' against silting over by a debris of received knowledge (see Kuo, p. 350) sums up their principle of seeing things in their own way and their doctrine of *chen* (truth to the self); Li's acceptance of all styles of writing, including those debarred from serious consideration by the orthodox for their vulgarity, gave the lead for the KAP rejection of an approved style and advocacy for creating individual styles: Li's esteem for popular literature was inherited by Chung-lang to the degree that he gave it as his opinion that only the songs of village women and children would survive from his age;[17] and Li's belief in the 'madness of creation'[18] was frequently echoed by the KAP, as for instance in Chung-lang's comparison of the act of writing to 'sounds produced when the wind is high' and 'shadows following the movement of the moon' when inspiration and situation coincide;[19] or this description of it, as 'a thousand words coming forth in an instant, like water converging eastwards, taking possession of the spirit'.[20]

Another person, whom Chung-lang addressed as 'teacher' in a poem (Kuo, p. 352), was Chiao Jo-hou (Chiao Hung 1541–1620). He anticipated the KAP in attacking the Seven Masters, and in his reverence for Su Shih and Po Chü-i. Again, a playwright of the previous generation, of whom Chung-lang wrote a very admiring biography, Hsü Wen-chang (Hsü Wei, 1521–93) said before them that imitation was only parroting (Kuo, p. 355), and this view T'ang Hsien-tsu (1550–1616), a contemporary of the Yüan brothers, also held, maintaining that it was impossible to recreate the spirit and qualities of Han and Sung and that it was therefore best to write as one's own nature dictated. He also stressed the primacy of inspiration, believing that style spontaneously followed in its wake.

[16] 'Miao Kao-shan fa ssu pei', quoted *Chung-kuo wen-hsüeh shih*, Academia Sinica, p. 927.
[17] 'Hsü Hsiao-hsiu shih', *Chin-tai san-wen hsüan*, p. 15.
[18] Propounded in 'Tsa shuo', *Fan shu* 3, Kuo, p. 351.
[19] In 'Hsing Su yüan ts'un kao yin', quoted Kuo, p. 378.
[20] 'Hsü Hsiao-hsiu shih'.

If, as we have seen, Chou thought less of the KAP as writers than of other individuals, and other people put forward the same arguments as they did, why did Chou see them particularly as not only precursors but mentors for the New Literature movement? The principal answer is a pedestrian one: that they also made up a movement, and were not isolated individuals. The other points of comparison were either equally general or more personal: personal in that, one suspects, they appealed to him as accomplished exponents of his favourite form, *hsiao-p'in-wen*, and were less cranky than the majority of the other people we have mentioned; general in that he felt they lived in an age similar to his own – a 'chaotic' one, as he described it in his preface to Chung-lang's works, and so faced at least some of the same problems; that their principal proposal matched the needs and temperament of modern writers, which was, as Chou said in *Yao wei chi* (p. 112) 'to have something to say, and want to say it well'; and that their chief target was *fu ku*, 'return to ancient ways', the danger of which Chou felt was ever present, and under the skirts of which he felt the hope of China becoming a modern, sane and civilized country might be smothered. They were also first class propagandists, as even the short extracts quoted give some hint of, and I suspect Chou liked the irreverence and occasional downright crudity of their invective.

The characteristics of the KAP which did make them, if not unique, at least very unusual, Chou ignored, as was consistent with his attitude of keeping his feet on the ground and professing dislike for abstruse theories. He expresses dislike for Chung-lang's not aesthetically unimportant dabbling in Ch'an and Pure Land Buddhism[21] in his preface to Chung-lang's works. Similarly, the key terms in Chung-lang's philosophy of literature, namely *chen, pien* 'change', *ch'ü* 'tone', and *yün* 'charm' (discussed by Kuo Shao-yü, pp. 367–79), are only palely reflected, if at all, in Chou Tso-jen's thinking.

[21] See Chang Ju-chao, 'Yüan Chung-lang ti fo-hsüeh ssu-hsiang' (Yüan Chung-lang's Buddhist Thought), in *Jen chien shih*, December 1934.

BIBLIOGRAPHY

Relevant Works of Chou Tso-jen

1 *Tzu-chi ti yüan-ti* 自己的園地 1923; enlarged 1928.

2 *Yü t'ien ti shu* 雨天的書 1925.

3 *I-shu yü sheng-huo* 藝術與生活 1926.

4 *Tse-hsieh chi* 澤瀉集, 1927.

5 *T'an lung chi* 談龍集, 1927.

6 *T'an hu chi* 談虎集, 2 vols., 1928.

7 *Yung jih chi* 永日集, 1929.

8 *K'an yün chi* 看雲集, 1932.

9 *Chung-kuo hsin wen-hsüeh ti yüan-liu* 中國新文學的源流, 1932.

10 *Chou Tso-jen shu-hsin* 周作人書信, 1933.

11 *K'u yü chai hsü pa wen* 苦雨齋序跋文, 1934.

12 *Yeh tu ch'ao* 夜讀抄, 1934.

13 *K'u ch'a sui-pi* 苦茶隨筆, 1935.

14 *K'u chu tsa chi* 苦竹雜記, 1936.

15 *Feng yü t'an* 風雨談, 1936.

16 *Kua tou chi* 瓜豆集, 1937.

17 *Chou Tso-jen tai-piao tso* 周作人代表作, 1937.

18 *Yao wei chi* 藥味集, 1942.

19 *Yao-t'ang tsa-wen* 藥堂雜文, 1944.

20 *Ping chu hou t'an* 秉燭後談, 1944.

21 *K'u k'ou kan k'ou* 苦口甘口, 1944.

22 *Kuo-ch'ü ti kung-tso* 過去的工作, 1959.

23 *Chih-t'ang i-yu wen-pien* 知堂乙酉文編, 1961.
24 *Chih-t'ang hui-hsiang lu* 知堂回想錄, 1970.

Dictionaries

Boorman, Howard, *Biographical Dictionary of Modern China*, New York, Columbia University Press, 1967.

Chang Ch'i-yün, ed., *Chung-wen ta tz'u-tien* 中文大辭典, 40 vols., Taipei, 1962–8.

Morohashi Tatsuji, *Dai Kan-Wa jiten* 大漢和辭典, 13 vols., Tokyo, 1955–60.

Classical Texts

Chu tzu chi ch'eng 諸子集成, 8 vols. Peking, 1954.

Han Ch'ang-li chi 韓昌黎集. Hong Kong, 1964.

Lun heng 論衡, by Wang Ch'ung 王充. *Lun heng chiao-shih* 論衡校釋, ed. Huang Hui 黃暉, Taipei, 1964.

Shih p'in 詩品, by Chung Jung 鍾嶸. *Shih p'in chu* 詩品注, ed. Ch'en Yen-chieh 陳延傑, Hong Kong, 1959.

Shih p'in 詩品, by Ssu-k'ung T'u 司空圖, ed. Yang Chia-lo 楊家駱, Taipei, 1962.

Ssu-k'u ch'üan-shu shu-mu 四庫全書書目, 10 vols., reprinted I-wen, Taipei, 1964.

Ssu-pu pei-yao 四部備要, Chung hua, Shanghai, 1927–36.

Ts'ang-lang shih-hua 滄浪詩話 by Yen yü 嚴羽. *Ts'ang-lang shih-hua chiao-shih* 滄浪詩話校釋, ed. Kuo Shao-yü 郭紹虞, Peking, 1962.

Wen shih t'ung i 文史通義, by Chang Hsüeh-ch'eng 章學誠. Hong Kong, 1964.

Wen hsin tiao lung 文心雕龍, by Liu Hsieh 劉勰. *Wen hsin tiao lung chu* 文心雕龍注, Taipei, 1958.

Wen hsüan 文選, by Chao-ming T'ai-tzu 昭明太子. Hong Kong, Shang-wu, 1960.

Yüan Chung-lang ch'üan-chi 袁中郎全集, by Yüan Hung-tao 袁宏道. Hong Kong, no date.

Collections

Chung-kuo hsin wen-hsüeh ta-hsi 中國新文學大系, ed. Chao Chia-pi 趙家璧, 1935. Hong Kong, 1962.

Chung-kuo wen-hsüeh p'i-p'ing lun-wen chi 中國文學批評論文集 ed. Wang Huan-piao 王煥鑣. Taipei, 1957.

Hsien-tai Chung-kuo san-wen hsüan 現代中國散文選, ed. Sun Hsi-chen 孫席珍. Peking, 1935.

Hsien-tai san-wen ch'ao 現代散文抄, ed. Shen Ch'i-wu 沈啟无, 1932. Hong Kong, 1957.

Li-tai shih-hua 歷代詩話, ed. Ho Wen-huan 何文煥. I-wen reprint, Taipei, 1956.

Wan-Ming hsiao-p'in hsüan-chu 晚明小品選注, ed. Chu Chien-hsin 朱劍心. Taipei, 1964.

Wen-hsüeh p'i-p'ing wen-hsüan 文學批評文選, ed. Yang Chia-lo. Taipei, 1953.

Wen-lun chiang-shu 文論講疏, ed. Hsü Wen-yü 許文雨, 1935. Taipei, 1967.

Modern Works in Chinese

A Ying 阿英 (Ch'ien Hsing-ts'un 錢杏邨), *Hsien-tai shih-liu chia hsiao-p'in* 現代十六家小品, Shanghai, 1939.

An-hui jen-min ch'u-pan she 安徽人民出版社, *T'ung-ch'eng p'ai yen-chiu lun-wen chi* 桐城派研究論文集, Anhwei, 1963.

Chang Chien 張健, *Chung-kuo wen-hsüeh san-lun* 中國文學散論, Taipei, 1967.

Chang Ch'i-yün 張其昀 ed., *Chung-kuo wen-hua lun-chi* 中國文化論集, Taipei, 1954.

Chiang Shu-ke 姜書閣, *T'ung-ch'eng wen-p'ai p'ing-shu* 桐城文派評述, 1928, reprinted Taipei, 1966.

Chiang Tsu-i 蔣祖怡, *Wang ch'ung ti wen-hsüeh li-lun* 王充的文學理論, Shanghai, 1962.

Ch'ien Mu 錢穆, *Chung-kuo wen-hua shih tao-lun* 中國文化史導論, Taipei, 1951.

——————— *Chung-kuo wen-hsüeh chiang-yen chi* 中國文學講演集, Hong Kong, 1963.

Chou Chen-fu 周振甫, *Shih tz'u li hua* 詩詞例話, Peking, 1962.

Chu Kuang-ch'ien 朱光潛, *T'an wen-hsüeh* 談文學, reprinted Taipei, 1958.

——————— *Wen-i hsin-li-hsüeh* 文藝心理學 reprinted Taipei, 1958.

Chu Tung-jun 朱東潤, *Chung-kuo wen-hsüeh p'i-p'ing shih ta-kang* 中國文學批評史大綱, reprinted Taipei, 1960.

Chung-kuo k'e-hsüeh-yüan wen-hsüeh yen-chiu-so 中國科學院文學研究所, *Chung-kuo wen-hsüeh shih* 中國文學史 (3 vols.), Peking, 1963.

Fang Hsiao-yüeh 方孝岳, *Chung-kuo wen-hsüeh p'i-p'ing* 中國文學批評, Shanghai, 1934.

Fu Keng-sheng 傅庚生, *Chung-kuo wen-hsüeh hsin-shang chü-yü* 中國文學欣賞舉隅, reprinted Hong Kong, 1969.

——————— *Chung-kuo wen-hsüeh p'i-p'ing t'ung-lun* 中國文學批評通論, Shanghai, 1947.

Ho Man-tzu 何滿子, *Lun Chin Sheng-t'an p'ing-kai Shui-hu chuan* 論金聖嘆評改水滸傳, Shanghai, 1954.

Hsü Fu-kuan 徐復觀, *Chung-kuo wen-hsüeh lun-chi* 中國文學論集, Taipei, 1966.

Hung Yen-ch'iu 洪炎秋, *Wen-hsüeh kai-lun* 文學概論, Taipei, 1957,

Jen Hsin 任卓, *T'an hsiao-p'in san-wen* 談小品散文, Hong Kong, 1957.

Juan Wu-ming 阮无名, *Chung-kuo hsin wen-t'an mi-lu* 中國新文壇秘錄, Shanghai, 1933.

Jung Chao-tsu 容肇祖, *Wei-Chin ti tzu-jan chu-i* 魏晉的自然主義 Taipei, 1966.

Kuo Shao-yü 郭紹虞, *Chung-kuo wen-hsüeh p'i-p'ing shih* 中國文學批評史, Hong Kong, no date.

Lu Hsün 魯迅 (Chou Shu-jen 周樹人), *Lu Hsün ch'üan-chi* 魯迅全集, Peking, 1961.

——— *Lu Hsün I-wen chi* 魯迅譯文集, Peking, 1959.

Li Ch'en-tung 李辰冬, *Wen-hsüeh hsin lun* 文學新論, Taipei, 1954.

Li Su-po 李素伯, *Hsiao-p'in san-wen yen-chiu* 小品散文研究, Shanghai, 1932.

Lo Ken-tse 羅根澤, *Chung-kuo wen-hsüeh p'i-p'ing shih* 中國文學批評史 (3 vols.), Shanghai, 1957–61.

Mao Tun 茅盾 (Shen Yen-ping 沈雁冰) ed., *Tso-chia lun* 作家論 Shanghai, 1936.

Pa Jen 巴人 (Wang Jen-shu 王任叔), *Lun Lu Hsün ti tsa-wen* 論魯迅的雜文, no place, 1940.

Su Hsüeh-lin 蘇雪林, *Chiu ke chung jen shen lien-ai wen-t'i* 九歌中的人神戀愛問題, Taipei, 1967.

T'ao Ming-chih 陶明志, *Chou Tso-jen lun* 周作人論, Shanghai, 1934.

Ts'ao Chü-jen 曹聚仁, *Hsien-tai wen-i shou-ts'e* 現代文藝手冊, Hong Kong, 1952.

T'u Kung-sui 涂公遂, *Wen-hsüeh kai-lun* 文學概論, Hong Kong, 1962.

Wang Meng-ou 王夢鷗, *Wen-hsüeh kai-lun* 文學概論, Taipei, 1964.

Wang Kuo-wei 王國維, *Sung Yüan hsi-ch'ü shih* 宋元戲曲史, reprinted Hong Kong, 1964.

——— *Jen-chien tz'u hua* 人間詞話, in Hsü Wen-yü's collection.

Wang Yao 王瑤, *Lu Hsün yü Chung-kuo wen-hsüeh* 魯迅與中國文學, Shanghai, 1952.

Japanese Works translated into Chinese

Aoki Masaru 青木正兒, *Chung-kuo ku-tai wen-i ssu-ch'ao lun* 中國古代文藝思潮論, trans. Wang Chün-yü 王俊瑜, reprinted Taipei, 1961.

———————— *Chung-kuo wen-hsüeh ssu-hsiang shih kang* 中國文學思想史綱, trans. Wang Fu-ch'üan 王馥泉, Shanghai, 1936.

Kuriyagawa Hakuson 廚川白村, *K'u-men ti hsiang-cheng* 苦悶的象征, trans. Lu Hsün, *Lu Hsün I-wen chi*, vol. 3.

Takeda Sakae 竹田復, *Chung-kuo wen-i ssu-hsiang* 中國文藝思想, trans. Sui Shu-sen 隋樹森, Hong Kong, 1966.

Watanabe Shūhō 渡邊秀方, *Chung-kuo che-hsüeh kai-lun* 中國哲學概論, trans. Liu K'an-yüan 劉侃元, Taipei, 1964.

English Translations

Birch, Cyril, *Anthology of Chinese Literature*, New York, 1965.

Lau, D. C., *Lao tzu*, Penguin Books, 1963.

Legge, James, *The Chinese Classics* (7 vols.), reprinted Taipei, 1966.

Shadick, Harold, *The Travels of Lao Ts'an*, Cornell University Press, 1952.

Shih, Vincent, *The Literary Mind and the Carving of Dragons*, New York, 1959.

Waley, Arthur, *The Book of Songs*, London, 1937.

Articles

Chang Ju-chao 張汝釗, 'Yüan Chung-lang ti fo-hsüeh ssu-hsiang' 袁中郎的佛學思想, *Jen-chien-shih* 人間世, December 1934.

Chung Ching-wen 鍾敬文, 'Shih t'an hsiao-p'in wen' 試談小品文 *Wen-hsüeh chou-pao* 文學週報, October 1928.

Kao Ming 高明, 'Chung-kuo hsiu-tz'u-hsüeh yen-chiu' 中國修辭學研究, *Chung-kuo yü-wen* 中國語文, Taipei, Vol. I, no. 6 and Vol. II, no. 2.

Pollard, D. E., 'Chou Tso-jen and cultivating one's garden', *Asia Major*, Vol. xi, pt. 2.

Wu Hung-i 吳宏一, 'Wang Ching-an ti ching-chieh shuo', 王靜安的境界說, *Chung-yang jih-pao* 中央日報, Taipei, 17 May 1967.

Works in English

Abrams, M. H., *The Mirror and the Lamp*, New York, 1958.

Atkins, J. W. H., *English Literary Criticism, Seventeenth and Eighteenth Centuries*, University Paperbacks, 1966.

Bishop, J. L., *Studies in Chinese Literature*, Cambridge, Mass., 1965.

Castro, Angela, 'Three Early Essays of Lu Hsün', London University M.Phil. thesis, 1968.

Chow Tse-tsung ed., *Wen-lin*, Wisconsin, 1968.

Follett, Wilson, *The Modern Novel*, London, 1923.

Hsia, T. A., *The Gate of Darkness*, Washington, 1968.

Liu, James J. Y., *The Art of Chinese Poetry*, London, 1962.

Mao Tse-tung, *Mao Tse-tung on Art and Literature*, Peking, 1960.

Nivison, David, *The Life and Thought of Chang Hsüeh-ch'eng*, Stanford, 1966.

Watt, Ian, *The Rise of the Novel*, Peregrine Books, 1956.

Wolff, Ernst, *Chou Tso-jen*, New York, 1971.

Yang, C. K., *Religion in Chinese Society*, University of California Press, 1967.

PEOPLE AND PUBLICATIONS NOT INCLUDED IN BIBLIOGRAPHY

Chang Chieh 張戒
Chang Ching 張景
Chang Hua 張華
Chang Hsüeh-ch'eng (Shih-chai) 章學誠（實齋）
Chang Ping-lin (T'ai-yen) 章炳麟（太炎）
Chang Tai (Tsung-tzu) 張岱（宗子）
Chen Te-hsiu 真德秀
Ch'en Hsien-chang 陳獻章
Ch'en Shih-tao 陳師道
Cheng Hsüan 鄭玄
Ch'eng I 程頤
Ch'eng Mien-chuang 程綿莊
Chiang K'ui 姜夔
Chiang Yen 江淹
Chiao Hsün 焦循
Chiao Hung (Jo-hou) 焦竑（弱侯）
Ch'ien Hsüan-t'ung 錢玄同
Chin Nung 金農
Chin Sheng 金聲
Chin Sheng-t'an 金聖嘆
Ch'in ting ssu shu wen 欽定四書文
Ching hua yüan 鏡花緣
Ching-ling 竟陵
Chou Tso-jen 周作人
Chou Tun-i 周敦頤

Chu Hsi 朱熹
Ch'u Tz'u 楚辭
Ch'ü Ta-chün 屈大均
Ch'ü Yüan 屈原
Ch'uang-tsao yüeh-k'an 創造月刊
Chung shuo 中說
Chung yung 中庸
Fan Yeh 范曄
Fang Chen-kuan 方貞觀
Fang Pao 方苞
Fang Tung-shu 方東樹
Feng Fei-ming 馮廢名
Han Shih 韓詩
Han Yü 韓愈
Ho I-hsing (Lan-kao) 郝懿行(蘭皐)
Ho I-sun 賀貽孫
Ho Yen 何晏
Hsi K'ang 嵇康
Hsiao Tzu-hsien 蕭子顯
Hsieh Fang-te 謝枋得
Hsieh Shih-hou 謝視侯
Hsiung Chu 熊錄
Hsü Kan 徐幹
Hsü Wei (Wen-chang) 徐渭(文長)
Hsüeh Hsüan 薛瑄
Hu Meng-hua 胡夢華
Huan Fan 桓範
Huang K'an 黃侃
Huang Ming shih liu chia hsiao p'in 皇明十六家小品
Huang T'ing-chien 黃庭堅
Huang Tsung-hsi (Li-chou) 黃宗羲(梨洲)
Hung Shui 洪水
I wen chih 藝文志
Jih chih lu 日知錄
Koizumi Yakumo 小泉八雲

Ku Wan-ch'uan 谷萬川
Ku wen yüeh hsüan 古文約選
K'uai-chi 會稽
Kui-ssu ts'un kao 癸巳存稿
Kui Yu-kuang 歸有光
Kung-an p'ai 公安派
K'ung Ying-ta 孔穎達
Li Ao 李翱
Li Chih (Cho-wu) 李贄（卓吾）
Li E 李諤
Li Han 李漢
Li Ke-fei 李格非
Li Kung 李塨
Li Shan 李善
Li Yü (Li-weng) 李漁（笠翁）
Liang Ch'i-ch'ao 梁啟超
Lin Shu 林紓
Liu Hai 劉海
Liu Hsien-t'ing 劉獻廷
Liu i chih 六藝志
Liu K'e-chuang 劉克莊
Liu Mien 柳冕
Liu Shih-p'ei 劉師培
Liu Ta-k'ui 劉大櫆
Liu T'ung-jen 劉同人
Lu Chi 陸機
Lü Po-kung 呂伯恭
Mao K'un 茅坤
Matsuo Bashō 松尾芭蕉
Mei Po-yen 梅伯言
Mei Tseng-liang 梅曾亮
Mei Yao-ch'en 梅堯臣
Mori Ōgai 森鷗外
Pei ying 背影
P'ei Tzu-yeh 裴子野

Piao-sheng wen chi 表聖文集
Shao Yung 邵雍
Shih huo chih 食貨志
Shih p'u hsü 詩譜序
Shu Po-hsiang 舒白香
Su Shih 蘇軾
Sui han t'ang shih hua 歲寒堂詩話
Sung Lien 宋濂
Ssu-k'ung T'u 司空圖
T'ang Hsien-tsu 湯顯祖
T'ang Shun-chih 唐順之
T'ang Sung pa ta chia wen ch'ao 唐宋八大家文抄
T'ao Ch'ung-tao 陶崇道
T'ao Ming-chün 陶明濬
Tiao ch'ung lun 雕蟲論
Ts'ao Chih 曹植
Tseng Kuo-fan 曾國藩
T'ung-ch'eng p'ai 桐城派
T'ung shu 通書
Wang An-shih 王安石
Wang Ch'ung 王充
Wang K'an 王侃
Wang K'en-t'ang 王肯堂
Wang Kuo-wei 王國維
Wang Pi 王弼
Wang Shih-chen 王士貞
Wang T'ung 王通
Wang Yüan-chi 王淵濟
Wen chang kui fan 文章軌範
Wen fu 文賦
Wen-hua p'i-p'an 文化批判
Wu Chih-hui 吳稚暉
Yang Hsiung 揚雄
Yao Nai 姚鼐
Yeh Shih 葉適

Yeh Sung-shih 葉松石
Yen Yü 嚴羽
Yen Yüan 顏元
Yokoi Yayū 横井也有
Yü Cheng-hsieh (Li-ch'u) 俞正燮（理初）
Yü P'ing-po 俞平伯
Yü Ta-fu 郁達夫
Yü Yüeh (Ch'ü-yüan) 俞樾（曲園）
Yüan Chen 元稹
Yüan Chung-tao 袁中道
Yüan Hung-tao (Chung-lang) 袁宏道（中郎）
Yüan Mei 袁枚
Yüan Tsung-tao 袁宗道

CHARACTER LIST FOR CHINESE TERMS

an-shih 暗示
ch'a-na chu-i 刹那主義
chen 真
chen-chih 真摯
chen-shih 真實
cheng 正
ch'eng 誠
ch'eng-hsin 誠信
chi 集
chi-hsing 即興
ch'i 氣
ch'i-mi 綺靡
ch'i-wei 氣味
ch'i-wei hsiang t'ou 氣味相投
chiao-hua 教化
chien-ming 簡明
chien-tan 簡單
ch'ien hou ch'i tzu 前後七子
chih ch'i pu k'e wei erh wei chih 知其不可為而為之
chih-su 質素
ch'ih-tu 尺牘
ching-chieh 境界
ch'ing 情
ch'ing chen ya cheng 清真雅正
ch'ing cheng ku ya 清正古雅

ch'ing-lang 清朗
ch'ing li ping ho 情理並合
ch'iung li erh chih yung 窮理而致用
cho 拙
chung hou 重厚
ch'ung tan 沖淡
ch'ü-wei 趣味
fan-k'ang-ti 反抗的
fei fu 肺腑
feng 風
feng chih 風致
feng ch'ü 風趣
feng hua hsüeh yüeh 風花雪月
fu shih yen chih 賦詩言志
fu te 賦得
hsiao p'in wen 小品文
hsien 閑
hsien shih 獻詩
hsin k'ou hsin wan chieh ch'eng lü tu 信口信腕,皆成律度
hsing 興
hsing ch'ü 興趣
hsing ling 性靈
hsiu tz'u li ch'i ch'eng 修辭立其誠
hsiung 胸
hsü-tzu 虛字
hsü yü 絮語
hua shih ping mao 華實並茂
hui wei 回味
i 義
i-wei 意味
jen-ch'ing-wei 人情味
jen-ch'ing wu-li 人情物理
kan fei 肝肺
kao 膏
kao miao 高妙

kou ch'üan hsing-ming yü luan shih 苟全性命于亂世
k'ou pu tse yen yen pu tse shih 口不擇言，言不擇事
ku 骨
k'u 苦
k'u tan 枯淡
ku wen 古文
kyogen 狂言
lan-shou 爛熟
lang-man t'an 浪漫談
li 理
ling-kan 靈感
liu ching tu 六經毒
lun 論
mei wen 美文
miao 妙
ming shih liu/p'ai 名士流/派
ming shuo 明說
ou-ch'eng 偶成
pa-ku-wen 八股文
p'ai hsieh t'i/wen 俳諧體/文
p'ai wen 俳文
p'ang men 旁門
pen se 本色
pi-chi 筆記
pien 變
pien feng 變風
p'ien wen 駢文
p'ing shuo 平說
p'ing-tan 平淡
p'ing-yung 平庸
pu ch'ien nu 不遷怒
pu feng 捕風
p'u 樸
p'u-chih 樸質
san-wen 散文

sao 騷
se 澀
se-wei (shibumi) 澀味
shen ju ch'ien ch'u 深入淺出
sheng-tiao 聲調
shih (poetry) 詩
shih (history) 史
shih-t'ieh 試帖
shih-tzu 實字
shih-ye 師爺
shih yen chih 詩言志
shih yüan ch'ing 詩緣情
shu 書
shu ch'ing 抒情
shuo-ch'u-ti 說出的
ssu wu hsieh 思無邪
sui-pi (zuihitsu) 隨筆
ta pu ching 大不敬
ta-yu shih 打油詩
tan erh wu wei 淡而無味
tan yüan 淡遠
tien shih 典實
tsa-chü 雜劇
tsa-kan 雜感
tsa-wen 雜文
tso-ch'u-ti 做出的
t'ung-jan 同然
t'ung-ta 通達
tzu 子
tzu-jan 自然
tzu-wei 滋味
tz'u 詞
tz'u ta erh i 辭達而已
wei 味
wei wai chih chih 味外之旨

wen 文
wen chih pin-pin 文質彬彬
wen ch'ing ping mao 文情並茂
wen i tsai tao 文以載道
wen jou tun hou 文柔敦厚
wen wai chih chih 文外之旨
ya 雅
ya cheng 雅正
ya chieh 雅潔
ya-chih-nai 亞支奶
yen chung yu wu 言中有物
yin yung hsing ch'ing 吟詠性情
yu pen 有本
yu pie-tse 有別擇
yü hsiang 餘香
yü yün 餘韻
yün 韻
yung wu 詠物

www.ingramcontent.com/pod-product-compliance
Lightning Source LLC
Chambersburg PA
CBHW021658110726
47902CB00007B/1981

* 9 7 8 0 5 2 0 3 3 6 9 9 5 *